C-1834   CAREER EXAMINATION SERIES

This is your
PASSBOOK for...

Materials Testing Technician

Test Preparation Study Guide
Questions & Answers

COPYRIGHT NOTICE

This book is SOLELY intended for, is sold ONLY to, and its use is RESTRICTED to individual, bona fide applicants or candidates who qualify by virtue of having seriously filed applications for appropriate license, certificate, professional and/or promotional advancement, higher school matriculation, scholarship, or other legitimate requirements of education and/or governmental authorities.

This book is NOT intended for use, class instruction, tutoring, training, duplication, copying, reprinting, excerption, or adaptation, etc., by:

1) Other publishers
2) Proprietors and/or Instructors of "Coaching" and/or Preparatory Courses
3) Personnel and/or Training Divisions of commercial, industrial, and governmental organizations
4) Schools, colleges, or universities and/or their departments and staffs, including teachers and other personnel
5) Testing Agencies or Bureaus
6) Study groups which seek by the purchase of a single volume to copy and/or duplicate and/or adapt this material for use by the group as a whole without having purchased individual volumes for each of the members of the group
7) Et al.

Such persons would be in violation of appropriate Federal and State statutes.

PROVISION OF LICENSING AGREEMENTS – Recognized educational, commercial, industrial, and governmental institutions and organizations, and others legitimately engaged in educational pursuits, including training, testing, and measurement activities, may address request for a licensing agreement to the copyright owners, who will determine whether, and under what conditions, including fees and charges, the materials in this book may be used them. In other words, a licensing facility exists for the legitimate use of the material in this book on other than an individual basis. However, it is asseverated and affirmed here that the material in this book CANNOT be used without the receipt of the express permission of such a licensing agreement from the Publishers. Inquiries re licensing should be addressed to the company, attention rights and permissions department.

All rights reserved, including the right of reproduction in whole or in part, in any form or by any means, electronic or mechanical, including photocopying, recording, or by any information storage and retrieval system, without permission in writing from the Publisher.

Copyright © 2025 by
National Learning Corporation

212 Michael Drive, Syosset, NY 11791
(516) 921-8888 • www.passbooks.com
E-mail: info@passbooks.com

PASSBOOK® SERIES

THE *PASSBOOK® SERIES* has been created to prepare applicants and candidates for the ultimate academic battlefield – the examination room.

At some time in our lives, each and every one of us may be required to take an examination – for validation, matriculation, admission, qualification, registration, certification, or licensure.

Based on the assumption that every applicant or candidate has met the basic formal educational standards, has taken the required number of courses, and read the necessary texts, the *PASSBOOK® SERIES* furnishes the one special preparation which may assure passing with confidence, instead of failing with insecurity. Examination questions – together with answers – are furnished as the basic vehicle for study so that the mysteries of the examination and its compounding difficulties may be eliminated or diminished by a sure method.

This book is meant to help you pass your examination provided that you qualify and are serious in your objective.

The entire field is reviewed through the huge store of content information which is succinctly presented through a provocative and challenging approach – the question-and-answer method.

A climate of success is established by furnishing the correct answers at the end of each test.

You soon learn to recognize types of questions, forms of questions, and patterns of questioning. You may even begin to anticipate expected outcomes.

You perceive that many questions are repeated or adapted so that you can gain acute insights, which may enable you to score many sure points.

You learn how to confront new questions, or types of questions, and to attack them confidently and work out the correct answers.

You note objectives and emphases, and recognize pitfalls and dangers, so that you may make positive educational adjustments.

Moreover, you are kept fully informed in relation to new concepts, methods, practices, and directions in the field.

You discover that you are actually taking the examination all the time: you are preparing for the examination by "taking" an examination, not by reading extraneous and/or supererogatory textbooks.

In short, this PASSBOOK®, used directedly, should be an important factor in helping you to pass your test.

MATERIALS TESTING TECHNICIAN

DUTIES
Performs routine testing of materials used in highway maintenance and construction and other materials submitted by various departments. You would direct and perform a variety of nondestructive tests on metal used for structural purposes, and on the completed members fabricated from such metals. You would direct inspection agencies such as testing laboratories or subcontractors, performing such tests during fabrication of steel and aluminum structures, and monitor their performance by performing random inspections and reviewing inspection documentation. You would also perform such nondestructive tests on existing bridges. You would inspect structural steel plants to ensure quality of materials and workmanship; review erection procedures; review and approve welding procedures; and prepare specifications for nondestructive tests (radiograph, magnetic particle, dye penetrant, hardness and ultrasonic). Does related work as required.

SCOPE OF THE EXAMINATION
The written test will cover knowledge, skills and abilities in such areas as:

1. Properties of engineering materials;
2. Principles, methods and apparatus used in the physical and chemical testing of materials;
3. Methods and materials for highway construction;
4. Understanding and interpreting construction plans and descriptive specifications; and
5. Math including algebra, geometry and trigonometry.

HOW TO TAKE A TEST

I. YOU MUST PASS AN EXAMINATION

A. WHAT EVERY CANDIDATE SHOULD KNOW

Examination applicants often ask us for help in preparing for the written test. What can I study in advance? What kinds of questions will be asked? How will the test be given? How will the papers be graded?

As an applicant for a civil service examination, you may be wondering about some of these things. Our purpose here is to suggest effective methods of advance study and to describe civil service examinations.

Your chances for success on this examination can be increased if you know how to prepare. Those "pre-examination jitters" can be reduced if you know what to expect. You can even experience an adventure in good citizenship if you know why civil service exams are given.

B. WHY ARE CIVIL SERVICE EXAMINATIONS GIVEN?

Civil service examinations are important to you in two ways. As a citizen, you want public jobs filled by employees who know how to do their work. As a job seeker, you want a fair chance to compete for that job on an equal footing with other candidates. The best-known means of accomplishing this two-fold goal is the competitive examination.

Exams are widely publicized throughout the nation. They may be administered for jobs in federal, state, city, municipal, town or village governments or agencies.

Any citizen may apply, with some limitations, such as the age or residence of applicants. Your experience and education may be reviewed to see whether you meet the requirements for the particular examination. When these requirements exist, they are reasonable and applied consistently to all applicants. Thus, a competitive examination may cause you some uneasiness now, but it is your privilege and safeguard.

C. HOW ARE CIVIL SERVICE EXAMS DEVELOPED?

Examinations are carefully written by trained technicians who are specialists in the field known as "psychological measurement," in consultation with recognized authorities in the field of work that the test will cover. These experts recommend the subject matter areas or skills to be tested; only those knowledges or skills important to your success on the job are included. The most reliable books and source materials available are used as references. Together, the experts and technicians judge the difficulty level of the questions.

Test technicians know how to phrase questions so that the problem is clearly stated. Their ethics do not permit "trick" or "catch" questions. Questions may have been tried out on sample groups, or subjected to statistical analysis, to determine their usefulness.

Written tests are often used in combination with performance tests, ratings of training and experience, and oral interviews. All of these measures combine to form the best-known means of finding the right person for the right job.

II. HOW TO PASS THE WRITTEN TEST

A. NATURE OF THE EXAMINATION

To prepare intelligently for civil service examinations, you should know how they differ from school examinations you have taken. In school you were assigned certain definite pages to read or subjects to cover. The examination questions were quite detailed and usually emphasized memory. Civil service exams, on the other hand, try to discover your present ability to perform the duties of a position, plus your potentiality to learn these duties. In other words, a civil service exam attempts to predict how successful you will be. Questions cover such a broad area that they cannot be as minute and detailed as school exam questions.

In the public service similar kinds of work, or positions, are grouped together in one "class." This process is known as *position-classification*. All the positions in a class are paid according to the salary range for that class. One class title covers all of these positions, and they are all tested by the same examination.

B. FOUR BASIC STEPS

1) Study the announcement

How, then, can you know what subjects to study? Our best answer is: "Learn as much as possible about the class of positions for which you've applied." The exam will test the knowledge, skills and abilities needed to do the work.

Your most valuable source of information about the position you want is the official exam announcement. This announcement lists the training and experience qualifications. Check these standards and apply only if you come reasonably close to meeting them.

The brief description of the position in the examination announcement offers some clues to the subjects which will be tested. Think about the job itself. Review the duties in your mind. Can you perform them, or are there some in which you are rusty? Fill in the blank spots in your preparation.

Many jurisdictions preview the written test in the exam announcement by including a section called "Knowledge and Abilities Required," "Scope of the Examination," or some similar heading. Here you will find out specifically what fields will be tested.

2) Review your own background

Once you learn in general what the position is all about, and what you need to know to do the work, ask yourself which subjects you already know fairly well and which need improvement. You may wonder whether to concentrate on improving your strong areas or on building some background in your fields of weakness. When the announcement has specified "some knowledge" or "considerable knowledge," or has used adjectives like "beginning principles of…" or "advanced … methods," you can get a clue as to the number and difficulty of questions to be asked in any given field. More questions, and hence broader coverage, would be included for those subjects which are more important in the work. Now weigh your strengths and weaknesses against the job requirements and prepare accordingly.

3) Determine the level of the position

Another way to tell how intensively you should prepare is to understand the level of the job for which you are applying. Is it the entering level? In other words, is this the position in which beginners in a field of work are hired? Or is it an intermediate or advanced level? Sometimes this is indicated by such words as "Junior" or "Senior" in the class title. Other jurisdictions use Roman numerals to designate the level – Clerk I, Clerk II, for example. The word "Supervisor" sometimes appears in the title. If the level is not indicated by the title, check the description of duties. Will you be working under very close supervision, or will you have responsibility for independent decisions in this work?

4) Choose appropriate study materials

Now that you know the subjects to be examined and the relative amount of each subject to be covered, you can choose suitable study materials. For beginning level jobs, or even advanced ones, if you have a pronounced weakness in some aspect of your training, read a modern, standard textbook in that field. Be sure it is up to date and has general coverage. Such books are normally available at your library, and the librarian will be glad to help you locate one. For entry-level positions, questions of appropriate difficulty are chosen – neither highly advanced questions, nor those too simple. Such questions require careful thought but not advanced training.

If the position for which you are applying is technical or advanced, you will read more advanced, specialized material. If you are already familiar with the basic principles of your field, elementary textbooks would waste your time. Concentrate on advanced textbooks and technical periodicals. Think through the concepts and review difficult problems in your field.

These are all general sources. You can get more ideas on your own initiative, following these leads. For example, training manuals and publications of the government agency which employs workers in your field can be useful, particularly for technical and professional positions. A letter or visit to the government department involved may result in more specific study suggestions, and certainly will provide you with a more definite idea of the exact nature of the position you are seeking.

III. KINDS OF TESTS

Tests are used for purposes other than measuring knowledge and ability to perform specified duties. For some positions, it is equally important to test ability to make adjustments to new situations or to profit from training. In others, basic mental abilities not dependent on information are essential. Questions which test these things may not appear as pertinent to the duties of the position as those which test for knowledge and information. Yet they are often highly important parts of a fair examination. For very general questions, it is almost impossible to help you direct your study efforts. What we can do is to point out some of the more common of these general abilities needed in public service positions and describe some typical questions.

1) General information

Broad, general information has been found useful for predicting job success in some kinds of work. This is tested in a variety of ways, from vocabulary lists to questions about current events. Basic background in some field of work, such as sociology or economics, may be sampled in a group of questions. Often these are principles which have become familiar to most persons through exposure rather than through formal training. It is difficult to advise you how to study for these questions; being alert to the world around you is our best suggestion.

2) Verbal ability

An example of an ability needed in many positions is verbal or language ability. Verbal ability is, in brief, the ability to use and understand words. Vocabulary and grammar tests are typical measures of this ability. Reading comprehension or paragraph interpretation questions are common in many kinds of civil service tests. You are given a paragraph of written material and asked to find its central meaning.

3) Numerical ability

Number skills can be tested by the familiar arithmetic problem, by checking paired lists of numbers to see which are alike and which are different, or by interpreting charts and graphs. In the latter test, a graph may be printed in the test booklet which you are asked to use as the basis for answering questions.

4) Observation

A popular test for law-enforcement positions is the observation test. A picture is shown to you for several minutes, then taken away. Questions about the picture test your ability to observe both details and larger elements.

5) Following directions

In many positions in the public service, the employee must be able to carry out written instructions dependably and accurately. You may be given a chart with several columns, each column listing a variety of information. The questions require you to carry out directions involving the information given in the chart.

6) Skills and aptitudes

Performance tests effectively measure some manual skills and aptitudes. When the skill is one in which you are trained, such as typing or shorthand, you can practice. These tests are often very much like those given in business school or high school courses. For many of the other skills and aptitudes, however, no short-time preparation can be made. Skills and abilities natural to you or that you have developed throughout your lifetime are being tested.

Many of the general questions just described provide all the data needed to answer the questions and ask you to use your reasoning ability to find the answers. Your best preparation for these tests, as well as for tests of facts and ideas, is to be at your physical and mental best. You, no doubt, have your own methods of getting into an exam-taking mood and keeping "in shape." The next section lists some ideas on this subject.

IV. KINDS OF QUESTIONS

Only rarely is the "essay" question, which you answer in narrative form, used in civil service tests. Civil service tests are usually of the short-answer type. Full instructions for answering these questions will be given to you at the examination. But in case this is your first experience with short-answer questions and separate answer sheets, here is what you need to know:

1) Multiple-choice Questions

Most popular of the short-answer questions is the "multiple choice" or "best answer" question. It can be used, for example, to test for factual knowledge, ability to solve problems or judgment in meeting situations found at work.

A multiple-choice question is normally one of three types—
- It can begin with an incomplete statement followed by several possible endings. You are to find the one ending which *best* completes the statement, although some of the others may not be entirely wrong.
- It can also be a complete statement in the form of a question which is answered by choosing one of the statements listed.

- It can be in the form of a problem – again you select the best answer.

Here is an example of a multiple-choice question with a discussion which should give you some clues as to the method for choosing the right answer:

When an employee has a complaint about his assignment, the action which will *best* help him overcome his difficulty is to
   A. discuss his difficulty with his coworkers
   B. take the problem to the head of the organization
   C. take the problem to the person who gave him the assignment
   D. say nothing to anyone about his complaint

In answering this question, you should study each of the choices to find which is best. Consider choice "A" – Certainly an employee may discuss his complaint with fellow employees, but no change or improvement can result, and the complaint remains unresolved. Choice "B" is a poor choice since the head of the organization probably does not know what assignment you have been given, and taking your problem to him is known as "going over the head" of the supervisor. The supervisor, or person who made the assignment, is the person who can clarify it or correct any injustice. Choice "C" is, therefore, correct. To say nothing, as in choice "D," is unwise. Supervisors have and interest in knowing the problems employees are facing, and the employee is seeking a solution to his problem.

2) True/False Questions

The "true/false" or "right/wrong" form of question is sometimes used. Here a complete statement is given. Your job is to decide whether the statement is right or wrong.

SAMPLE: A roaming cell-phone call to a nearby city costs less than a non-roaming call to a distant city.

This statement is wrong, or false, since roaming calls are more expensive.

This is not a complete list of all possible question forms, although most of the others are variations of these common types. You will always get complete directions for answering questions. Be sure you understand *how* to mark your answers – ask questions until you do.

V. RECORDING YOUR ANSWERS

Computer terminals are used more and more today for many different kinds of exams.

For an examination with very few applicants, you may be told to record your answers in the test booklet itself. Separate answer sheets are much more common. If this separate answer sheet is to be scored by machine – and this is often the case – it is highly important that you mark your answers correctly in order to get credit.

An electronic scoring machine is often used in civil service offices because of the speed with which papers can be scored. Machine-scored answer sheets must be marked with a pencil, which will be given to you. This pencil has a high graphite content which responds to the electronic scoring machine. As a matter of fact, stray dots may register as answers, so do not let your pencil rest on the answer sheet while you are pondering the correct answer. Also, if your pencil lead breaks or is otherwise defective, ask for another.

Since the answer sheet will be dropped in a slot in the scoring machine, be careful not to bend the corners or get the paper crumpled.

The answer sheet normally has five vertical columns of numbers, with 30 numbers to a column. These numbers correspond to the question numbers in your test booklet. After each number, going across the page are four or five pairs of dotted lines. These short dotted lines have small letters or numbers above them. The first two pairs may also have a "T" or "F" above the letters. This indicates that the first two pairs only are to be used if the questions are of the true-false type. If the questions are multiple choice, disregard the "T" and "F" and pay attention only to the small letters or numbers.

Answer your questions in the manner of the sample that follows:

32. The largest city in the United States is
     A. Washington, D.C.
     B. New York City
     C. Chicago
     D. Detroit
     E. San Francisco

1) Choose the answer you think is best. (New York City is the largest, so "B" is correct.)
2) Find the row of dotted lines numbered the same as the question you are answering. (Find row number 32)
3) Find the pair of dotted lines corresponding to the answer. (Find the pair of lines under the mark "B.")
4) Make a solid black mark between the dotted lines.

VI. BEFORE THE TEST

Common sense will help you find procedures to follow to get ready for an examination. Too many of us, however, overlook these sensible measures. Indeed, nervousness and fatigue have been found to be the most serious reasons why applicants fail to do their best on civil service tests. Here is a list of reminders:

- Begin your preparation early – Don't wait until the last minute to go scurrying around for books and materials or to find out what the position is all about.
- Prepare continuously – An hour a night for a week is better than an all-night cram session. This has been definitely established. What is more, a night a week for a month will return better dividends than crowding your study into a shorter period of time.
- Locate the place of the exam – You have been sent a notice telling you when and where to report for the examination. If the location is in a different town or otherwise unfamiliar to you, it would be well to inquire the best route and learn something about the building.
- Relax the night before the test – Allow your mind to rest. Do not study at all that night. Plan some mild recreation or diversion; then go to bed early and get a good night's sleep.
- Get up early enough to make a leisurely trip to the place for the test – This way unforeseen events, traffic snarls, unfamiliar buildings, etc. will not upset you.
- Dress comfortably – A written test is not a fashion show. You will be known by number and not by name, so wear something comfortable.

- Leave excess paraphernalia at home – Shopping bags and odd bundles will get in your way. You need bring only the items mentioned in the official notice you received; usually everything you need is provided. Do not bring reference books to the exam. They will only confuse those last minutes and be taken away from you when in the test room.
- Arrive somewhat ahead of time – If because of transportation schedules you must get there very early, bring a newspaper or magazine to take your mind off yourself while waiting.
- Locate the examination room – When you have found the proper room, you will be directed to the seat or part of the room where you will sit. Sometimes you are given a sheet of instructions to read while you are waiting. Do not fill out any forms until you are told to do so; just read them and be prepared.
- Relax and prepare to listen to the instructions
- If you have any physical problem that may keep you from doing your best, be sure to tell the test administrator. If you are sick or in poor health, you really cannot do your best on the exam. You can come back and take the test some other time.

VII. AT THE TEST

The day of the test is here and you have the test booklet in your hand. The temptation to get going is very strong. Caution! There is more to success than knowing the right answers. You must know how to identify your papers and understand variations in the type of short-answer question used in this particular examination. Follow these suggestions for maximum results from your efforts:

1) Cooperate with the monitor

The test administrator has a duty to create a situation in which you can be as much at ease as possible. He will give instructions, tell you when to begin, check to see that you are marking your answer sheet correctly, and so on. He is not there to guard you, although he will see that your competitors do not take unfair advantage. He wants to help you do your best.

2) Listen to all instructions

Don't jump the gun! Wait until you understand all directions. In most civil service tests you get more time than you need to answer the questions. So don't be in a hurry. Read each word of instructions until you clearly understand the meaning. Study the examples, listen to all announcements and follow directions. Ask questions if you do not understand what to do.

3) Identify your papers

Civil service exams are usually identified by number only. You will be assigned a number; you must not put your name on your test papers. Be sure to copy your number correctly. Since more than one exam may be given, copy your exact examination title.

4) Plan your time

Unless you are told that a test is a "speed" or "rate of work" test, speed itself is usually not important. Time enough to answer all the questions will be provided, but this does not mean that you have all day. An overall time limit has been set. Divide the total time (in minutes) by the number of questions to determine the approximate time you have for each question.

5) Do not linger over difficult questions

If you come across a difficult question, mark it with a paper clip (useful to have along) and come back to it when you have been through the booklet. One caution if you do this – be sure to skip a number on your answer sheet as well. Check often to be sure that you have not lost your place and that you are marking in the row numbered the same as the question you are answering.

6) Read the questions

Be sure you know what the question asks! Many capable people are unsuccessful because they failed to *read* the questions correctly.

7) Answer all questions

Unless you have been instructed that a penalty will be deducted for incorrect answers, it is better to guess than to omit a question.

8) Speed tests

It is often better NOT to guess on speed tests. It has been found that on timed tests people are tempted to spend the last few seconds before time is called in marking answers at random – without even reading them – in the hope of picking up a few extra points. To discourage this practice, the instructions may warn you that your score will be "corrected" for guessing. That is, a penalty will be applied. The incorrect answers will be deducted from the correct ones, or some other penalty formula will be used.

9) Review your answers

If you finish before time is called, go back to the questions you guessed or omitted to give them further thought. Review other answers if you have time.

10) Return your test materials

If you are ready to leave before others have finished or time is called, take ALL your materials to the monitor and leave quietly. Never take any test material with you. The monitor can discover whose papers are not complete, and taking a test booklet may be grounds for disqualification.

VIII. EXAMINATION TECHNIQUES

1) Read the general instructions carefully. These are usually printed on the first page of the exam booklet. As a rule, these instructions refer to the timing of the examination; the fact that you should not start work until the signal and must stop work at a signal, etc. If there are any *special* instructions, such as a choice of questions to be answered, make sure that you note this instruction carefully.

2) When you are ready to start work on the examination, that is as soon as the signal has been given, read the instructions to each question booklet, underline any key words or phrases, such as *least, best, outline, describe* and the like. In this way you will tend to answer as requested rather than discover on reviewing your paper that you *listed without describing*, that you selected the *worst* choice rather than the *best* choice, etc.

3) If the examination is of the objective or multiple-choice type – that is, each question will also give a series of possible answers: A, B, C or D, and you are called upon to select the best answer and write the letter next to that answer on your answer paper – it is advisable to start answering each question in turn. There may be anywhere from 50 to 100 such questions in the three or four hours allotted and you can see how much time would be taken if you read through all the questions before beginning to answer any. Furthermore, if you come across a question or group of questions which you know would be difficult to answer, it would undoubtedly affect your handling of all the other questions.

4) If the examination is of the essay type and contains but a few questions, it is a moot point as to whether you should read all the questions before starting to answer any one. Of course, if you are given a choice – say five out of seven and the like – then it is essential to read all the questions so you can eliminate the two that are most difficult. If, however, you are asked to answer all the questions, there may be danger in trying to answer the easiest one first because you may find that you will spend too much time on it. The best technique is to answer the first question, then proceed to the second, etc.

5) Time your answers. Before the exam begins, write down the time it started, then add the time allowed for the examination and write down the time it must be completed, then divide the time available somewhat as follows:
   - If 3-1/2 hours are allowed, that would be 210 minutes. If you have 80 objective-type questions, that would be an average of 2-1/2 minutes per question. Allow yourself no more than 2 minutes per question, or a total of 160 minutes, which will permit about 50 minutes to review.
   - If for the time allotment of 210 minutes there are 7 essay questions to answer, that would average about 30 minutes a question. Give yourself only 25 minutes per question so that you have about 35 minutes to review.

6) The most important instruction is to *read each question* and make sure you know what is wanted. The second most important instruction is to *time yourself properly* so that you answer every question. The third most important instruction is to *answer every question*. Guess if you have to but include something for each question. Remember that you will receive no credit for a blank and will probably receive some credit if you write something in answer to an essay question. If you guess a letter – say "B" for a multiple-choice question – you may have guessed right. If you leave a blank as an answer to a multiple-choice question, the examiners may respect your feelings but it will not add a point to your score. Some exams may penalize you for wrong answers, so in such cases *only*, you may not want to guess unless you have some basis for your answer.

7) Suggestions
   a. Objective-type questions
      1. Examine the question booklet for proper sequence of pages and questions
      2. Read all instructions carefully
      3. Skip any question which seems too difficult; return to it after all other questions have been answered
      4. Apportion your time properly; do not spend too much time on any single question or group of questions

5. Note and underline key words – *all, most, fewest, least, best, worst, same, opposite,* etc.
6. Pay particular attention to negatives
7. Note unusual option, e.g., unduly long, short, complex, different or similar in content to the body of the question
8. Observe the use of "hedging" words – *probably, may, most likely,* etc.
9. Make sure that your answer is put next to the same number as the question
10. Do not second-guess unless you have good reason to believe the second answer is definitely more correct
11. Cross out original answer if you decide another answer is more accurate; do not erase until you are ready to hand your paper in
12. Answer all questions; guess unless instructed otherwise
13. Leave time for review

   b. Essay questions
   1. Read each question carefully
   2. Determine exactly what is wanted. Underline key words or phrases.
   3. Decide on outline or paragraph answer
   4. Include many different points and elements unless asked to develop any one or two points or elements
   5. Show impartiality by giving pros and cons unless directed to select one side only
   6. Make and write down any assumptions you find necessary to answer the questions
   7. Watch your English, grammar, punctuation and choice of words
   8. Time your answers; don't crowd material

8) Answering the essay question

Most essay questions can be answered by framing the specific response around several key words or ideas. Here are a few such key words or ideas:

M's: manpower, materials, methods, money, management
P's: purpose, program, policy, plan, procedure, practice, problems, pitfalls, personnel, public relations

   a. Six basic steps in handling problems:
   1. Preliminary plan and background development
   2. Collect information, data and facts
   3. Analyze and interpret information, data and facts
   4. Analyze and develop solutions as well as make recommendations
   5. Prepare report and sell recommendations
   6. Install recommendations and follow up effectiveness

   b. Pitfalls to avoid
   1. *Taking things for granted* – A statement of the situation does not necessarily imply that each of the elements is necessarily true; for example, a complaint may be invalid and biased so that all that can be taken for granted is that a complaint has been registered

2. *Considering only one side of a situation* – Wherever possible, indicate several alternatives and then point out the reasons you selected the best one
3. *Failing to indicate follow up* – Whenever your answer indicates action on your part, make certain that you will take proper follow-up action to see how successful your recommendations, procedures or actions turn out to be
4. *Taking too long in answering any single question* – Remember to time your answers properly

IX. AFTER THE TEST

Scoring procedures differ in detail among civil service jurisdictions although the general principles are the same. Whether the papers are hand-scored or graded by machine we have described, they are nearly always graded by number. That is, the person who marks the paper knows only the number – never the name – of the applicant. Not until all the papers have been graded will they be matched with names. If other tests, such as training and experience or oral interview ratings have been given, scores will be combined. Different parts of the examination usually have different weights. For example, the written test might count 60 percent of the final grade, and a rating of training and experience 40 percent. In many jurisdictions, veterans will have a certain number of points added to their grades.

After the final grade has been determined, the names are placed in grade order and an eligible list is established. There are various methods for resolving ties between those who get the same final grade – probably the most common is to place first the name of the person whose application was received first. Job offers are made from the eligible list in the order the names appear on it. You will be notified of your grade and your rank as soon as all these computations have been made. This will be done as rapidly as possible.

People who are found to meet the requirements in the announcement are called "eligibles." Their names are put on a list of eligible candidates. An eligible's chances of getting a job depend on how high he stands on this list and how fast agencies are filling jobs from the list.

When a job is to be filled from a list of eligibles, the agency asks for the names of people on the list of eligibles for that job. When the civil service commission receives this request, it sends to the agency the names of the three people highest on this list. Or, if the job to be filled has specialized requirements, the office sends the agency the names of the top three persons who meet these requirements from the general list.

The appointing officer makes a choice from among the three people whose names were sent to him. If the selected person accepts the appointment, the names of the others are put back on the list to be considered for future openings.

That is the rule in hiring from all kinds of eligible lists, whether they are for typist, carpenter, chemist, or something else. For every vacancy, the appointing officer has his choice of any one of the top three eligibles on the list. This explains why the person whose name is on top of the list sometimes does not get an appointment when some of the persons lower on the list do. If the appointing officer chooses the second or third eligible, the No. 1 eligible does not get a job at once, but stays on the list until he is appointed or the list is terminated.

X. HOW TO PASS THE INTERVIEW TEST

The examination for which you applied requires an oral interview test. You have already taken the written test and you are now being called for the interview test – the final part of the formal examination.

You may think that it is not possible to prepare for an interview test and that there are no procedures to follow during an interview. Our purpose is to point out some things you can do in advance that will help you and some good rules to follow and pitfalls to avoid while you are being interviewed.

What is an interview supposed to test?

The written examination is designed to test the technical knowledge and competence of the candidate; the oral is designed to evaluate intangible qualities, not readily measured otherwise, and to establish a list showing the relative fitness of each candidate – as measured against his competitors – for the position sought. Scoring is not on the basis of "right" and "wrong," but on a sliding scale of values ranging from "not passable" to "outstanding." As a matter of fact, it is possible to achieve a relatively low score without a single "incorrect" answer because of evident weakness in the qualities being measured.

Occasionally, an examination may consist entirely of an oral test – either an individual or a group oral. In such cases, information is sought concerning the technical knowledges and abilities of the candidate, since there has been no written examination for this purpose. More commonly, however, an oral test is used to supplement a written examination.

Who conducts interviews?

The composition of oral boards varies among different jurisdictions. In nearly all, a representative of the personnel department serves as chairman. One of the members of the board may be a representative of the department in which the candidate would work. In some cases, "outside experts" are used, and, frequently, a businessman or some other representative of the general public is asked to serve. Labor and management or other special groups may be represented. The aim is to secure the services of experts in the appropriate field.

However the board is composed, it is a good idea (and not at all improper or unethical) to ascertain in advance of the interview who the members are and what groups they represent. When you are introduced to them, you will have some idea of their backgrounds and interests, and at least you will not stutter and stammer over their names.

What should be done before the interview?

While knowledge about the board members is useful and takes some of the surprise element out of the interview, there is other preparation which is more substantive. It *is* possible to prepare for an oral interview – in several ways:

1) Keep a copy of your application and review it carefully before the interview

This may be the only document before the oral board, and the starting point of the interview. Know what education and experience you have listed there, and the sequence and dates of all of it. Sometimes the board will ask you to review the highlights of your experience for them; you should not have to hem and haw doing it.

2) Study the class specification and the examination announcement

Usually, the oral board has one or both of these to guide them. The qualities, characteristics or knowledges required by the position sought are stated in these documents. They offer valuable clues as to the nature of the oral interview. For example, if the job involves supervisory responsibilities, the announcement will usually indicate that knowledge of modern supervisory methods and the qualifications of the candidate as a supervisor will be tested. If so, you can expect such questions, frequently in the form of a hypothetical situation which you are expected to solve. NEVER go into an oral without knowledge of the duties and responsibilities of the job you seek.

3) Think through each qualification required

Try to visualize the kind of questions you would ask if you were a board member. How well could you answer them? Try especially to appraise your own knowledge and background in each area, *measured against the job sought*, and identify any areas in which you are weak. Be critical and realistic – do not flatter yourself.

4) Do some general reading in areas in which you feel you may be weak

For example, if the job involves supervision and your past experience has NOT, some general reading in supervisory methods and practices, particularly in the field of human relations, might be useful. Do NOT study agency procedures or detailed manuals. The oral board will be testing your understanding and capacity, not your memory.

5) Get a good night's sleep and watch your general health and mental attitude

You will want a clear head at the interview. Take care of a cold or any other minor ailment, and of course, no hangovers.

What should be done on the day of the interview?

Now comes the day of the interview itself. Give yourself plenty of time to get there. Plan to arrive somewhat ahead of the scheduled time, particularly if your appointment is in the fore part of the day. If a previous candidate fails to appear, the board might be ready for you a bit early. By early afternoon an oral board is almost invariably behind schedule if there are many candidates, and you may have to wait. Take along a book or magazine to read, or your application to review, but leave any extraneous material in the waiting room when you go in for your interview. In any event, relax and compose yourself.

The matter of dress is important. The board is forming impressions about you – from your experience, your manners, your attitude, and your appearance. Give your personal appearance careful attention. Dress your best, but not your flashiest. Choose conservative, appropriate clothing, and be sure it is immaculate. This is a business interview, and your appearance should indicate that you regard it as such. Besides, being well groomed and properly dressed will help boost your confidence.

Sooner or later, someone will call your name and escort you into the interview room. *This is it.* From here on you are on your own. It is too late for any more preparation. But remember, you asked for this opportunity to prove your fitness, and you are here because your request was granted.

What happens when you go in?

The usual sequence of events will be as follows: The clerk (who is often the board stenographer) will introduce you to the chairman of the oral board, who will introduce you to the other members of the board. Acknowledge the introductions before you sit down. Do not be surprised if you find a microphone facing you or a stenotypist sitting by. Oral interviews are usually recorded in the event of an appeal or other review.

Usually the chairman of the board will open the interview by reviewing the highlights of your education and work experience from your application – primarily for the benefit of the other members of the board, as well as to get the material into the record. Do not interrupt or comment unless there is an error or significant misinterpretation; if that is the case, do not hesitate. But do not quibble about insignificant matters. Also, he will usually ask you some question about your education, experience or your present job – partly to get you to start talking and to establish the interviewing "rapport." He may start the actual questioning, or turn it over to one of the other members. Frequently, each member undertakes the questioning on a particular area, one in which he is perhaps most competent, so you can expect each member to participate in the examination. Because time is limited, you may also expect some rather abrupt switches in the direction the questioning takes, so do not be upset by it. Normally, a board member will not pursue a single line of questioning unless he discovers a particular strength or weakness.

After each member has participated, the chairman will usually ask whether any member has any further questions, then will ask you if you have anything you wish to add. Unless you are expecting this question, it may floor you. Worse, it may start you off on an extended, extemporaneous speech. The board is not usually seeking more information. The question is principally to offer you a last opportunity to present further qualifications or to indicate that you have nothing to add. So, if you feel that a significant qualification or characteristic has been overlooked, it is proper to point it out in a sentence or so. Do not compliment the board on the thoroughness of their examination – they have been sketchy, and you know it. If you wish, merely say, "No thank you, I have nothing further to add." This is a point where you can "talk yourself out" of a good impression or fail to present an important bit of information. Remember, *you close the interview yourself.*

The chairman will then say, "That is all, Mr. _____, thank you." Do not be startled; the interview is over, and quicker than you think. Thank him, gather your belongings and take your leave. Save your sigh of relief for the other side of the door.

How to put your best foot forward

Throughout this entire process, you may feel that the board individually and collectively is trying to pierce your defenses, seek out your hidden weaknesses and embarrass and confuse you. Actually, this is not true. They are obliged to make an appraisal of your qualifications for the job you are seeking, and they want to see you in your best light. Remember, they must interview all candidates and a non-cooperative candidate may become a failure in spite of their best efforts to bring out his qualifications. Here are 15 suggestions that will help you:

1) Be natural – Keep your attitude confident, not cocky

If you are not confident that you can do the job, do not expect the board to be. Do not apologize for your weaknesses, try to bring out your strong points. The board is interested in a positive, not negative, presentation. Cockiness will antagonize any board member and make him wonder if you are covering up a weakness by a false show of strength.

2) Get comfortable, but don't lounge or sprawl

Sit erectly but not stiffly. A careless posture may lead the board to conclude that you are careless in other things, or at least that you are not impressed by the importance of the occasion. Either conclusion is natural, even if incorrect. Do not fuss with your clothing, a pencil or an ashtray. Your hands may occasionally be useful to emphasize a point; do not let them become a point of distraction.

3) Do not wisecrack or make small talk

This is a serious situation, and your attitude should show that you consider it as such. Further, the time of the board is limited – they do not want to waste it, and neither should you.

4) Do not exaggerate your experience or abilities

In the first place, from information in the application or other interviews and sources, the board may know more about you than you think. Secondly, you probably will not get away with it. An experienced board is rather adept at spotting such a situation, so do not take the chance.

5) If you know a board member, do not make a point of it, yet do not hide it

Certainly you are not fooling him, and probably not the other members of the board. Do not try to take advantage of your acquaintanceship – it will probably do you little good.

6) Do not dominate the interview

Let the board do that. They will give you the clues – do not assume that you have to do all the talking. Realize that the board has a number of questions to ask you, and do not try to take up all the interview time by showing off your extensive knowledge of the answer to the first one.

7) Be attentive

You only have 20 minutes or so, and you should keep your attention at its sharpest throughout. When a member is addressing a problem or question to you, give him your undivided attention. Address your reply principally to him, but do not exclude the other board members.

8) Do not interrupt

A board member may be stating a problem for you to analyze. He will ask you a question when the time comes. Let him state the problem, and wait for the question.

9) Make sure you understand the question

Do not try to answer until you are sure what the question is. If it is not clear, restate it in your own words or ask the board member to clarify it for you. However, do not haggle about minor elements.

10) Reply promptly but not hastily

A common entry on oral board rating sheets is "candidate responded readily," or "candidate hesitated in replies." Respond as promptly and quickly as you can, but do not jump to a hasty, ill-considered answer.

11) Do not be peremptory in your answers

A brief answer is proper – but do not fire your answer back. That is a losing game from your point of view. The board member can probably ask questions much faster than you can answer them.

12) Do not try to create the answer you think the board member wants

He is interested in what kind of mind you have and how it works – not in playing games. Furthermore, he can usually spot this practice and will actually grade you down on it.

13) Do not switch sides in your reply merely to agree with a board member

Frequently, a member will take a contrary position merely to draw you out and to see if you are willing and able to defend your point of view. Do not start a debate, yet do not surrender a good position. If a position is worth taking, it is worth defending.

14) Do not be afraid to admit an error in judgment if you are shown to be wrong

The board knows that you are forced to reply without any opportunity for careful consideration. Your answer may be demonstrably wrong. If so, admit it and get on with the interview.

15) Do not dwell at length on your present job

The opening question may relate to your present assignment. Answer the question but do not go into an extended discussion. You are being examined for a *new* job, not your present one. As a matter of fact, try to phrase ALL your answers in terms of the job for which you are being examined.

Basis of Rating

Probably you will forget most of these "do's" and "don'ts" when you walk into the oral interview room. Even remembering them all will not ensure you a passing grade. Perhaps you did not have the qualifications in the first place. But remembering them will help you to put your best foot forward, without treading on the toes of the board members.

Rumor and popular opinion to the contrary notwithstanding, an oral board wants you to make the best appearance possible. They know you are under pressure – but they also want to see how you respond to it as a guide to what your reaction would be under the pressures of the job you seek. They will be influenced by the degree of poise you display, the personal traits you show and the manner in which you respond.

ABOUT THIS BOOK

This book contains tests divided into Examination Sections. Go through each test, answering every question in the margin. We have also attached a sample answer sheet at the back of the book that can be removed and used. At the end of each test look at the answer key and check your answers. On the ones you got wrong, look at the right answer choice and learn. Do not fill in the answers first. Do not memorize the questions and answers, but understand the answer and principles involved. On your test, the questions will likely be different from the samples. Questions are changed and new ones added. If you understand these past questions you should have success with any changes that arise. Tests may consist of several types of questions. We have additional books on each subject should more study be advisable or necessary for you. Finally, the more you study, the better prepared you will be. This book is intended to be the last thing you study before you walk into the examination room. Prior study of relevant texts is also recommended. NLC publishes some of these in our Fundamental Series. Knowledge and good sense are important factors in passing your exam. Good luck also helps. So now study this Passbook, absorb the material contained within and take that knowledge into the examination. Then do your best to pass that exam.

EXAMINATION SECTION

EXAMINATION SECTION
TEST 1

DIRECTIONS: Each question or incomplete statement is followed by several suggested answers or completions. Select the one that BEST answers the question or completes the statement. *PRINT THE LETTER OF THE CORRECT ANSWER IN THE SPACE AT THE RIGHT.*

1. Before splicing together the ends of two steel columns, the ends are *usually*   1._____

    A. coped   B. milled   C. broached   D. blocked

2. Of the following heat treatment processes, the one that brings steel to the LOWEST hardness is   2._____

    A. tempering   B. normalizing
    C. annealing   D. nitriding

3. A riveted girder consists of flange angles, flange plates, web, and stiffeners. Of the structural members listed above, the one that would MOST likely be crimped is the   3._____

    A. flange angles   B. flange plates
    C. web   D. stiffeners

4. In the installation of steel studs on the flange of a beam with an automatic-end welder, the ceramic part that is removed from the stud after the completion of the welding process is known as a   4._____

    A. yoke   B. batten   C. collar   D. ferrule

5. Of the following, the machine that should be used to make an angle from a flat plate is the   5._____

    A. shaper   B. turret lathe
    C. brake   D. mandrel press

6. According to the AISC Code, the MINIMUM edge distance permitted for drilled holes in structural steel plate when the edges of the plate are sheared and when 5/8" diameter bolts are to be used is   6._____

    A. 7/8"   B. 1 1/8"   C. 1 1/2"   D. 1 3/4"

7. Of the following welding processes, the one that is presently MOST widely used in the fabrication of structural steel is _____ welding.   7._____

    A. friction   B. braze   C. arc   D. forge

8. The COMMON fabrication practice for structural steel is to make rivet holes _____ the size of the rivet.   8._____

    A. 1/32" smaller than   B. equal to
    C. 1/32" larger than   D. 1/16" larger than

9. The tool that should be used to taper the top of a hole in a steel plate is a   9._____

    A. boring bar   B. reamer
    C. spot facer   D. countersink

10. The type of rivet head MOST often used for structural steel is the _____ head.

    A. truss
    B. flat
    C. button
    D. wagon box

11.

    WELD

    STEEL PLATE

    1¼"

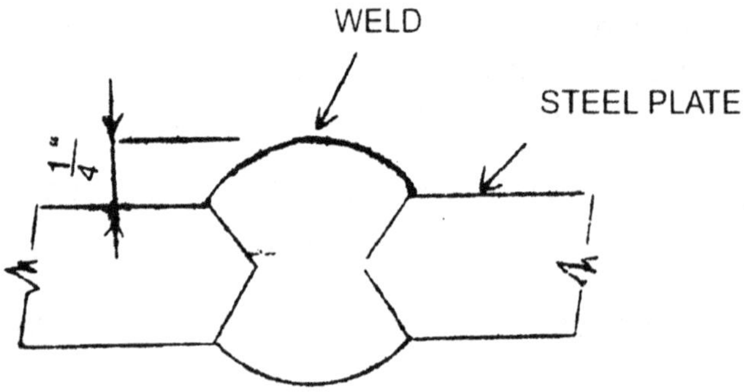

    The sketch shown above is a profile of a type of defective weld. This type of defect is known as

    A. insufficient throat
    B. overlap
    C. excessive convexity
    D. excessive concavity

12. Of the following profiles of welds shown in cross-section, the one that shows an undercut is

    A.    B.    C.    D.

13. Of the following measuring devices, the one that gives the MOST precise measurement of thickness is the

    A. micrometer caliper
    B. machinists steel scale
    C. combination square
    D. protractor

14. Of the following methods, the BEST one to use in order to check the curvature of a curved steel beam is the

    A. chord-offset
    B. radius-offset
    C. tangent-offset
    D. deflection angle-chord

15. A testing machine that measures hardness is the

    A. Riehle
    B. Tinius Olsen
    C. Scott
    D. Brinnel

16. Brittleness of steel is measured by the _____ Test.

    A. Rockwell   B. Charpy   C. Proctor   D. Spark

17. The micrometer reading shown at the right is
    A. .318"
    B. .346"
    C. .377"
    D. .392"

17._____

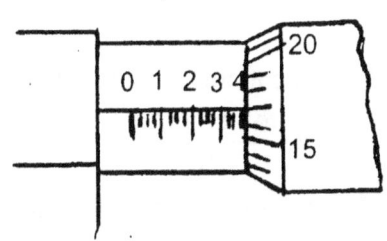

18.

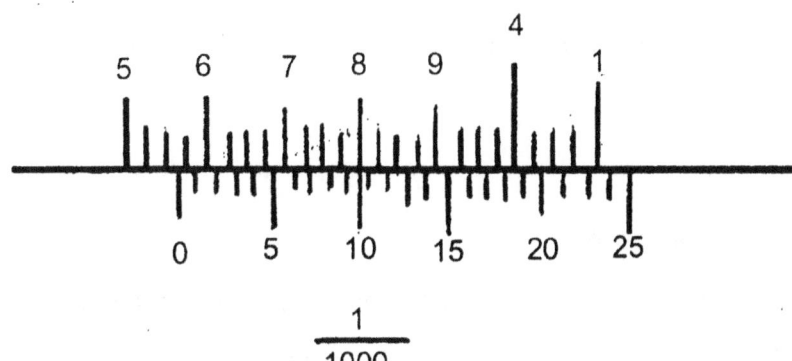

$$\frac{1}{1000}$$

The reading on the height gauge, with vernier shown above, is MOST NEARLY

A. A.3.274 B. 3.560 C. 4.615 D. 4.916

18._____

19.

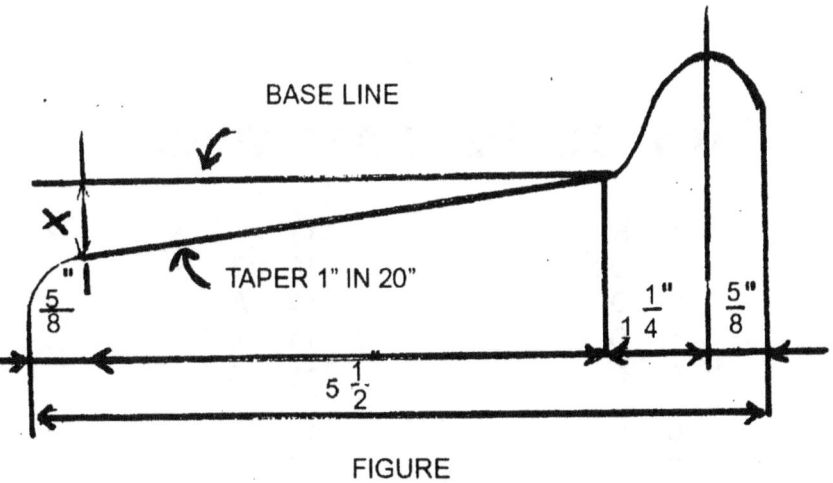

FIGURE

The distance X in the figure shown above is MOST NEARLY

A. 3/32" B. 1/8" C. 5/32" D. 3/16"

19._____

20. Of the following atmospheric conditions, the one under which it is MOST harmful to store welding electrodes is

    A. dampness B. dryness C. heat D. cold

20._____

21. Of the following, the BEST tool to use to check the length of the circumference of the tread of a new railroad car wheel is a

    A. trammel   B. tape
    C. back-to-back gage   D. protractor

21._____

22. Specifications state that the tolerance for camber of a steel beam is equal to

    $1/8" \times \dfrac{\text{total length}}{5}$

    The tolerance for camber for a beam 30 feet long is

    A. 1/2"   B. 5/8"   C. 3/4"   D. 7/8"

23. The MAIN reason for making a ladle analysis of steel is to determine the _____ of the steel.

    A. chemical composition
    B. corrosion rate
    C. fatigue limit
    D. expansion and contraction

24. The machine that is NOT used in the physical testing of steel products is the

    A. Tinnius Olsen   B. Riehle
    C. Brinnel   D. Scott

25. An electrode has a designation of E7018. The digit that designates the position or positions it is suitable for is the

    A. 7   B. 0   C. 1   D. 8

KEY (CORRECT ANSWERS)

1.	B	11.	C
2.	C	12.	B
3.	D	13.	A
4.	D	14.	A
5.	C	15.	D
6.	B	16.	B
7.	C	17.	D
8.	D	18.	B
9.	D	19.	C
10.	C	20.	A

21. B
22. C
23. A
24. D
25. C

TEST 2

DIRECTIONS: Each question or incomplete statement is followed by several suggested answers or completions. Select the one that BEST answers the question or completes the statement. *PRINT THE LETTER OF THE CORRECT ANSWER IN THE SPACE AT THE RIGHT.*

1. A test that is NON-DESTRUCTIVE is the _____ test. 1._____
   A. ultrasonic
   B. tensile
   C. charpy
   D. strip

2. The symbol shown below that represents the cross-section of steel is 2._____

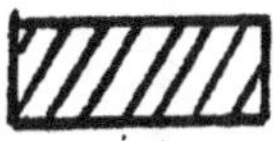

3. The turn-of-nut method is to be used to tighten A325 bolts. The outer faces of the bolted parts are parallel to each other and perpendicular to the bolt axis (bevel washers not used). The additional required nut rotation from the *snug tight* condition is a _____ turn. 3._____
   A. 1/4   B. 1/2   C. 3/4   D. full

4. In the tensile testing of bolts, which of the following strength measurements are recorded? 4._____
   A. Yield point and ultimate strength
   B. Elastic limit and ultimate strength
   C. Yield point and fracture strength
   D. Elastic limit and fracture strength

5. In a guided bend test for weld ductility, the weld specimen is bent through an angle of 5._____
   A. 45°   B. 90°   C. 135°   D. 180°

6. The type of butt weld shown above is a double 6._____
   A. bevel   B. J   C. U   D. V

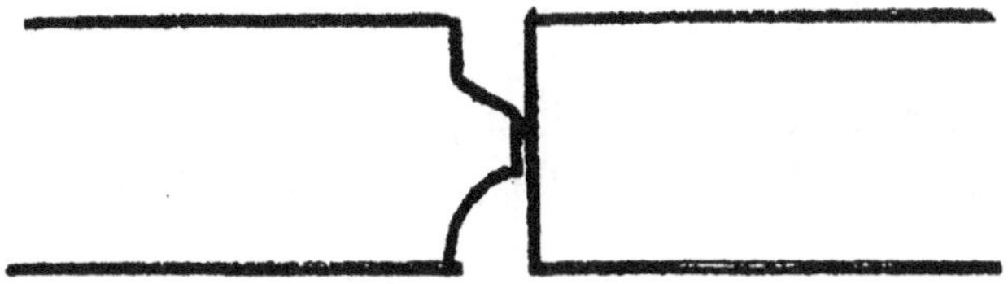

7. The conventional sign that represents a countersunk and chipped shop rivet is 7._____

8. The structural shape represented by the designation C15 x 40 is 8._____

9. Galvanizing of steel, when specified for grating, means coating the steel with   9.___

   A. lead   B. titanium   C. zinc   D. tin

10. The shop coat of paint MOST often specified for structural steel is   10.___

    A. vermiculite   B. red lead
    C. vinyl resin   D. latex

11. A contract states that the material in steel piles and splices shall conform to structural   11.___
    steel specification ASTM A36. The 36 in the specification refers to the _____ steel.

    A. thickness of the
    B. minimum length of rolled section of
    C. weight per foot of the
    D. yield point of the

12. A rectangular bar, 1 3/4" thick, must have a minimum area of .36 square inches. Of the   12.___
    following, the MINIMUM acceptable width of the bar is

    A. 3/32"   B. 5/32"   C. 7/32"   D. 9/32"

13. The rounded interior corners of structural steel shapes are called   13.___

    A. fillets   B. kerfs   C. dogs   D. chamfers

14. A structural steel member having a designation of 18H5 is a   14.___

    A. girt   B. purlin   C. joist   D. lintel

15. A hexagonal steel gusset plate is shown on a shop drawing with six equally spaced holes   15.___
    on the circumference of a 9-inch diameter circle. The distance between the centers of the
    adjacent holes is

    A. 4"   B. 4 1/4"   C. 4 1/2"   D. 4 3/4"

16. Shown at the right is a sketch of the top of a bolt.   16.___
    The marking A490 on the head of the bolt is the _____ number of the
    bolt.
    A. heat
    B. shipment
    C. hardness
    D. specification

Questions 17-19.

   DIRECTIONS: The drawing shown below refers to Questions 17 through 19. These questions
                should be answered in accordance with this drawing.

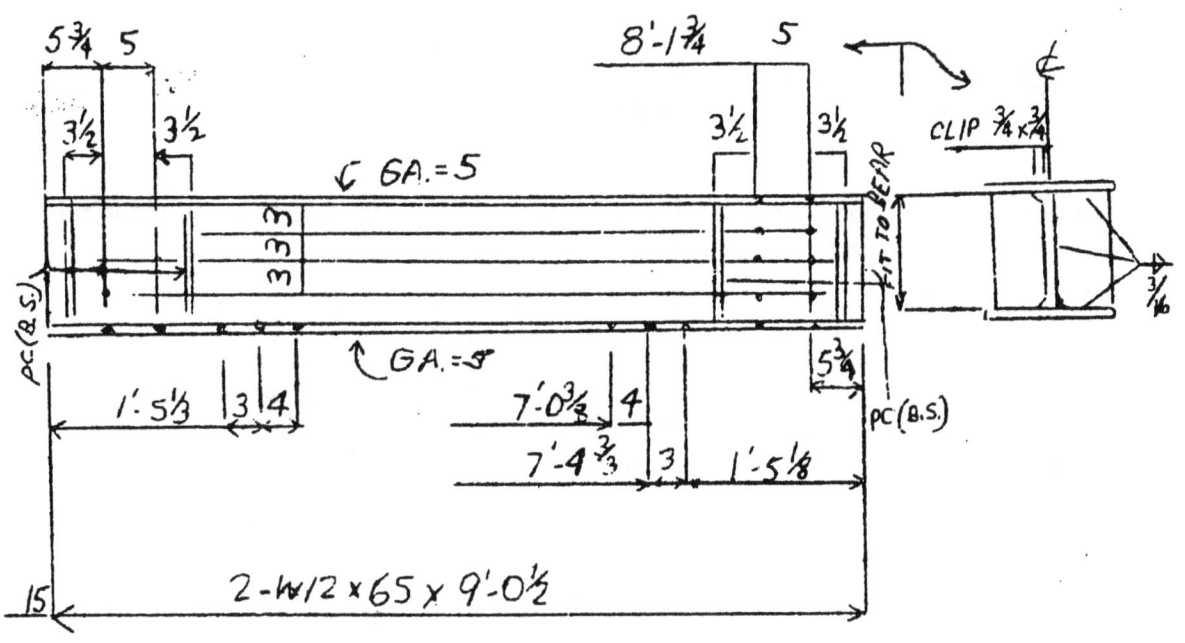

17. The welding symbol shown on the above diagram designates a _____ weld. 17._____

    A. spot   B. plug   C. butt   D. fillet

18. The abbreviation GA. appearing on the drawing means 18._____

    A. gage   B. galvanize   C. gap   D. gam

19. In the designation pc(B.S.) appearing on the shop drawing, the B.S. means 19._____

    A. billet steel   B. bearing steel
    C. both sides   D. beam stiffener

20. A specification states that in the shop assembly of structural steel, the parts of riveted structural members shall be well pinned and firmly drawn together with bolts before riveting is commenced. The pins used for aligning and holding the fabricated steel in place before bolting are known as _____ pins. 20._____

    A. linch   B. drift   C. clevis   D. finnegan

21. Of the following items relating to a written weekly report on the status of a fabrication contract, the MOST important item is that the report should be 21._____

    A. brief   B. accurate
    C. subjective   D. creative

22. Of the following, in preparing a monthly report of the work inspected in a steel fabrication shop, the BEST source of data is 22._____

    A. the contract CPM diagram   B. the fabricator's log book
    C. the shop drawings   D. his diary

23. Of the following items, the one that is LEAST important in qualifying a steel fabricator is the number of

    A. strikes suffered by the company in the last five years
    B. paid holidays given employees
    C. years the firm has been in existence
    D. miles the plant is from the nearest railroad

24. In writing a shop accident report, it is generally BEST to make each sentence in the report _____ and with _____ idea(s).

    A. long; one
    B. long; many
    C. short; one
    D. short; many

25. A specification states that gratings which show black or uncoated spots, *dross,* improper or insufficient galvanizing or any other defects shall be rejected.
    In the above specification, *dross* means

    A. dirt   B. gloss   C. flat   D. clear

KEY (CORRECT ANSWERS)

1. A		11. D
2. B		12. C
3. C		13. A
4. A		14. C
5. D		15. C
6. B		16. D
7. D		17. D
8. D		18. A
9. C		19. C
10. B		20. B

21. B
22. D
23. B
24. C
25. A

EXAMINATION SECTION
TEST 1

DIRECTIONS: Each question or incomplete statement is followed by several suggested answers or completions. Select the one that BEST answers the question or completes the statement. *PRINT THE LETTER OF THE CORRECT ANSWER IN THE SPACE AT THE RIGHT.*

1. The material that is MOST often made from gypsum is

   A. lime
   C. grout
   B. mortar
   D. plaster of paris

2. Of the following types of utility pipes, the one for which the slope of the line is USUALLY most important is a ___ line.

   A. sewer   B. gas   C. water   D. steam

3. Piles, as related to building construction, are located *most likely* in the

   A. foundation
   C. structural frame
   B. roof
   D. wall

4. The scale of a drawing is 1/8" = 1'0". A rectangle on the drawing actually measures 7 1/8" x 6 1/4".
   This represents the true area, in square feet, of *most nearly*

   A. 72   B. 144   C. 1375   D. 2850

5. The architectural symbol for brick as it would appear in section is USUALLY

   A.   B.   C.   D.

6.

   The length of AB is, in feet, *most nearly*

   A. 130   B. 135   C. 140   D. 145

7. An inspector estimated that a paving job would require 30 cubic yards of concrete. The volume of the concrete actually used was 27.5 cubic yards.
   The percentage of error in the inspector's estimate is *most nearly*

   A. 4 1/2   B. 9   C. .08   D. .09

8. The frame and cover of a sewer manhole is USUALLY made of

   A. stainless steel
   C. Monel metal
   B. cast iron
   D. structural steel

9. Sleeves are used around anchor bolts that bolt steel columns to footings PRIMARILY to
   A. allow for minor lateral adjustments of anchor bolts
   B. provide better bearing of base plate on the footing
   C. provide greater bond between anchor bolt and footing
   D. allow the proper setting of the column as to elevation

10. The weld MOST commonly used to permanently connect the end of a structural steel angle to a plate as shown above is a _____ weld.
    A. tack   B. fillet   C. butt   D. plug

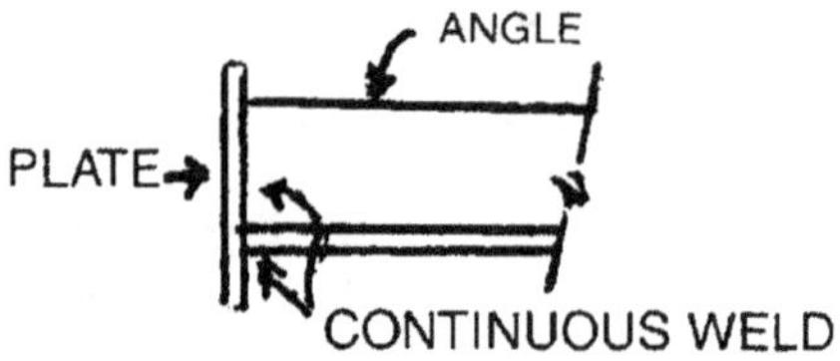

11. Cement is composed PRIMARILY of the following materials heated to fusion:
    A. Gypsum and sand
    B. Gypsum and limestone
    C. Clay and limestone
    D. Sand and clay

12. The capacity of storage batteries or its useful life is USUALLY expressed in
    A. amperes
    B. watts
    C. watt-hours
    D. ampere-hours

13. A transistor depends for its functioning on the flow of electrons through a
    A. gas   B. vapor   C. solid   D. vacuum

14. A bi-metallic element is made up by riveting a brass and iron strip together. When subjected to high temperature, the element will
    A. vibrate
    B. bend
    C. remain the same length
    D. shorten

15. Expansion bolts would *most likely* be used to attach electric equipment to walls made of
    A. concrete   B. hollow-tile   C. wood   D. steel

16. Of the following prefixes commonly used with electrical units, the one which would indicate one-millionth of a unit is
    A. mega   B. kilo   C. micro   D. milli

17. The voltage in volts, across the 2.4 ohms resistance in the circuit shown above is *most nearly* equal to
    A. 32   B. 48   C. 60   D. 72

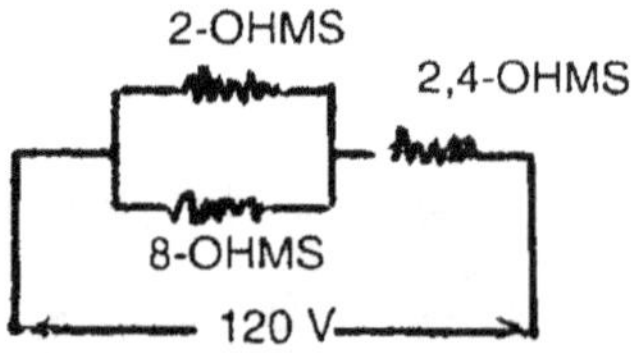

18. The term *bell and spigot in* plumbing refers to

    A. soil pipes
    B. faucets
    C. hot water risers
    D. overflow alarm

19. The drafting symbol —⋈— on a line piping diagram USUALLY indicates a _____ valve.

    A. ball B. globe C. check D. gate

20. The babbit metals are used

    A. for dies and cutting tools
    B. for high speed shafts
    C. in the manufacture of gears
    D. as bearing metals

21. The safety device that can be used instead of a fuse to protect a piece of electrical equipment in case of overload is a

    A. toggle switch
    B. circuit shunt
    C. circuit rheostat
    D. circuit breaker

22. A device that is used to convert mechanical energy into electrical energy is USUALLY called a

    A. battery
    B. generator
    C. motor
    D. transformer

23. A pitot tube is used for measuring water

    A. density
    B. velocity
    C. temperature
    D. volatility

24. $\sqrt[x]{a^y}$ is equal to

    A. $a^{\frac{y}{x}}$ B. a^{x+y} C. $a^{\frac{y}{x}}$ D. a^{y-x}

25. Of the following, an approved means of obtaining the area of an irregular figure is by means of a

    A. slide caliper
    B. micrometer
    C. planimeter
    D. pantograph

KEY (CORRECT ANSWERS)

1. D
2. A
3. A
4. D
5. B

6. B
7. B
8. B
9. A
10. B

11. C
12. D
13. C
14. B
15. A

16. C
17. D
18. A
19. C
20. D

21. D
22. B
23. B
24. C
25. C

———

TEST 2

DIRECTIONS: Each question or incomplete statement is followed by several suggested answers or completions. Select the one that BEST answers the question or completes the statement. *PRINT THE LETTER OF THE CORRECT ANSWER IN THE SPACE AT THE RIGHT.*

1. Of the following, the BEST reason for using vibrators in concrete construction is to

   A. increase the slump of the concrete
   B. remove excess water
   C. retard the setting of the concrete
   D. consolidate the concrete

2. Specifications state that column dowels are embedded 24 diameters in the footing. The length of embedment for a number 8 bar in the footing is, in inches, *most nearly*

   A. 6   B. 12   C. 18   D. 24

3. A *tremie* is USUALLY used to

   A. weigh large quantities of sand
   B. support precast girders
   C. deposit concrete under water
   D. measure ground elevation very accurately

4. Of the following woods, the one that is the HARDEST is

   A. Hickory   B. Douglas Fir
   C. Southern Pine   D. Sitka Spruce

5. The total weight of a 10 WF 45 beam 8 feet long is, in pounds, *most nearly*

   A. 45   B. 80   C. 360   D. 450

6. The thickness 17 gage steel can be BEST checked with a

   A. finely divided steel scale
   B. depth gage
   C. hermaphrodite caliper
   D. micrometer

7. A specification for mixing concrete states *the minimum time of mixing concrete shall be one minute per cubic yard after all material, including the water, has been placed in the drum and the drum shall be reversed for an additional two minutes.*
   According to the above statement, the MINIMUM time for mixing a 3 cubic yard batch of concrete is *most nearly* _____ minutes.

   A. 3   B. 5   C. 8   D. 9

8. Of the following species of lumber, the one *most likely* used for wood formwork for concrete is

   A. birch   B. pine   C. oak   D. maple

9. Of the following, the one that is NOT a lightweight aggregate is

   A. hematite
   B. perlite
   C. expanded shale
   D. pumice

10. Of the following, the MOST important factor that an individual must fulfill in order to insure his own safety on a construction job is to

    A. work slowly
    B. be familiar with the specifications
    C. wear clothing to suit climatic conditions
    D. be alert

11. A wall alongside of a ramp is 7'6" high at one end and 12'0" high at the other end. The length of the wall is 32'0".
    The area of one face of the wall, in square feet, is *most nearly*

    A. 310 B. 311 C. 312 D. 313

12. The equation $x^2 + y^2 = r^2$ is that of a

    A. parabola
    B. ellipse
    C. straight line
    D. circle

13. A round rod with a right-handed thread is to be coupled with another rod of the same diameter but with a left-handed thread.
    Of the following attachments, the one which is MOST appropriate to use is a(n)

    A. turnbuckle
    B. thimble
    C. clevis
    D. eye bolt

14. In the two simultaneous equations
    (3x + y = 17)
    (2x - y = 8),
    the value of *y* is

    A. 1 B. 2 C. 3 D. 4

15. Leaks in gas piping may be BEST located by the use of

    A. cigarette lighter
    B. miner's lamp
    C. heated filament
    D. soapy water solution

16. The value of *x* that will satisfy the equation $x^3 - x^2 - 4 = 0$ is

    A. 3 B. 2 C. 1 D. -1

17. The number of board feet in a board 24 feet long, one foot wide, and 2 inches thick is _____ board feet.

    A. 4 B. 12 C. 24 D. 48

18. The distinguishing characteristic of safety shoes is

    A. their color
    B. their height
    C. the use of spikes on the sole
    D. the use of a steel toe box

19. For a 20 foot ladder, the base should extend back from the face of the wall *approximately*   19.____
    A. 3'   B. 5'   C. 7'   D. 10'

20. π/2 radian is equivalent to, in degrees,   20.____
    A. 22 1/2   B. 45   C. 90   D. 180

21. Of the following conventional cross-hatching, the one that is for brass is   21.____
    A.   B.   C.   D.

22. The $2\sqrt{690}$ is *most nearly*   22.____
    A. 26.25   B. 26.27   C. 26.29   D. 26.30

23. The line $y = 2x + 8$ intersects the *x* axis at   23.____
    A. -4   B. +4   C. -2   D. +8

24. If the radius of the circle shown is 5", the area of the shaded area, in square inches, is *most nearly*   24.____
    A. 6.1   B. 7.1   C. 7.6   D. 8.1

25. A cone has a base whose area is A and its altitude is h. The volume of this cone is   25.____
    A. Ah   B. 1/2 Ah   C. 1/3 Ah   D. 1/4 Ah

KEY (CORRECT ANSWERS)

1. D
2. D
3. C
4. A
5. C

6. D
7. B
8. B
9. A
10. D

11. C
12. D
13. A
14. B
15. D

16. B
17. D
18. D
19. B
20. C

21. A
22. B
23. A
24. B
25. C

———

TEST 3

DIRECTIONS: Each question or incomplete statement is followed by several suggested answers or completions. Select the one that BEST answers the question or completes the statement. *PRINT THE LETTER OF THE CORRECT ANSWER IN THE SPACE AT THE RIGHT.*

1. A street has a grade of 1 1/2%.
   The distance the street rises in 1 1/2 miles is, in feet, *most nearly*

   A. 79.20   B. 98.75   C. 103.50   D. 118.80

2. The elevation of a steel member shown above represents a

   A. tee   B. channel   C. rail   D. zee

3. A circular tank is 12 feet in diameter and 9 feet high. The depth of water in the tank is 1/3 from the top. There are 7 1/2 gallons in a cubic foot.
   The number of gallons of water in the tank is *most nearly*

   A. 4820   B. 5070   C. 5320   D. 5570

4. If log of 2 = 0.3010 and log of 3 = 0.4772, then the log of 36 equals

   A. 0.7782   B. 1.0792   C. 1.2554   D. 1.5564

5. If there are 43,560 square feet in an acre, the number of acres in a tract 2 miles long by 3.2 miles wide is *most nearly*

   A. 3750   B. 4100   C. 4350   D. 4600

6. A foundation for a building consists of 9 concrete footings 8 ft. by 6 ft. by 18 inches deep.
   The total number of cubic yards of concrete in the footings is *most nearly*

   A. 12   B. 24   C. 36   D. 72

7. A drawing showing the longitudinal slope in elevation of a street is known as

   A. perspective   B. plan
   C. profile   D. route

8. On a drawing showing front, rear, and side elevations, and roof plan, the projected views are *most likely*

   A. isogonic   B. orthographic
   C. isographic   D. isometric

9. A note on a drawing reads *#6 bottom bars 6'0" long, 6" o.c.* "The #6 means *most nearly* _____ diameter.

   A. 6/8"   B. 0.6"   C. 6/16"   D. 6/32"

10. The signs of the sine, cosine, and tangent of an angle are all positive in Quadrant

    A. I   B. II   C. III   D. IV

11. The sum of three interior angles of a four-sided parcel of land add up to 115°, The fourth interior angle, in degrees, is *most nearly*

    A. 25   B. 75   C. 245   D. 295

12. Of the following print processes, the one that is LEAST like blue printing is

    A. Van Dyke   B. black and white
    C. Ozalid   D. multilith

13. Railroad curves would *most likely* be used to draw

    A. arcs of large radii
    B. ellipses
    C. circles of small radii
    D. circles of large radii

14. Concrete test cylinders are USUALLY tested in

    A. bending   B. buckling
    C. compression   D. shear

15. The invert of a sewer is the elevation of the _____ surface.

    A. bottom of the inside   B. top of the outside
    C. bottom of the outside   D. top of the inside

16. The symbol ┼┼┼┼┼┼┼┼┼┼┼┼┼ on a topographic map USUALLY represents a(n)

    A. abandoned highway   B. underground stream
    C. single track railroad   D. picket fence

17. Terrazzo would *most likely* be found on a(n)

    A. interior wall   B. exterior wall
    C. ceiling   D. floor

18. Well points are USUALLY used in construction to

    A. provide water for cleaning the area under construction
    B. dewater the area under construction
    C. provide water for the concrete used in construction
    D. provide adequate drinking water where other sources are not available

19. A flexible pavement is a

    A. shoulder of compacted clay
    B. pavement containing an air entraining ingredient
    C. pavement of concrete without reinforcing
    D. pavement of graded granular materials with bitumen

20. Closely spaced contour lines on a topographic map USUALLY indicate a   20.____

    A. small contour interval   B. large contour interval
    C. steep slope   D. mild slope

21. If concrete weighs 150#/cubic foot, then the weight of a 15'0" long, 36" I.D. and 3" wall   21.____
    thickness concrete pipe is *most nearly* (I.D. - inside diameter) _____ lbs.

    A. 5300   B. 5500   C. 5700   D. 6000

22. Of the following mixes, the one that is *most likely* to be used as mortar for brickwork is   22.____
    cement(,)

    A. and water   B. sand and water
    C. lime and water   D. gypsum and water

23. The pattern of brickwork is USUALLY called the   23.____

    A. bond   B. lay   C. coursing   D. register

24. The MOST important precaution to be observed in the storage of cement is to protect the   24.____
    cement against

    A. heat   B. dampness
    C. corrosion   D. decomposition

25. Lead was poured into the joint between two pipes. The material composition of each pipe   25.____
    was *most likely*

    A. cast iron   B. vitrified clay
    C. asbestos cement   D. concrete

KEY (CORRECT ANSWERS)

1. D		11. C	
2. D		12. D	
3. B		13. A	
4. D		14. C	
5. B		15. A	
6. B		16. C	
7. C		17. D	
8. B		18. B	
9. A		19. D	
10. A		20. C	

21. C
22. B
23. A
24. B
25. A

TEST 4

DIRECTIONS: Each question or incomplete statement is followed by several suggested answers or completions. Select the one that BEST answers the question or completes the statement. *PRINT THE LETTER OF THE CORRECT ANSWER IN THE SPACE AT THE RIGHT.*

1. The main danger of having oil on the surface of steel reinforcing bars is PRIMARILY that the

    A. setting time of the concrete will be too great
    B. bond between steel and concrete will be weakened
    C. concrete will be weakened
    D. steel will corrode

2. The Brinell number of a metal is GENERALLY a measure of its

    A. hardness   B. ductility
    C. tensile strength   D. malleability

3. Masonite is a

    A. gypsum product   B. cement product
    C. wood product   D. coal tar derivative

4. A stairway has 9 treads. It NORMALLY would have _____ risers.

    A. 8   B. 9   C. 10   D. 11

5. A beam projecting from a wall is called a _____ beam.

    A. dolly   B. stringer
    C. cantilever   D. lally

6. In a paint mixture, the pigment is added PRIMARILY to supply

    A. hardness   B. color   C. body   D. toughness

7. The chemical formula for sand is

    A. $CaCO_3$ B. CaO C. Al_2O_3 D. SiO_2

8. If steel is galvanized, it is coated with

    A. copper   B. zinc   C. tin   D. lead

9. A hod is MOST often used by a

    A. rigger   B. plumber
    C. carpenter   D. plasterer

10. An engine is delivering 300 horsepower. The equivalent delivery, in kilowatts, is *most nearly* (1 HP = 746 watts)

    A. 175   B. 200   C. 225   D. 250

11. Of the following drafting pencils, the one that has the SOFTEST lead is

    A. 3B   B. HB   C. H   D. F

12. Two applications at 0.4 gallons per square yard of bituminous material on a 1/2 mile of road 18 feet wide would require *most nearly* _____ gallons.

    A. 425   B. 3,875   C. 4,225   D. 38,000

13. Rock excavation is to be paid for at a unit price of $25/cubic yard.
    Of the following, the cost of rock between Sta. 3+35 and Sta. 8+65 for a width of 45 feet and a depth of five feet is *most nearly*

    A. $75,000   B. $110,000   C. $220,000   D. $330,000

14. Three 40 foot long piles are driven so that their top elevations are 79.6', 81.7', and 80.2' before being cut off at elevation 75.5'.
    If the contract unit price is $4.50 per foot in place, then the payment to the contractor is *most nearly*

    A. $405.00   B. $472.50   C. $540.00   D. $600.00

15. To void a contract means *most nearly* to _____ it.

    A. reinstate   B. nullify   C. amend   D. redeem

16. Of the following, the MOST important characteristic of a good inspector on construction work is

    A. punctuality
    B. good penmanship
    C. superior physical strength
    D. keen observation

17. The BEST method of making assignments of technicians would be ordinarily to make them according to the technician's

    A. seniority
    B. desire to do the work
    C. ability to do the work
    D. attitude towards other employees

18. Of the following, the BEST way to correct a mistake made by your subordinate is to

    A. correct the mistake yourself and privately explain correction to subordinate
    B. correct the mistake yourself and say nothing to subordinate
    C. give it to another subordinate to correct
    D. belittle him and then have him correct the mistake

19. If a draftsman cannot possibly complete a drawing on time, then the BEST action for him to take is

    A. work during lunchtime
    B. work overtime
    C. ask an employee to assist you
    D. notify the supervisor

20. Of the following, the BEST thing for a supervisor to do when a subordinate has done a very good job is to

    A. tell him to take it easy
    B. praise his work
    C. reduce his work load
    D. say nothing because he may become conceited

21. Of the following, the method MOST often used to keep a record of progress of construction of a project is a _____ chart.

    A. bar   B. pie   C. polar   D. Venn

22. Of the following, the BEST method of getting an employee who is not working up to his capacity to produce more work is to

    A. have another employee criticize his production
    B. privately criticize his production but encourage him to produce more
    C. criticize his production before his associates
    D. criticize his production and threaten to fire him

23. The ability of an employee to take the first step and follow through on a job is known as

    A. demeanor   B. indolence
    C. initiative   D. individuality

24. Of the following behavior characteristics of a supervisor, the one that is *most likely* to lower the morale of the men he supervises is

    A. diligence   B. favoritism
    C. punctuality   D. thoroughness

25. Of the following, the MOST important item in a good engineering report is

    A. brevity   B. promptness
    C. accuracy   D. good grammar

KEY (CORRECT ANSWERS)

1. B
2. A
3. C
4. C
5. C

6. B
7. D
8. B
9. D
10. C

11. A
12. C
13. B
14. B
15. B

16. D
17. C
18. A
19. D
20. B

21. A
22. B
23. C
24. B
25. C

EXAMINATION SECTION
TEST 1

DIRECTIONS: Each question or incomplete statement is followed by several suggested answers or completions. Select the one that BEST answers the question or completes the statement. *PRINT THE LETTER OF THE CORRECT ANSWER IN THE SPACE AT THE RIGHT.*

1. A bill of materials lists two 15 [34 x 25'6", two 15 [34 x 31'6", and three 12 WF 27 x 31'6". The total weight of the listed steel in pounds is *most nearly*

    A. 5,850 B. 6,020 C. 6,170 D. 6,430

    1.____

2.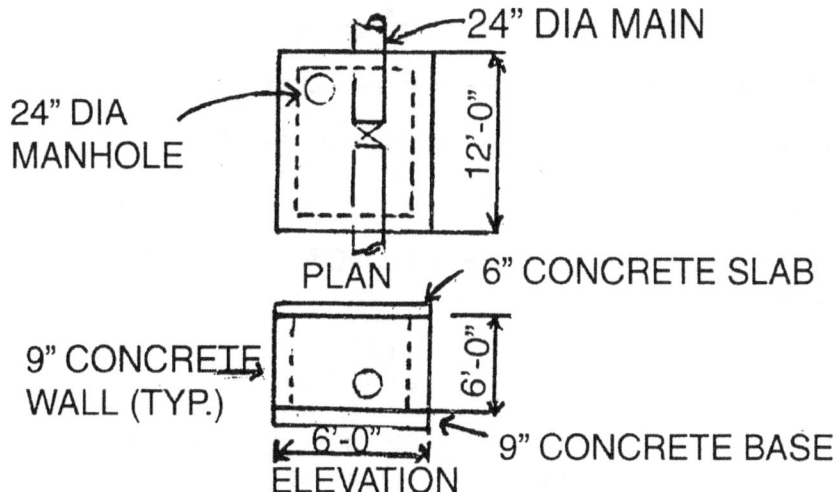

    The number of cubic feet of concrete in the above shown concrete valve chamber is *most nearly*

    A. 200.6 B. 212.4 C. 215.2 D. 232.0

    2.____

3. A flow of 20 million gallons/day is *most nearly* equal to (7.48 gallons = 1 cu. ft.)

    A. 24 c.f.s B. 31 c.f.s. C. 36 c.f.s. D. 42 c.f.s.

    3.____

4.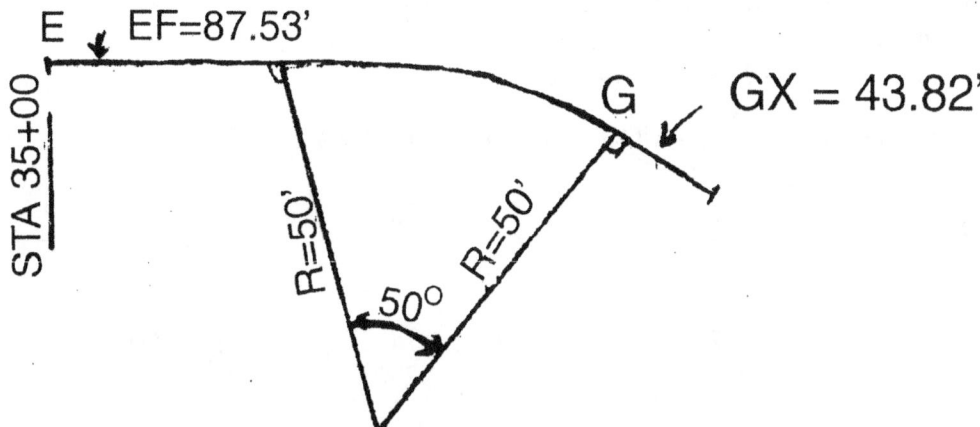

    In the above shown layout for a sidewalk curb (EFGX), the stationing at X in feet would be *most nearly* STA.

    A. 37 + 20 B. 36 + 75 C. 36 + 00 D. 35 + 17

    4.____

5. The number of board feet in 10 pieces of 2" x 8" x 18'6" lumber is *most nearly*

   A. 37   B. 185   C. 247   D. 502

6. The $\sqrt{835}$ is *most nearly* equal to

   A. 28.75   B. 28.80   C. 28.85   D. 28.90

7. 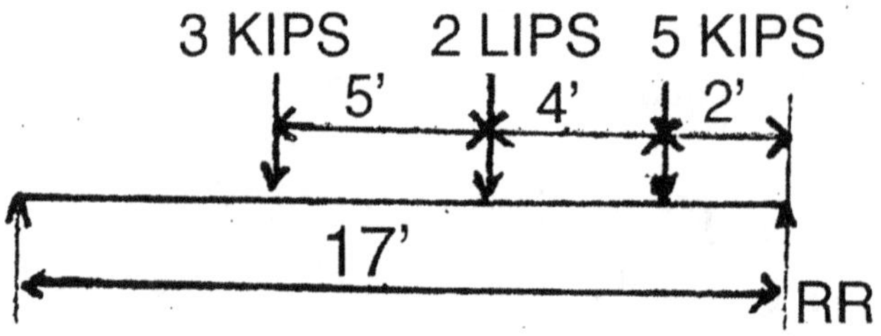
   In the sketch shown above, the reaction R_R is, in Kips, *most nearly*

   A. 6.4   B. 6.8   C. 7.2   D. 7.5

8. Of the following structural steel shapes, the one that is MOST often used as a stringer on a flight of stairs is a(n)

   A. channel
   B. angle
   C. tee
   D. wide flange

9. The hydrostatic pressure in a 24" diameter ductile iron water main is 75 p.s.i. If the thickness of the iron is 1/2", then the tension in the iron due to the hydrostatic pressure, in p.s.i., is *most nearly*

   A. 1,800   B. 2,000   C. 2,200   D. 2,400

10. When no reference is made to a code, standard or specification, the standards of the A.S.T.M. shall govern.
    In the above stated specification, A.S.T.M. means

    A. Accepted Standards of Trade Manufacturers
    B. Applicable Specifications Tentatively Maintained
    C. Automotive Society Technical Manuals
    D. American Society of Testing Materials

11. Of the following valves, the type MOST often used in the water mains of the water distribution system is the _____ valve.

    A. globe   B. gate   C. angle   D. plug

12. The chemical symbol for spelter is

    A. Sn   B. Zn   C. Pb   D. Ag

13.

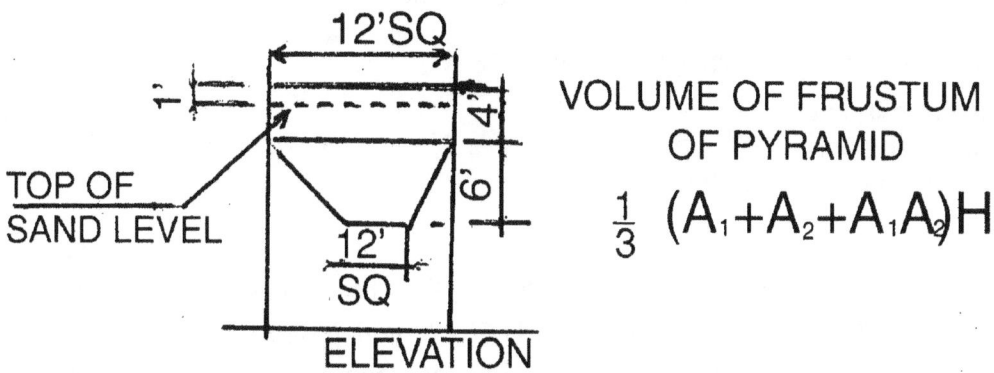

VOLUME OF FRUSTUM OF PYRAMID

$$\frac{1}{3}(A_1+A_2+A_1A_2)H$$

The volume of sand in the hopper shown above in cubic feet is *most nearly*

A. 725 B. 750 C. 775 D. 800

14. The ends of wood fence posts that are to be set into the ground are MOST often treated with

A. creosote B. red lead
C. varnish D. aluminum

15.

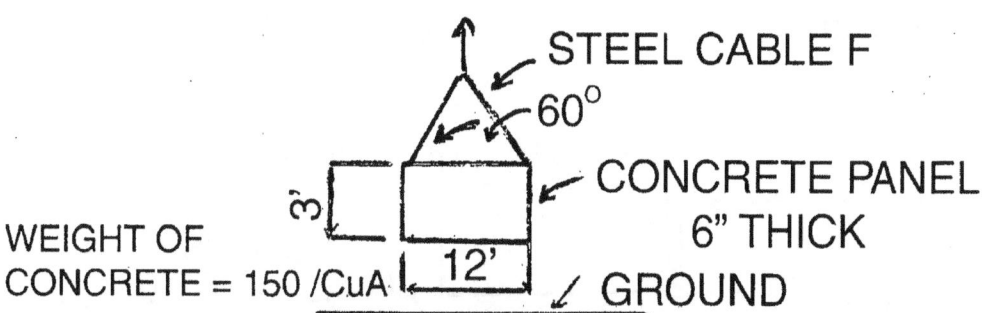

STEEL CABLE F
60°
CONCRETE PANEL 6" THICK
GROUND

WEIGHT OF CONCRETE = 150 /CuA

The tension, in pounds, in the steel cable F in the diagram on the preceding page is *most nearly*

A. 1,350 B. 1,565 C. 1,800 D. 2,400

16. If the allowable load in single shear for an unfinished bolt is 10,000 p.s.i., then the MINIMUM number of 7/8" diameter bolts to resist a shear of 30,000 pounds is *most nearly*

A. 3 B. 4 C. 5 D. 6

17. The chemical formula for soda ash is

A. Na_2CO_3 B. KOH C. Na_2SO_4 D. K_2CO_3

18. The temperature of 45° C is equivalent to (9/5° C + 32 = ° F)

A. -7° F B. 81° F C. 102° F D. 113° F

19. A unit of electric power is the

A. dielectric B. erg C. watt D. angstrom

20. In a 1:1.5:7 mortar mix, the 1.5 represents the proportion of

A. sand B. cement C. lime D. kalite

21. The purpose of a step-up transformer is to raise

    A. the current only
    B. the voltage only
    C. the voltage and lower the current
    D. both the voltage and the current

22. If the latent heat of fusion of ice when it melts at 32° is 144 Btu/pound, then the cooling effect, in Btu, of the melting of 1 ton of ice per day is *most nearly*

    A. 62,000 B. 124,000 C. 288,000 D. 576,000

23. A device that is sensitive to the degree of moisture in the air is a(n)

    A. aquastat   B. rheostat
    C. damperstat   D. hygrostat

24. Of the following types of pipe joints, the one that is MOST often used on sewer pipe lines is

    A. victaulic   B. dresser
    C. bell and spigot   D. flanged

25. In the sketch shown on the preceding page, the fitting F is called a _____ cock.

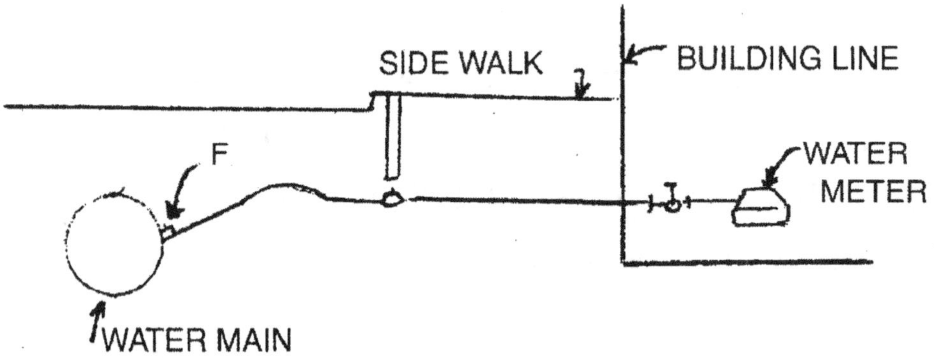

    A. compression   B. key
    C. bibb   D. corporation

26. If a fan delivers 4800 C.F.M. of air, then the velocity, in feet per second, of the air in a 34" x 16" duct is *most nearly*

    A. 21.2 B. 23.4 C. 26.7 D. 28.2

27. Of the following types of pipes of the same diameter, the one that is LEAST corrosion resistant is

    A. copper   B. steel
    C. wrought iron   D. brass

Questions 28-29.

DIRECTIONS: Questions 28 and 29 refer to the following sketch.

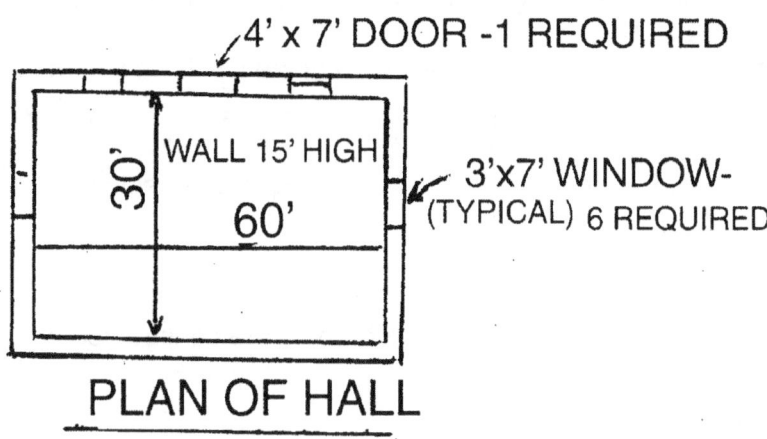

PLAN OF HALL

28. If a gallon of paint covers 350 square feet, then the number of gallons required to paint the interior walls of the above hall with one coat is

    A. 6   B. 7   C. 8   D. 9

29. Without accounting for waste, the number of 9" x 9" pieces of tile needed for the hall floor is

    A. 3,150   B. 3,200   C. 3,250   D. 3,300

30. One radian is *most nearly* equal to

    A. 57.3°   B. 58.4°   C. 69.6°   D. 70.2°

31.

    PLAN

    In the plan shown above, the pipe invert elevation 25 feet from MH2 is *most nearly*

    A. 75.82'   B. 75.93'   C. 76.32'   D. 76.59'

32. In a 6 x 19 wire rope, the 6 indicates the

    A. diameter of wire rope   B. number of strands
    C. number of wires   D. gage of the wire

33. The quadrant in which the sine and cosine are negative is the

    A. first   B. second   C. third   D. fourth

34. When converted to inches, 0.6927 feet is *most nearly*

    A. 8 1/4   B. 8 9/32   C. 8 5/16   D. 8 11/32

35. The distance between two existing points on the ground is measured with a 100 ft. steel tape and found to be 1012.60 ft.
If the tape is .04 ft. too long, then the true length of the line is, in feet, *most nearly*

   A. 1012.15   B. 1012.00   C. 1012.75   D. 1013.00

36. With the weight of steel being equal to 490#/cu. ft., the cross-sectional area of an 18 WF 96 steel beam is, in square inches, *most nearly*

   A. 26.3   B. 27.4   C. 28.2   D. 30.5

37. In specifications containing the statement, scrubbers are constructed of PVC, the term PVC refers to

   A. plain vitrified clay
   B. polyvinyl chloride
   C. patented vanadium copper
   D. pliable varnished canvas

38. The piece of wood shown below used to strike off excess concrete from the surface of a freshly poured concrete slab is known as a

   A. scabbard   B. batten
   C. batter board   D. screed

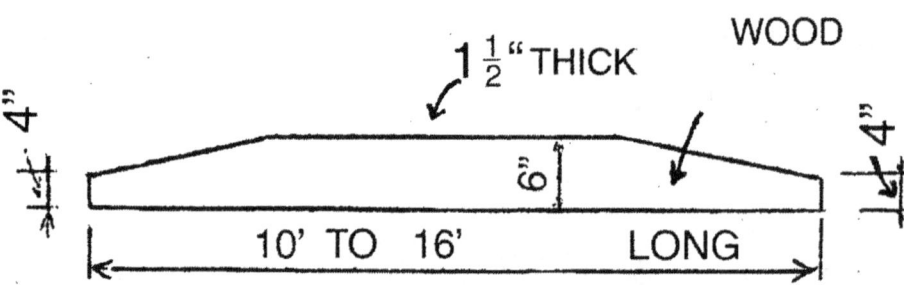

Questions 39-40.

DIRECTIONS: Questions 39 and 40 refer to the sketch below.

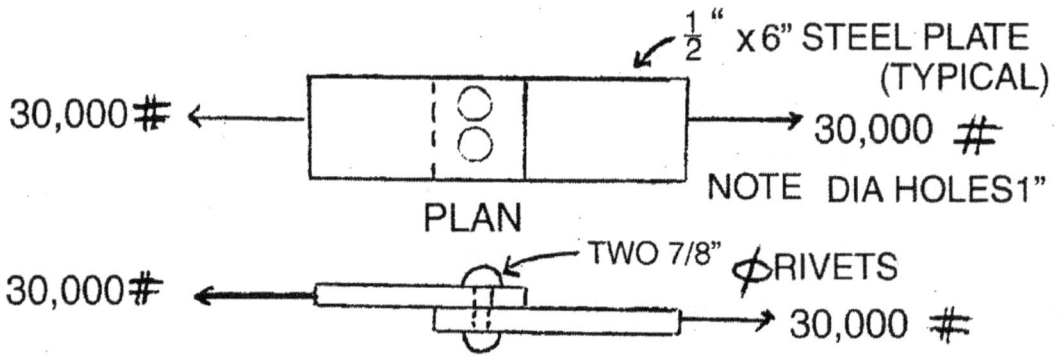

39. The shearing unit stress, in p.s.i., in each rivet is *most nearly*

   A. 12,500   B. 15,000   C. 20,000   D. 25,000

40. The MAXIMUM tensile unit stress, in p.s.i., in each plate is *most nearly* 40.____

  A. 10,000   B. 12,500   C. 15,000   D. 20,000

KEY (CORRECT ANSWERS)

1. D	11. B	21. C	31. A
2. D	12. B	22. C	32. B
3. B	13. C	23. D	33. C
4. B	14. A	24. C	34. C
5. C	15. B	25. D	35. D
6. D	16. C	26. A	36. C
7. B	17. A	27. B	37. B
8. A	18. D	28. C	38. D
9. A	19. C	29. B	39. D
10. D	20. C	30. A	40. C

TEST 2

DIRECTIONS: Each question or incomplete statement is followed by several suggested answers or completions. Select the one that BEST answers the question or completes the statement. *PRINT THE LETTER OF THE CORRECT ANSWER IN THE SPACE AT THE RIGHT.*

Questions 1-2.

DIRECTIONS: Questions 1 and 2 refer to the sketch shown below.

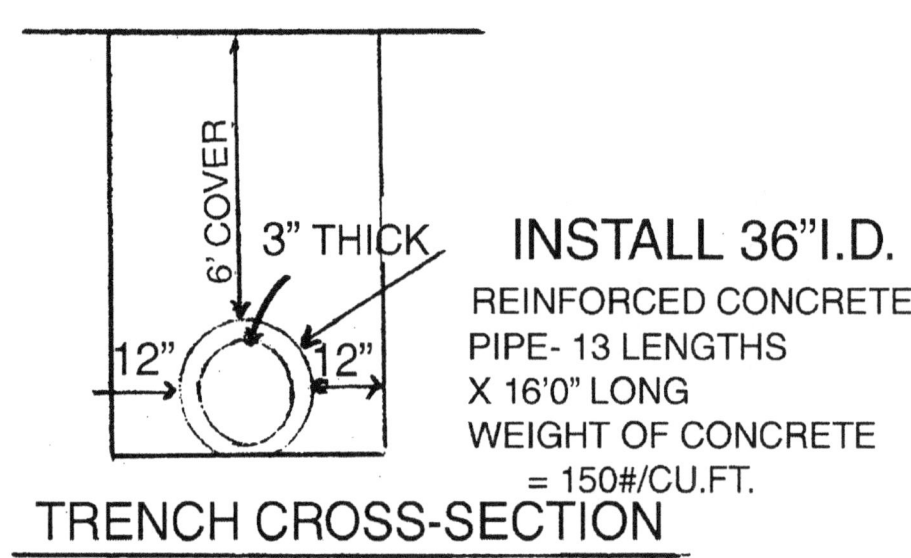

TRENCH CROSS-SECTION

1. The number of cubic yards of material excavated from the trench shown above is *most nearly*

   A. 402   B. 451   C. 543   D. 725   1.___

2. The weight of each length of concrete pipe, in tons, is *most nearly*

   A. 2.75   B. 3.00   C. 3.25   D. 3.50   2.___

3. Three wet samples of sand weigh 35#, 42#, and 37#, respectively. The amount of water in each sample is 10%, 15%, and 12%, respectively, of its dry weight.
   The average weight of the three dry samples is, in pounds, *most nearly*   3.___

   A. 33.2   B. 33.4   C. 33.6   D. 33.8

4. The value of $\dfrac{3+\sqrt{y}}{3-\sqrt{y}} - \dfrac{3-\sqrt{y}}{3+\sqrt{y}}$ is equal to   4.___

   A. 9   B. $\dfrac{\sqrt{y}}{3}$ C. $\dfrac{12\sqrt{y}}{9-y}$ D. $\dfrac{12y}{24-y^2}$

5. The value of $\dfrac{1535}{6!}$ is most nearly

   A. 2.1   B. 45.5   C. 255.0   D. 507.0

6. The equation $\dfrac{X^2}{A^2} - \dfrac{Y^2}{B^2} = 1$ represents a(n)

   A. hyperbola   B. parabola   C. catenary   D. ellipse

7. The equation $y = b^{-x}$ is equivalent to the equation

   A. $x = \log_b \dfrac{y}{a}$
   B. $x = -\log_b \dfrac{y}{a}$
   C. $y = \log_b \dfrac{x}{a}$
   D. $y = -\log_b \dfrac{x}{a}$

8.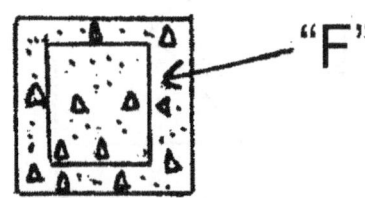

   In the beam cross-section shown above, the reinforcing bar "F" is called

   A. hanger   B. clamp   C. chair   D. stirrup

9. Type K is used to designate _____ tubing.

   A. steel   B. aluminum
   C. copper   D. ductile iron

10.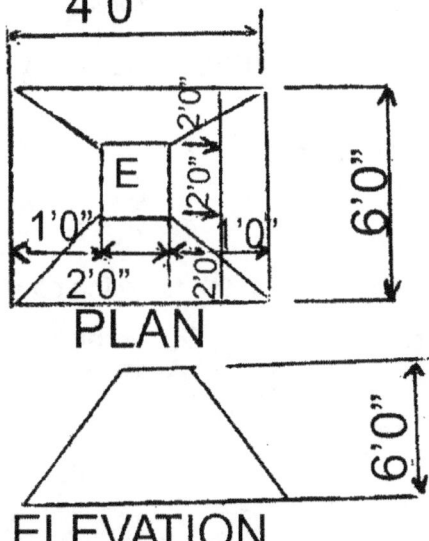

    The true length of line EF shown in the sketch on the preceding page is, in feet and inches, most nearly

| A. 6'3" | B. 6'5" | C. 6'7" | D. 6'9" |

11. Honeycomb is a defect that is MOST often found in _____ work.

    A. brick B. steel C. false D. concrete

12. The Brinell Number of a metal indicates its

    A. hardness
    C. porosity
    B. tenacity
    D. compressibility

13. A transite pipe is made MOSTLY of

    A. asphaltum
    C. bitumastic
    B. clay
    D. asbestos

14.

[Sketch: 10 Foot Ladder leaning against a wall on a level surface, with X being the distance from the base of the ladder to the wall.]

In the above sketch, the safest distance, X, to set the base of the ladder from the wall is, in feet, *most nearly*

    A. 3.0 B. 2.5 C. 2.0 D. 1.5

15. The emergency exit bolt sets put on the inside of doors to provide positive exit from a building by a slight pressure on any part of the cross bar are known as _____ bolts.

    A. fire B. exit C. panic D. tap

16. The thickness of light gage sheet steel is BEST measured with

    A. outside calipers
    B. dividers and an engineer's scale
    C. a micrometer
    D. a protractor

17. The beveled edge X on the plan shown [on the following page] of a column is called a

    A. camber B. reglet C. cornice D. chamfer

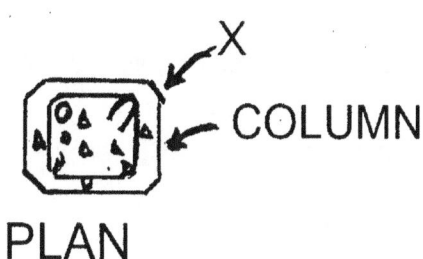

PLAN

18.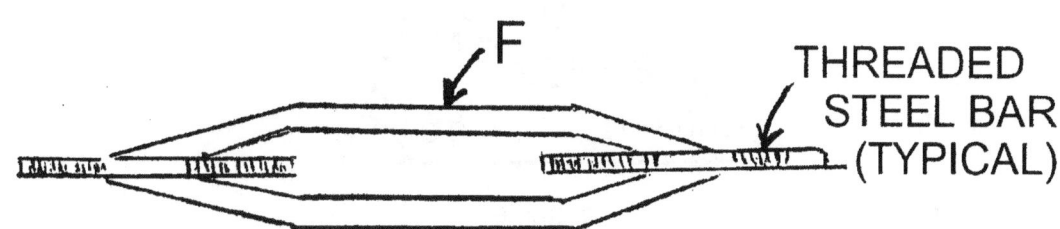

The fitting F shown above is called a

A. cleat B. clevis
C. coupling D. turnbuckle

19. A water pump operating under a head of 120 feet delivers 400 gpm. The horsepower delivered by the pump is *most nearly* ($HP = \dfrac{Qwh}{33,000}$; 1 cu. ft. = 7.5 gallons)

A. 11 B. 12 C. 13 D. 14

20.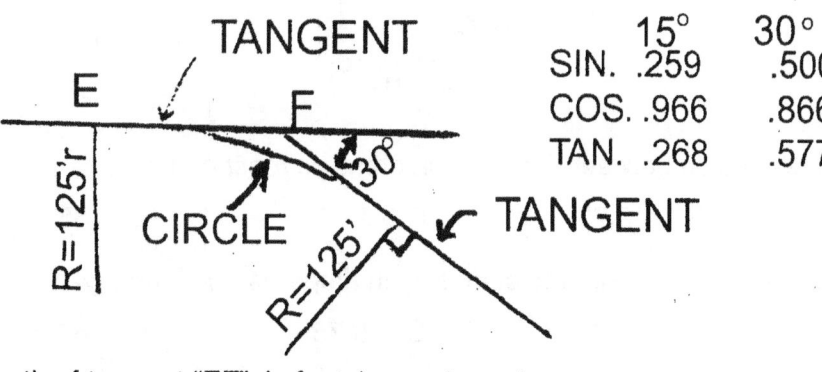

	15°	30°
SIN.	.259	.500
COS.	.966	.866
TAN.	.268	.577

The length of tangent "EF", in feet, is *most nearly*

A. 11 B. 22 C. 33 D. 62.5

21. The soft material placed between two flanges of a water pipe to prevent leakage is called a

A. gasket B. shim C. plinth D. cove

22. A 6" diameter water main is reduced to a 4" diameter main.
If the velocity of the water in the 6" main is 3 feet per second, then the velocity of the water in the 4" main is, in feet per second,

A. 2.50 B. 6.00 C. 6.75 D. 8.25

23. A wooden strip or mortar placed on a wall or ceiling at intervals to gage the thickness of plastering is called a   23.___

   A. scupper B. screed C. skein D. slab

24. Lines on a topographical drawing connecting points of equal elevation are called   24.___

   A. hachures B. parallels C. flats D. contours

25.   25.___

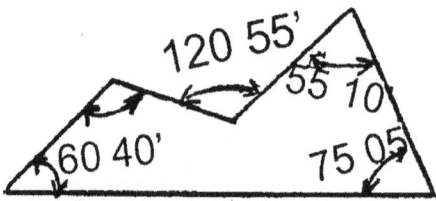

   In the sketch shown above, the unknown angle X is

   A. 110°00' B. 170°00' C. 220°00' D. 250°00'

Questions 26-27.

DIRECTIONS: Questions 26 and 27 refer to the diagram shown below.

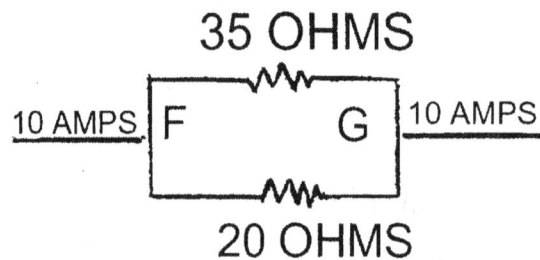

26. The combined resistance between F and G, in ohms, is *most nearly*   26.___

   A. 6.37 B. 12.75 C. 27.5 D. 55.

27. The current flowing in the 20 ohm resistance is, in amperes, *most nearly*   27.___

   A. 3.64 B. 4.62 C. 5.75 D. 6.36

28.   28.___

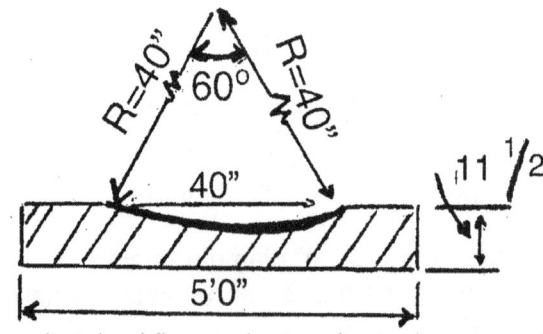

The area of the cross-hatched figure shown above, in square inches, is *most nearly*

A. 545   B. 568   C. 575   D. 582

29. A venturi meter is a device that measures

    A. specific gravity   B. surface tension
    C. flow   D. viscosity

30. Of the following, the device MOST often used in measuring cross-sectional areas shown on an engineering drawing is a

    A. pantograph   B. French curve
    C. geodimeter   D. planimeter

31.

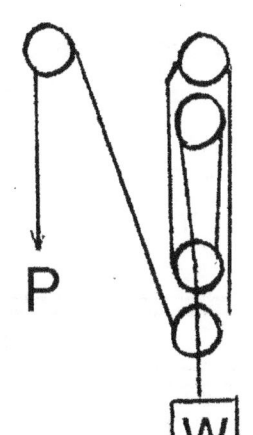

If W weighs 150 pounds, then the pull, P, required to keep the weight W in equilibrium is, in pounds, *most nearly*

    A. 25   B. 30   C. 35   D. 40

32.

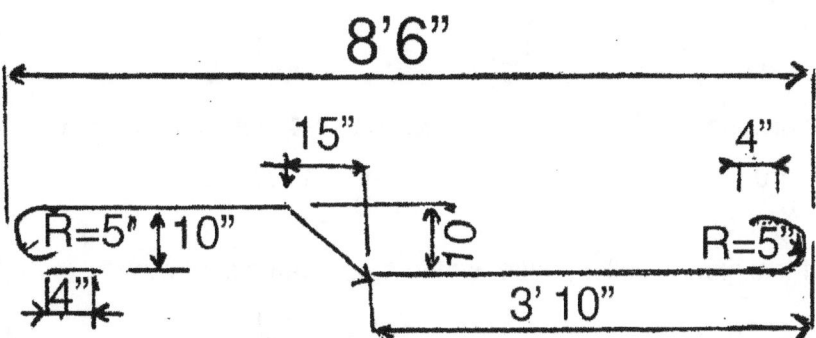

The total length of the rebar shown above is, in feet and inches, *most nearly*

    A. 8'4"   B. 9' 6 1/2"   C. 10'7"   D. 11' 2 1/2"

33. The symbol  on an engineering drawing represents

    A. common brick   B. loose insulation
    C. glass   D. cinder concrete

34. The symbol ____⌒____ on an engineering drawing represents a(n)

   A. outlet
   B. air circuit breaker
   C. rheostat
   D. condenser

35. If the bearing of a line is N 30° E, the clockwise azimuth from the south is

   A. 120°   B. 130°   C. 150°   D. 210°

36. Threads on a lag bolt are

   A. V-shaped
   B. round
   C. square
   D. elliptical

37. The structural steel shape MOST often used as a purlin is a(n)

   A. channel
   B. Tee section
   C. Z-section
   D. angle

38.

   F ←⌐

   [elevation view of member]

   F ←⌐

   ELEVATION

   In the Elevation shown on the preceding page, Section F - F would appear as in

   A. ⌐⌐   B. ⌐⌐   C. ⌠   D. ⌐⌐

39. The scale which shows the dimensions drawn to 1/4 of its actual size is

   A. 1/4" = 1'0"
   B. 1 1/2" - 1'0"
   C. 2' = 1'0"
   D. 3" = 1'0"

40. On an electrical plan, a ceiling outlet would *most likely* be shown as

   A. ⊢▢   B. [C]   C. ⊕   D. ⊗

KEY (CORRECT ANSWERS)

1.	A	11.	D	21.	A	31.	B
2.	B	12.	A	22.	C	32.	D
3.	D	13.	D	23.	B	33.	A
4.	C	14.	B	24.	D	34.	B
5.	A	15.	C	25.	A	35.	D
6.	A	16.	C	26.	B	36.	A
7.	B	17.	D	27.	D	37.	A
8.	D	18.	D	28.	A	38.	B
9.	C	19.	B	29.	C	39.	D
10.	D	20.	C	30.	D	40.	C

EXAMINATION SECTION
TEST 1

DIRECTIONS: Each question or incomplete statement is followed by several suggested answers or completions. Select the one that BEST answers the question or completes the statement. *PRINT THE LETTER OF THE CORRECT ANSWER IN THE SPACE AT THE RIGHT.*

1. The quadrant in which the cosine and tangent are both negative is the
   A. first   B. second   C. third   D. fourth

2.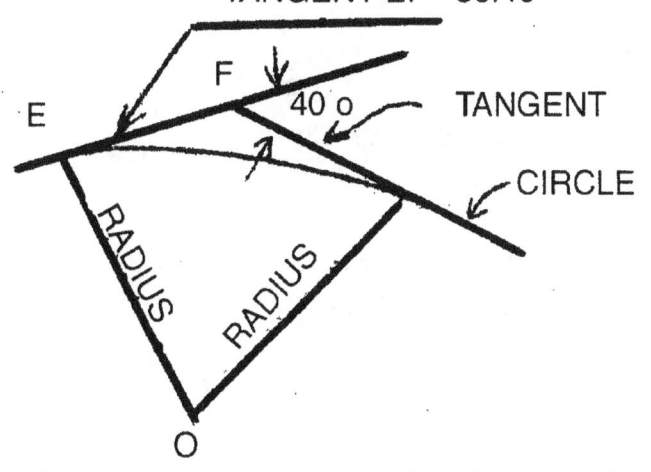

	20°	40°
sin.	.342	.643
cos.	.940	.766
tan.	.364	.839

   In the sketch shown above, the length of the radius OE, in feet, is MOST NEARLY
   A. 100   B. 103   C. 106   D. 109

3. 32 x 72 is equal to
   A. $3^8 \times 2^3$ B. $3^2 \times 2^8$ C. $3^2 \times 2^6$ D. $3^3 \times 2^8$

4. When 0.5313 feet is converted to inches, it is MOST NEARLY
   A. 6 5/16"   B. 6 3/8"   C. 6 13/32"   D. 6 1/4"

5. The supplement of the angle 62° is an angle of
   A. 28°   B. 38°   C. 118°   D. 162°

6. The numerical value of $\frac{7200}{6!}$ is MOST NEARLY
   A. 6   B. 8   C. 10   D. 12

7. The $\sqrt{543}$ is MOST NEARLY equal to
   A. 23.20   B. 23.25   C. 23.30   D. 23.35

8. $\dfrac{x-2}{x^2-6x+8}$ can be reduced to

   A. $\dfrac{1}{x-2}$ B. $\dfrac{x-2}{x-4}$ C. $\dfrac{1}{x-4}$ D. $\dfrac{1}{x+4}$

9. If Log 2 is .301 and Log 3 is .477, then Log 72 is MOST NEARLY

   A. 1.705   B. 1.857   C. 1.943   D. 2.001

10. The number of radians MOST NEARLY equal to 172° is

    A. 2.0   B. 2.5   C. 3.0   D. 3.5

11. $(x+3y)(x-y)$ is equal to

    A. $x^2 + 2xy - 3y^2$
    B. $x^2 + 4xy - 3y^2$
    C. $x^2 - 3y^2$
    D. $x^2 + 4xy + 3y^2$

12. The $\cos(x+70°)$ is equal to

    A. $\cos(20°-x)$
    B. $\cos(20°+x)$
    C. $\sin(20°-x)$
    D. $\sin(20°+x)$

13. If $f = k(\dfrac{1}{r})^2$, then 1 is equal to

    A. $r\dfrac{\sqrt{f}}{k}$ B. $\dfrac{\sqrt{rf}}{k}$ C. $\dfrac{\sqrt{k}}{rf}$ D. $\dfrac{\sqrt{fk}}{r}$

14. If $X = \text{arc}\cos\dfrac{\sqrt{3}}{2}$, then X, in degrees, is

    A. 30   B. 45   C. 60   D. 90

15. If $Z = 3$ and $Y = 2$ and $Y^3Z^2 + 2Y^2Z - Y^0Z^2 + 8Y^3 = X$, then X equals

    A. 84   B. 86   C. 88   D. 90

16. A motor-driven pump consists of a motor whose efficiency is 72% and a pump having an efficiency of 25%.
    The combined efficiency of the pump and its motor is MOST NEARLY

    A. 18%   B. 33%   C. 45%   D. 97%

17. The weight, in pounds, of a 1/4" steel plate 6 feet by 9 feet is MOST NEARLY (weight of steel = 480 lbs./cu.ft.)

    A. 500   B. 520   C. 540   D. 560

18. The number of cubic yards of concrete in a 9-foot long storm sewer pipe which has an inside diameter of 17 feet and a wall thickness of 15" is MOST NEARLY

    A. 24   B. 26   C. 28   D. 30

19. An off-shore pile has been driven so that 5/12 of its length is in silt, 3/8 of its length is in water, and the remaining 9 1/2 feet of its length is above water. The length of the pile, in feet, is MOST NEARLY

    A. 35   B. 40   C. 45   D. 50

20.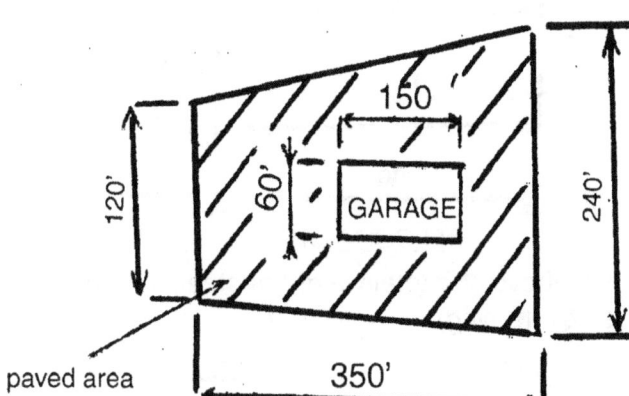

    Plan

    In the Plan shown above, the total number of square yards of asphalt in the paved area outside the garage is MOST NEARLY

    A. 3,000   B. 4,000   C. 5,000   D. 6,000

21. If the total temperature rise permitted for a certain device is 10° centigrade, the permissible temperature rise, in degrees fahrenheit, is

    A. 5.5   B. 10.0   C. 18.0   D. 50.0

22.

    In the Plan shown above, the total number of linear feet of 1 1/2" diameter pipe is MOST NEARLY

    A. 105   B. 125   C. 150   D. 175

23. To a fuel oil tank that is 1/8 full, 550 gallons of oil are added. The tank is then 1/2 full. The capacity of the tank, in gallons, is MOST NEARLY

    A. 1260   B. 1350   C. 1470   D. 1520

24.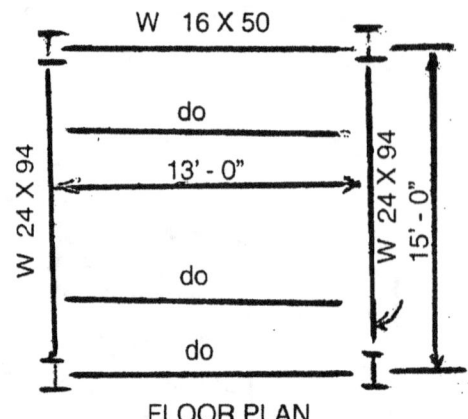

FLOOR PLAN

In the Floor Plan shown above, the total weight of steel, in pounds, is MOST NEARLY (neglect losses caused by framing)

A. 5100 B. 5200 C. 5300 D. 5400

25. When a valve is suddenly closed on a flow of water, the wave of increased pressure transmitted back through the pipe is COMMONLY called

A. the schottky effect
B. a standing wave
C. scattering
D. water hammer

KEY (CORRECT ANSWERS)

1. B   11. A
2. A   12. C
3. B   13. A
4. B   14. A
5. C   15. C

6. C   16. A
7. C   17. C
8. C   18. A
9. B   19. C
10. C   20. D

21. C
22. D
23. C
24. D
25. D

TEST 2

DIRECTIONS: Each question or incomplete statement is followed by several suggested answers or completions. Select the one that BEST answers the question or completes the statement. *PRINT THE LETTER OF THE CORRECT ANSWER IN THE SPACE AT THE RIGHT.*

1. The Section shown at the right of a building material represents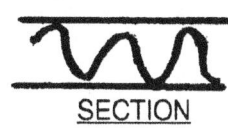

   A. slate
   B. earth
   C. glazed tile
   D. insulation

   1.____

2. The welding symbol shown at the right designates a _____ weld.

   A. fillet
   B. plug
   C. spot
   D. bevel

   2.____

3. The structural shape shown at the right represents a _____ shape.

   A. W   B. S   C. HP   D. MC

   3.____

4. Of the following, the grade of pencil MOST likely to be used for lettering dimensions, and arrowheads on an engineering drawing is

   A. H   B. 3H   C. 6H   D. 9H

   4.____

5. The electrical symbol at the right shown on an electrical wiring diagram USUALLY represents a(n)

   A. amplifier   B. coil
   C. capacitor   D. circuit breaker

   5.____

6. The meaning of the abbreviation *USC&GS* appearing on a line and grade map is: United States _____ Survey.

   A. Curb and Grade   B. City and Government
   C. County and Government   D. Coast and Geodetic

   6.____

7. The scale which shows an object drawn to one-quarter of its actual size is

   A. 1/4" = 1'0"   B. 1 1/2" = 1'0"
   C. 2" = 1'0"   D. 3" = 1'0"

   7.____

8. The alloy of tin, antimony, and copper, which is frequently used for machine bearings, is COMMONLY known as 8._____

   A. babbit   B. brass   C. bronze   D. bismuth

9. For the Elevation shown at the right, the Section X-X would be 9._____

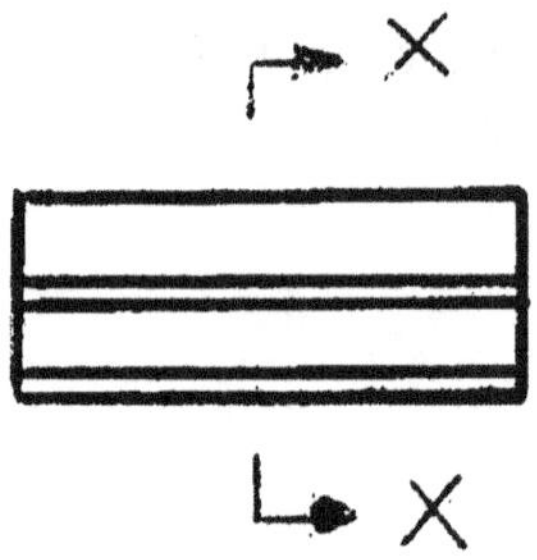

   ELEVATION

   A.    B.

   C.    D.

10. The symbol  ⚠ shown on a topographic map represents a 10._____

    A. bench mark   B. triangulation station
    C. mountain peak   D. cave shaft

11. The designations *AA* and *AAA* are used to specify _____ pipe. 11._____

    A. cast iron   B. aluminum
    C. copper   D. lead

12. In a 1:2 1/4:3 concrete mix, the *2 1/4* represents the proportion of 12._____

    A. water   B. sand   C. cement   D. aggregate

13. Brass is an alloy whose CHIEF components are copper and 13._____

    A. zinc   B. lead   C. tin   D. aluminum

14. The metal GENERALLY used to galvanize steel wire mesh is 14._____

    A. tin   B. cadmium   C. magnesium   D. zinc

15. The ends of wooden stair posts that are buried in the ground are MOST often treated with 15._____

    A. trisodium phosphate   B. creosote
    C. lime   D. kerosene

16. Of the following terms, the one which BEST describes the transfer of heat through a vacuum is

    A. radiation
    B. convection
    C. conduction
    D. cavitation

17. The compound MOST often used by a glazier to seal glass in a wooden frame is

    A. neat cement
    B. asphaltum
    C. putty
    D. gypsum

18. Of the following, the material LEAST likely to be used as a foundation pile is

    A. cast iron
    B. steel
    C. concrete
    D. wood

19. The effective diameter of a #6 reinforcing bar is MOST NEARLY

    A. 1/4"   B. 1/2"   C. 3/4"   D. 1"

20. *Honeycomb* is a defect MOST often found in

    A. concrete   B. brick   C. steel   D. aluminum

21. The weight of a full bag of Portland cement is MOST NEARLY _____ pounds.

    A. 64   B. 74   C. 84   D. 94

22. A pyrometer is COMMONLY used to measure

    A. temperature
    B. pressure
    C. acceleration
    D. acidity

23. Terrazzo is MOST often specified for

    A. walls   B. ceilings   C. pilasters   D. floors

24. Transite pipe is also known as _____ pipe.

    A. asbestos cement
    B. PVC
    C. Orangeburg
    D. plastic

25. Lightweight concrete is MOST often made by using a lightweight

    A. sand   B. cement   C. aggregate   D. liquid

KEY (CORRECT ANSWERS)

1.	D	11.	D
2.	D	12.	B
3.	D	13.	A
4.	A	14.	D
5.	D	15.	B
6.	D	16.	A
7.	D	17.	C
8.	A	18.	A
9.	B	19.	C
10.	B	20.	A

21.	D
22.	A
23.	D
24.	A
25.	C

EXAMINATION SECTION
TEST 1

DIRECTIONS: Each question or incomplete statement is followed by several suggested answers or completions. Select the one that BEST answers the question or completes the statement. *PRINT THE LETTER OF THE CORRECT ANSWER IN THE SPACE AT THE RIGHT.*

1. Of the following, the metal MOST often used in transformer wiring is 1._____

    A. copper B. aluminum C. silver D. steel

2. Of the following, the computer language MOST frequently used to solve engineering problems is 2._____

    A. COBOL B. COMIT C. SNOBOL D. FORTRAN

3. A 3/4" diameter steel bolt 4 inches long threaded at one end for insertion into a tapped hole and the other end threaded for a nut is known as a(n) _____ bolt. 3._____

    A. nipple B. acorn C. stud D. expansion

4. The Brinnel Test is a test for the 4._____

    A. density of water B. hardness of a metal
    C. permeability of sand D. purity of water

5. The term *3000 pound concrete* represents the ultimate strength of concrete attained at the end of _____ days. 5._____

    A. 3 1/2 B. 7 C. 14 D. 28

6. The technique of using arrow diagrams in the planning and scheduling of construction work is called the _____ method. 6._____

    A. CPM B. ADP C. APM D. CAP

7. Of the following personality traits, the one that BEST describes the ability of a subordinate who skillfully and promptly solves difficult problems is 7._____

    A. conscientious B. meticulous
    C. zestful D. resourceful

8. Of the following, the action that is generally BEST for a principal engineering technician to take when a subordinate turns in a completed job is to 8._____

    A. say nothing
    B. make a few favorable comments about his work
    C. take him out for lunch
    D. ask him why he took so long to do the job

9. An applicant is to be hired for a provisional position requiring drafting ability. Of the following, the BEST method of evaluating the applicant's drafting skill is by 9._____

    A. the number of years of experience he has as a draftsman
    B. asking him to make a sample drawing
    C. interviewing him about his drafting experience
    D. telephoning the engineering firms he worked for as a draftsman

2 (#1)

10. Of the following, the MOST important item in a good daily construction report is

    A. penmanship B. length
    C. language   D. accuracy

11. In the winter, while working in the field in a park area, a drowning man is pulled out of a lake. He is not breathing when rescued.
    The FIRST thing to do to the victim is to

    A. remove his wet clothes and put him in a blanket
    B. bring him to a warm shelter
    C. remove water from his lungs
    D. give him mouth-to-mouth resuscitation

12. Assume that an extension ladder has been extended to 16 feet and is to be placed against a vertical wall. The safest horizontal distance between the base of this ladder and the wall, in feet, is MOST NEARLY

    A. 1   B. 2   C. 4   D. 6

13. Of the following drafting symbols, the one that indicates a safety device is

    A. ⊣⊢   B. ─o‿o─   C. ─◇─   D. ─⊛─

14. A panic bolt is a safety device used MOST often on

    A. doors   B. pumps
    C. motors   D. power lines

15. Of the following, the organization whose MAJOR purpose is to examine and test devices, systems, and materials for safety is the

    A. American Society of Testing Materials
    B. Underwriters Laboratories
    C. National Association of Suggestion Systems
    D. General Services Administration

16. A stud is MOST NEARLY similar to a

    A. rafter   B. girder   C. stringer   D. column

17. In the sketch shown at the right, the reaction RL, in kips, is MOST NEARLY

    A. 10.1
    B. 11.3
    C. 12.5
    D. 13.5

18. A tachometer is a device that measures 18.____

    A. GPM   B. RPM   C. CFS   D. PSF

19. The horizontal structural member set over a door to carry the weight of the material above it is called a 19.____

    A. lintel   B. joist   C. stud   D. pylon

20. In the sketch shown at the right, the bearing of line GH is 20.____

    A. N5°E
    B. N5°W
    C. S5°E
    D. S5°W

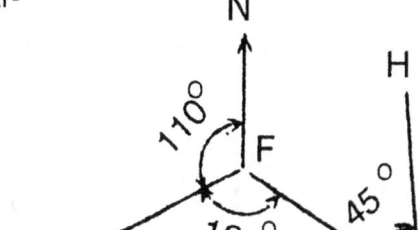

KEY (CORRECT ANSWERS)

1.	A	11.	D
2.	D	12.	C
3.	C	13.	B
4.	B	14.	A
5.	D	15.	B
6.	A	16.	D
7.	D	17.	C
8.	B	18.	B
9.	B	19.	A
10.	D	20.	B

TEST 2

DIRECTIONS: Each question or incomplete statement is followed by several suggested answers or completions. Select the one that BEST answers the question or completes the statement. *PRINT THE LETTER OF THE CORRECT ANSWER IN THE SPACE AT THE RIGHT.*

1. The TOTAL horizontal pressure, in pounds, on the face of a vertical sluice gate 6 feet high and 5 feet wide whose top is set 15 feet below the surface of water is MOST NEARLY

    A. 32,200　　B. 33,700　　C. 44,200　　D. 45,100

2. The unit used to measure the intensity of sound is the

    A. farad　　B. decibel　　C. henry　　D. lumen

3. A steel plate, 1 foot square and 1 inch thick, is completely immersed in water. If steel weighs 480 lbs/cubic foot in air, the weight of this steel plate in water will be MOST NEARLY _____ lbs.

    A. 5.2　　B. 20.6　　C. 34.8　　D. 45.1

4. Of the following, the valve that allows a liquid to flow in one direction ONLY is a _____ valve.

    A. butterfly　　B. gate　　C. globe　　D. check

5. Pipes that carry streams under roadway embankments are known as

    A. flumes　　B. weirs　　C. raceways　　D. culverts

6. To which one of the following is a horsepower MOST closely related?

    A. Farads　　B. Watts　　C. Poundals　　D. Newtons

7.

    In the sketch shown above, the combined resistance of the three individual resistors is _____ ohms.

    A. 6　　B. 11　　C. 17　　D. 20

8. A shaft two feet in diameter is rotating with a velocity of one revolution per second. The linear velocity of a point on the rim of the shaft, in feet per second, is MOST NEARLY

    A. 1.00　　B. 2.00　　C. 3.14　　D. 6.28

9. If the current in a 120-volt circuit is 6 amperes, the TOTAL resistance of the circuit is MOST NEARLY _____ ohms.

    A. 6　　B. 12　　C. 20　　D. 120

10. Water flows through a 4" diameter pipe at a rate of 6 feet per second.
    If the pipe increases to a diameter of 8", then the velocity of the water in the 8" pipe is, in feet per second, MOST NEARLY

    A. 1.5   B. 2.0   C. 2.5   D. 3.0

11. A slump test is used in making

    A. mortar   B. plaster   C. putty   D. concrete

12. Of the following, the one which is MOST NEARLY the modulus of elasticity of steel is 30 X

    A. 10^2 B. 10^4 C. 10^6 D. 10^8

13. A wooden stairway has 8 risers. The number of treads this stairway would NORMALLY have is

    A. 6   B. 7   C. 8   D. 9

14. An air conditioner has a rated capacity of 1 1/2 tons.
    This capacity is equivalent to the removal of _____ BTU/hr.

    A. 12,000   B. 18,000   C. 24,000   D. 30,000

15. A horizontal opening in a roof having a hinged cover used as a means of access to the roof is known as a

    A. bulkhead   B. shaftway   C. scuttle   D. kiosk

16. A 1/8 cast iron bend will change the direction of the piping to which it is connected by

    A. 22 1/2°   B. 33°   C. 45°   D. 66°

17. A rheostat is a variable

    A. resistor   B. inductance
    C. relay   D. capacitor

18. The diameter of a shaft is given as 2.000" .003". This means that

    A. the diameter of the shaft must be 2.000" to be acceptable
    B. 1.996" is an acceptable diameter for this shaft
    C. the tolerance is 1/100 of an inch
    D. 2.003" is an acceptable diameter

19. If a 100-foot long steel tape expands 0.06" for a rise of 10°F, then the expansion of an 80-foot long steel tape for a rise of 60F is MOST NEARLY

    A. 0.29"   B. 0.35"   C. 0.41"   D. 0.47"

20. A block 3' x 4' x 5' weighs 1800 pounds. If it is placed on the ground in such position that its height is 3 feet, then the pressure it exerts on the ground, in pounds per square foot, is MOST NEARLY

    A. 30   B. 90   C. 120   D. 150

KEY (CORRECT ANSWERS)

1. B
2. B
3. C
4. D
5. D

6. B
7. A
8. D
9. C
10. A

11. D
12. C
13. B
14. B
15. C

16. C
17. A
18. D
19. A
20. B

EXAMINATION SECTION
TEST 1

DIRECTIONS: Each question or incomplete statement is followed by several suggested answers or completions. Select the one that BEST answers the question or completes the statement. *PRINT THE LETTER OF THE CORRECT ANSWER IN THE SPACE AT THE RIGHT.*

1. Spontaneous combustion is started by the accumulation of heat from slow 1.____

   A. resonance
   B. electrolysis
   C. cooling
   D. oxidation

2. Power may be defined as 2.____

   A. force times distance
   B. mass times acceleration
   C. mass times velocity
   D. the rate of doing work

3. The British thermal unit (BTU) is the amount of heat needed to 3.____

   A. warm one pound of water one Fahrenheit degree
   B. maintain a temperature of 68° F in one pound of water
   C. melt one pound of ice
   D. change one pound of water to steam

4. A temperature of 60° C is, in °F, 4.____

   A. 150   B. 140   C. 120   D. 108

5. An inclined plane 6 feet long and 4 inches high has a *theoretical* mechanical advantage of 5.____

   A. 1.5   B. 10   C. 18   D. 24

6. If the velocity of an object is doubled, its kinetic energy is 6.____

   A. doubled
   B. quadrupled
   C. quartered
   D. halved

7. The volume of a given weight of dry gas is inversely proportional to its pressure, *provided* the temperature 7.____

   A. increases
   B. decreases
   C. remains constant
   D. is within the ambient range

8. Water, at a pressure of one atmosphere (760 mm of mercury), boils at a temperature of 8.____

   A. 460°R   B. 21°F   C. 100°C   D. 4°C

9. The angle of declination is the number of degrees that a compass needle varies from 9.____

   A. the equator
   B. mean sea level
   C. true south
   D. true north

10. If the pressure of a gas is kept constant, the volume will vary _____ the absolute temperature

    A. *inversely* as
    B. *directly* as
    C. *inversely* as the square of
    D. *directly* as the square of

11. A hygrometer is an instrument used to determine

    A. absolute pressure
    B. specific gravity
    C. relative humidity
    D. time

12. The separation of white light into its component colors by means of a triangular glass prism is known as

    A. dispersion
    B. reflection
    C. diffraction
    D. magnification

13. A hydraulic press has a small piston 3/8" in diameter and a large piston 1 1/2" in diameter. If a force of 50 pounds is applied to the small piston, the force on the large piston would be _____ pounds.

    A. 1600 B. 800 C. 200 D. 25

14. Brass is an alloy which consists PRIMARILY of

    A. zinc and copper
    B. beryllium and asbestos
    C. bromine and iron
    D. copper and steel

15. The gases produced by the electrolysis of sodium chloride in water solution are

    A. sulfur dioxide and oxygen
    B. carbon monoxide and helium
    C. hydrogen and chlorine
    D. bromine and methane

16. The chemical symbol for potassium is

    A. K B. P C. PO D. Na

17. Carbon tetrachloride has a specific gravity of 1.6. Water weighs 62.4 pounds per cubic foot.
    The pressure intensity, in pounds per square inch gage, at the bottom of a tank 10 feet deep full of carbon tetrachloride is MOST NEARLY

    A. 6.93 B. 16.0 C. 624.0 D. 997.9

18. The resultant of two 80-l forces acting at right angles to each other is MOST NEARLY _____ pounds.

    A. 0 B. 57 C. 113 D. 160

19. If it requires a force of 40 pounds to drag a 240-pound block of concrete across the floor, then the coefficient of friction is MOST NEARLY

    A. 0.17 B. 0.25 C. 6.0 D. 200

20. If electricity costs 8 cents per kilowatt hour, then the cost of burning twelve 75-watt and five 60-watt bulbs for 10 hours is _____ cents. 20.____

    A. 62   B. 88   C. 96   D. 124

21. A steel rail is 60 feet long at 10° C. 21.____
    If the coefficient of linear expansion is 0.000013/C°, then the length of the rail, at 50° C, is MOST NEARLY _____ feet.

    A. 59.969   B. 60.003   C. 60.031   D. 62.328

22. A square tank 12 feet high having a perimeter of 40 feet is filled with water weighing 62.4 pounds per cubic foot. The total horizontal force on one side of the tank due to the water pressure is MOST NEARLY _____ pounds. 22.____

    A. 58,000   B. 45,000   C. 36,000   D. 13,000

23. A barge 30 feet long and 20 feet wide floats in sea water weighing 64 pounds per cubic foot. The barge sinks 6 inches when a truck is driven aboar 23.____
    The weight of the truck is MOST NEARLY _____ pounds.

    A. 21,800   B. 19,200   C. 7,900   D. 6,300

24. Assume that a mercury barometer indicates an atmospheric pressure of 29 inches and that mercury weighs 848 pounds per cubic foot. 24.____
    The atmospheric pressure, in pounds per square inch, under these conditions is MOST NEARLY

    A. 15.0   B. 14.7   C. 14.2   D. 13.2

25. An electric iron draws 12 amperes on a 110-volt circuit. If electricity costs 5 cents per kilowatt-hour, the cost to operate the iron for 6 hours is _____ cents. 25.____

    A. 40   B. 56   C. 22   D. 110

KEY (CORRECT ANSWERS)

1. D
2. D
3. A
4. B
5. C

6. B
7. C
8. C
9. D
10. B

11. C
12. A
13. B
14. A
15. C

16. A
17. A
18. C
19. A
20. C

21. C
22. B
23. B
24. C
25. A

TEST 2

DIRECTIONS: Each question or incomplete statement is followed by several suggested answers or completions. Select the one that BEST answers the question or completes the statement. *PRINT THE LETTER OF THE CORRECT ANSWER IN THE SPACE AT THE RIGHT.*

1. Ohm's Law states that the intensity of an electric current varies *directly* as the electromotive force and *inversely* as the

    A. potential
    B. resistance
    C. voltage
    D. energy

    1.____

2. A step-up transformer has a turn ratio of 1 to 20. If 110 volts A.C. is applied to the primary, then the voltage on the secondary is _____ volts.

    A. 4400 B. 2200 C. 220 D. 55

    2.____

3. Wire A has a resistance of 30 ohms. Wire B, made of the same material, is the same length as A and has a diameter twice as large as The resistance of wire B is _____ ohms.

    A. 60 B. 30 C. 15 D. 7.5

    3.____

4. If an observer sees the flash of a cannon 2 seconds before he hears the sound, the *approximate* distance between the observer and the cannon is _____ feet.

    A. 186,000 B. 10,720 C. 2,180 D. 600

    4.____

5. The pH of vinegar is MOST NEARLY

    A. 212 B. 10^2 C. 12 D. 2.8

    5.____

6. The value of 9 3/4 inches, expressed in feet, is MOST NEARLY

    A. 0.67 B. 0.75 C. 0.813 D. 1.15

    6.____

7. When $\frac{x}{3} - 2$ is subtracted from $\frac{x+6}{3}$, the answer is

    A. 0 B. 2 C. -2 D. 4

    7.____

8. The length of a rectangle is 4 times the width. If the area of the rectangle is 324 square feet, the dimensions of the rectangle, in feet, are

    A. 4 x 81 B. 8 x 41 C. 9 x 36 D. 12 x 27

    8.____

9. The reciprocal of $\frac{25x^2}{y}$ is

    A. $-\frac{y}{25x^2}$ B. $-\frac{25x^2}{y}$ C. $\frac{y}{25x^2}$ D. $\frac{25y}{x^2}$

    9.____

10. If $\frac{3a-1}{4} = 2$, then a equals

    A. 2　　　B. 3　　　C. 4　　　D. 9

11. An angle E is 60 degrees larger than its supplement. The number of degrees in angle E is

    A. 270　　　B. 120　　　C. 60　　　D. 30

12. The three angles of a triangle are in the ratio of 2:3:4. If one of the angles is 60°, the other two angles are

    A. 30° and 90°　　　B. 20° and 100°
    C. 40° and 80°　　　D. 50° and 70°

13. y varies inversely with x^2. If y = 12 when x = 2, then when x = 4, y is equal to

    A. 2　　　B. 3　　　C. 4　　　D. 6

14. If the base angle of an isosceles triangle is four times the vertex angle, the number of degrees in the vertex angle is

    A. 13　　　B. 20　　　C. 27.5　　　D. 30

15. The angle of a sector of a circle is 160 degrees and the radius of the circle is 12 inches. The area of the sector, in square inches, is

    A. 144π　　　B. 64π　　　C. 32π　　　D. 24π

16. The number 8^6 is the same as the number

    A. 2^{48}　　　B. 2^{15}　　　C. 2^{18}　　　D. 4^{16}

17. Assume that a circle has a radius of 70 feet. The perimeter of this circle is MOST NEARLY _____ feet.

    A. 219.8　　　B. 439.6　　　C. 690　　　D. 15,306

18. The numerical value of $9^{3/2}$ is

    A. 18　　　B. 27　　　C. 36　　　D. 81

19. The numerical value of $\sqrt{640}$ is MOST NEARLY

    A. 80　　　B. 25.3　　　C. 24.3　　　D. 20

20. The number of radians in the arc of a circle whose central angle is 120° is

    A. $2/3\,\pi$　　　B. π　　　C. $3/2\,\pi$　　　D. 4

21. The value of $5\sqrt{12} - 2\sqrt{27}$ is equal to

   A. $4\sqrt{3}$ B. $3\sqrt{5}$ C. $5\sqrt{2}$ D. $3\sqrt{15}$

22. The area of an equilateral triangle whose side is 8 is

   A. 32   B. $16\sqrt{3}$ C. 24   D. $8\sqrt{3}$

23. The logarithm to the base 10 of 1000 is

   A. 100   B. 1.6   C. 2.718   D. 3

24. The cosine of 15° is

   A. $\dfrac{2}{\sqrt{3}}$ B. $-\dfrac{\sqrt{3}}{2}$ C. $-\dfrac{1}{2}$ D. $-\dfrac{1}{\sqrt{2}}$

25. The interior angle between two adjacent sides of a regular hexagon is

   A. 180°   B. 120°   C. 90°   D. 60°

KEY (CORRECT ANSWERS)

1. B
2. B
3. D
4. C
5. D
6. C
7. D
8. C
9. C
10. B
11. B
12. C
13. B
14. B
15. B
16. C
17. B
18. B
19. B
20. A
21. A
22. B
23. D
24. B
25. B

EXAMINATION SECTION
TEST 1

DIRECTIONS: Each question or incomplete statement is followed by several suggested answers or completions. Select the one that BEST answers the question or completes the Statement. *PRINT THE LETTER OF THE CORRECT ANSWER IN THE SPACE AT THE RIGHT.*

1. When efflorescence is caused by poor workmanship, it would *generally* be the fault of a(n)   1.____

   A. mason
   B. painter
   C. wire lather
   D. iron worker

2. Of the following, the tool that should be used to accurately check that the gage of steel is in accordance with specifications is a(n)   2.____

   A. combination square
   B. micrometer
   C. engineers scale
   D. invar tape

3. Of the following types of wood, the one that is classified as a softwood is   3.____

   A. redwood   B. ash   C. cherry   D. oak

4. Of the following utility lines, the one that must ALWAYS be carefully checked for slope before backfilling the trench is   4.____

   A. water   B. sewer   C. gas   D. steam

5. A 6"-sixteenth bell and spigot cast-iron fitting has a deflection angle of   5.____

   A. 8 1/8°   B. 11 1/4°   C. 22 1/2°   D. 45°

6.   6.____

   In the sketch shown above, the SAFEST horizontal distance X to set the base of the ladder is

   A. 4.5'   B. 6.5'   C. 8.5'   D. 10.5'

7. Of the following plumbing fixtures, the one that is used PRIMARILY to prevent obnoxious and/or poisonous gases from entering a building is a   7.____

   A. corporation cock
   B. trap
   C. sill cock
   D. ball cock

8. Of the following types of fire extinguishers, the one that should NOT be used to extinguish a burning gasoline fire is

   A. soda acid
   B. dry chemical
   C. carbon dioxide
   D. liquified gas

9. While in the field on a very cold day, your fingers become frostbitten.
   Of the following, the BEST action for you to take is to go indoors and

   A. have someone rub your fingers
   B. take an alcoholic drink
   C. bathe fingers in water that is about 95°F
   D. bathe the fingers in a solution of cold epsom salts

10. While in the field, you are bitten on the hand by a stray cat.
    Of the following, the BEST action for you to take is to

    A. apply iodine to wound
    B. suck blood from the wound
    C. go to the doctor at once
    D. wash wound with soap and water

11. The plenum box shall not be less than #20 USSG sheet steel. In the above specification, #20 refers to the _____ of the sheet steel.

    A. density
    B. hardness
    C. weight
    D. thickness

12. A galvanized surface is a surface finish that would be specified for

    A. steel   B. aluminum   C. brass   D. bronze

13. All valves 3" and over in size located at pumps, tanks, and major equipment shall be of the O.S. & Y. type flanged. In the above specification, the abbreviation O.S. & Y. means outside

    A. saddle and yardarm
    B. sheave and yardstick
    C. seat and yawl
    D. screw and yoke

14. Tubes shall be formed of hot finished seamless (A.S.T.M. A83) or electric resistance welded (A.S.T.M. A178) open hearth steel. In the above specification, A.S.T.M. means

    A. American Society for Testing Materials
    B. Association of Steel Treatment Manufacturers
    C. Approved Systems for Treating Metals
    D. Accepted Steel Treatment Methods

15. All miscellaneous metal work before leaving the shop shall be cleaned of all scale, rust, and dirt and shall be given one shop coat of red lead.
    Miscellaneous metal used in the specification above refers, in general, to

    A. angles
    B. I beams
    C. rivets, welding, and general bolting
    D. steel other than structural steel

16. A temporary structure or platform built to enable workmen to reach high places is known as

    A. scarfing
    B. scantling
    C. scaling
    D. staging

17. Of the following, the one that is NOT a part of a stairway is a

    A. muntin   B. balustrade   C. nosing   D. newel

18. In reinforced concrete, the effective diameter of a #4 reinforcing bar is *most nearly*

    A. 1/4"   B. 1/2"   C. 3/4"   D. 1"

19. In a 1:1:1 3/4 concrete mix, the *1 3/4* represents the proportion of

    A. gravel
    B. Portland cement
    C. sand
    D. water

20. After concrete for a sidewalk is poured, the top surface is rarely at the exact elevation required. The process of striking off the excess concrete in order to bring it to the right elevation is called

    A. floating
    B. trowelling
    C. brooming
    D. screeding

21.

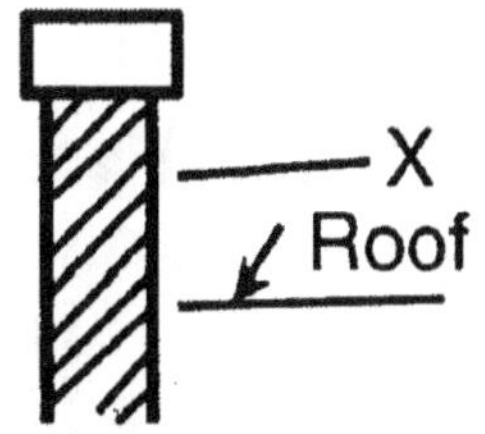

    ELEVATION

    In the Elevation shown above, the wall X is called a

    A. pillar   B. pilaster   C. parapet   D. pylon

22. In concrete form work, the horizontal pieces of lumber that are set parallel to the plywood sheets are called

    A. nailers   B. walers   C. cleats   D. spreaders

23.

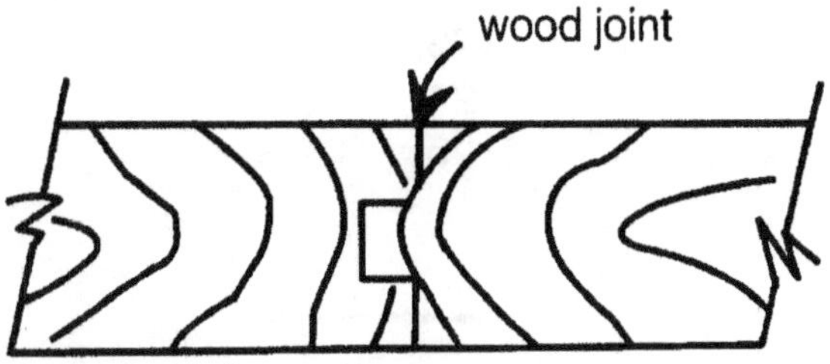

    The wood joint shown above is known as a

    A. tongue and groove
    B. dove tail
    C. ship lap
    D. scarf joint

24. Transite is commonly used as siding for industrial buildings. This material consists MAINLY of _____ and cement.

    A. asbestos   B. vermiculite
    C. haydite   D. scoria

25.

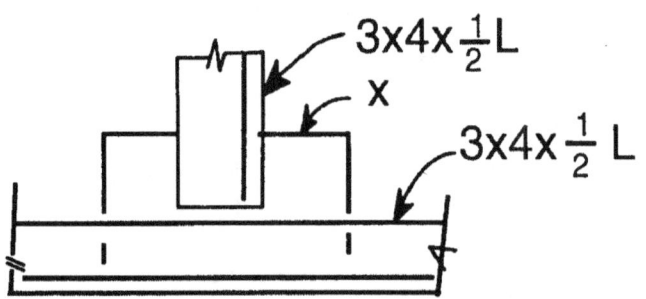

The plate X shown above is known as a _____ plate.

    A. sole   B. gusset   C. batten   D. toe

KEY (CORRECT ANSWERS)

1.	A	11.	D
2.	B	12.	A
3.	A	13.	D
4.	B	14.	A
5.	C	15.	D
6.	A	16.	D
7.	B	17.	A
8.	A	18.	B
9.	C	19.	A
10.	C	20.	D

21. C
22. B
23. A
24. A
25. B

TEST 2

DIRECTIONS: Each question or incomplete statement is followed by several suggested answers or completions. Select the one that BEST answers the question or completes the statement. *PRINT THE LETTER OF THE CORRECT ANSWER IN THE SPACE AT THE RIGHT.*

Questions 1-4.

DIRECTIONS: In each of the following groups of drawings, the top view and front elevation of an object are shown on the left. At the right are four drawings, one of which represents the end elevation of the object as seen from the right. Select the drawing which represents the correct end elevation and mark in the space at the right the letter of this drawing.

The first group is shown as an example only.

The correct answer in this group is C.

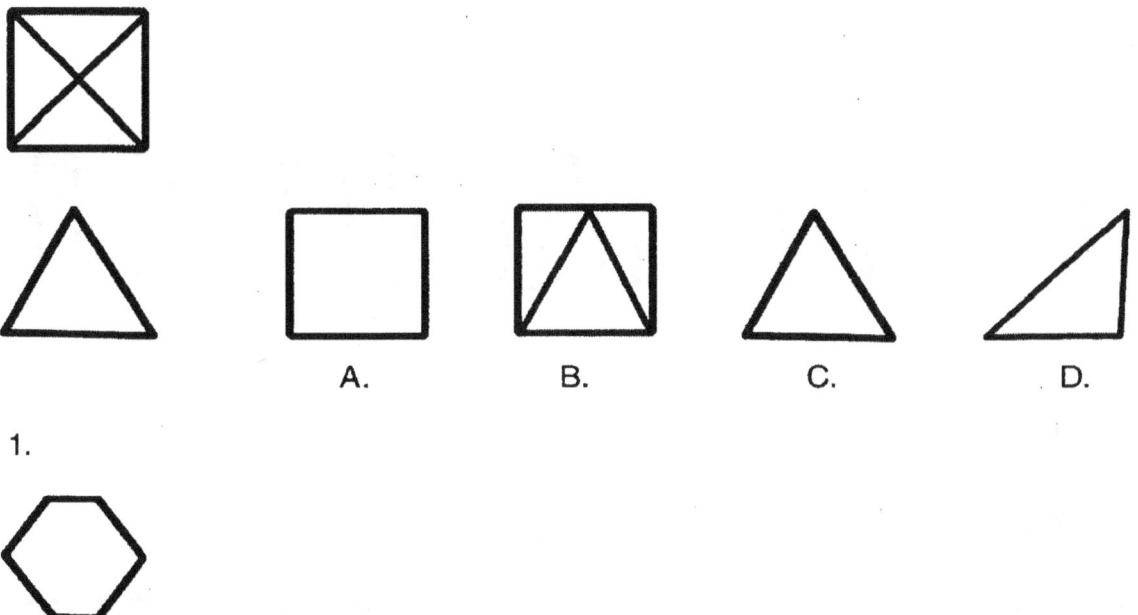

1.   1.____

65

2.

 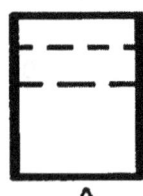   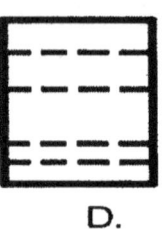
A.   B.   C.   D.

3.

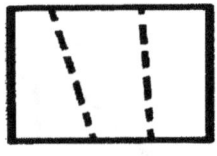    
A.   B.   C.   D.

4.

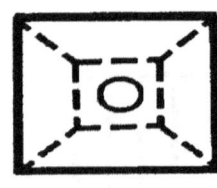  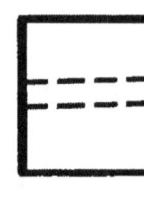 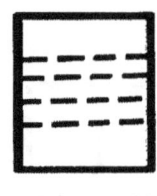 
A.   B.   C.   D.

5. The range of pencils usually recommended for doing line-work on drafting paper is
   A. 6B to 3B   B. 2B to F   C. 2H to 4H   D. 5H to 7H

6. The scale which indicates that dimensions are drawn to 1/6 of its actual size is

   A. $\frac{1}{2}" = 1'0"$ B. $1" = 1'0"$

   C. $1\frac{1}{2}" = 1'0"$ D. $2" = 1'0"$

7. On an electrical plan, a floor outlet would be shown as

   A. 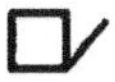 ▢✓   B. 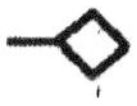 ◇   C. ⊙   D. ▣

8. The drafting symbol ▨ represents a section of

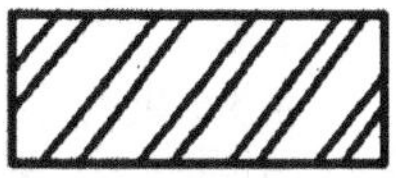

   A. aluminum   B. cast iron   C. lead   D. steel

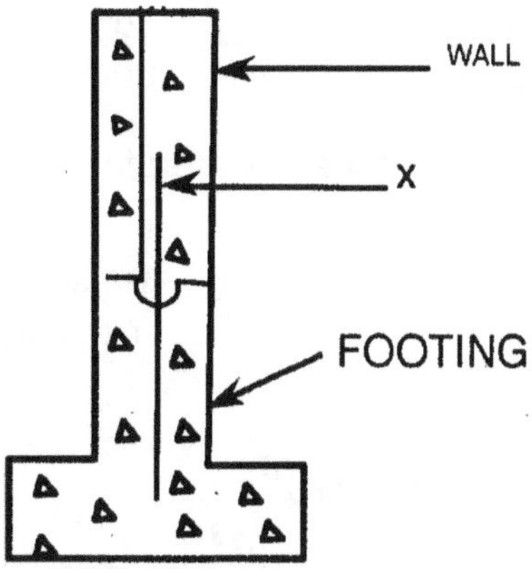

9. In the Section shown above, the reinforcing bar marked X is known as a

   A. reglet   B. dowel   C. bollard   D. clevis

10. The piping symbol ⟶|N|⟶ represents a _____ valve.

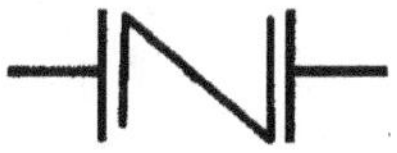

    A. check   B. gate   C. float   D. globe

11. The piping symbol 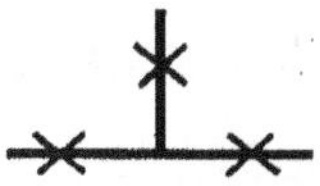 represents a _____ tee.

    A. bell and spigot   B. screwed
    C. welded   D. flanged

12. The electrical symbols shown above represent

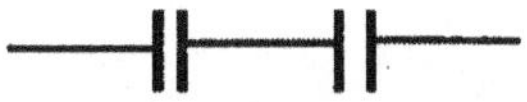

    A. inductors   B. capacitors
    C. conductors   D. batteries

13. A plumbing drawing is drawn to a scale of 1/8" = 1 foot. A vertical cold water riser measuring 6 1/2" on the drawing would be equivalent to _____ feet of pipe.

    A. 32   B. 42   C. 52   D. 62

14. Contour lines are shown on a drawing.
    This drawing is *most likely* a

    A. plan   B. elevation
    C. section   D. profile

15. A scale on a map reads 1:24000.
    Of the following scales, the one that is EQUIVALENT to this scale is

    A. 1" = 24000'   B. 1' = 24000"   C. 1" = 2000'   D. 1" = 2000"
    E. 5.0   F. 10.0   G. 12.5   H. 15.0
    I. 30   J. 45   K. 60   L. 75

16. The arrangement of equipment shown below used for determining the value of an unknown resistance is called a

    A. diamond circuit   B. Wheatstone Bridge
    C. volt ohmmeter   D. Y circuit

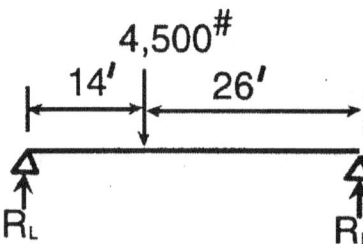

17. In the sketch shown below, the upward force R_R is *most nearly* _____ lbs.

    A. 1500   B. 1525   C. 1550   D. 1575

18. In the sketch shown below, the tension T in the cable is *most nearly* _____ lbs.

    A. 250   B. 300   C. 400   D. 500

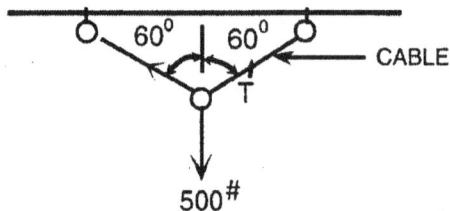

Sin 60° = .866
Cos 60° = .500
Tan 60° = 1.732

19. Nails used to fasten 2 x 4's and other wood structural members are known as

    A. common nails   B. case-hardened nails
    C. box nails   D. brads

20. Vertical 2 x 4 wood members in a wood frame residence are known as

   A. studs   B. stringers   C. purlins   D. bridging

21. The total number of amperes in a 120-volt line feeding a 1.5 KW electric heating appliance is *most nearly*

   A. 5.0   B. 10.0   C. 12.5   D. 15.0

22. In the sketch shown below, the voltage drop across the 6-ohm resistance is _____ volts.

   A. 30   B. 45   C. 60   D. 75

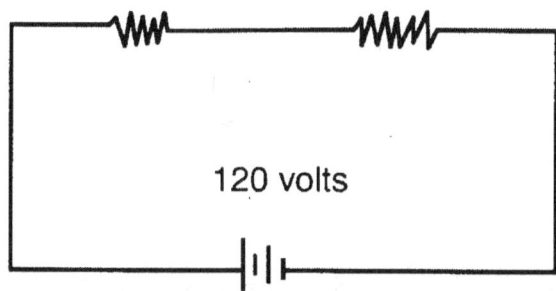

23. The arrangement of equipment shown below used for determining the value of an unknown resistance is called a

   A. diamond circuit
   C. volt ohmmeter
   B. Wheatstone Bridge
   D. Y circuit

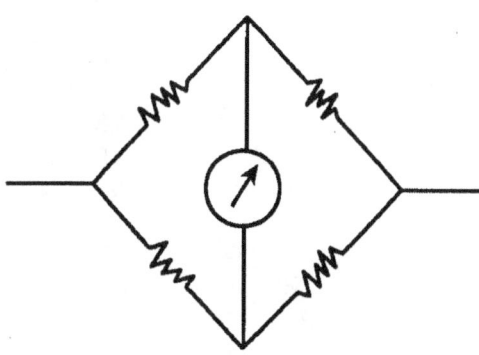

24. Water flows through a section of pipe 10" in diameter with a velocity of 1.5 feet per second. If the diameter of the pipe then decreases to 6", the velocity of the water in the 6" pipe will be *most nearly* _____ fps.

   A. 3   B. 4   C. 5   D. 6

25. The flashing block shown in Section below is also known as a   25. ____

   A. coping   B. scupper   C. fascia   D. reglet

SECTION

KEY (CORRECT ANSWERS)

1.	A	11.	C
2.	C	12.	B
3.	D	13.	C
4.	A	14.	A
5.	C	15.	C
6.	D	16.	C
7.	C	17.	D
8.	D	18.	D
9.	B	19.	A
10.	A	20.	A

21. C
22. A
23. B
24. B
25. D

EXAMINATION SECTION
TEST 1

DIRECTIONS: Each question or incomplete statement is followed by several suggested answers or completions. Select the one that BEST answers the question or completes the statement. *PRINT THE LETTER OF THE CORRECT ANSWER IN THE SPACE AT THE RIGHT.*

1. The angles of a triangle are in the ratio 1:3:5. Find the number of degrees in the SMALLEST angle.

    A. 60   B. 40   C. 30   D. 20

    1.____

2. The number 0.000036 may be written as

    A. 3.6^{-5} B. 3.6×10^{-4} C. 3.6×10^{-5} D. 3.6^{-6}

    2.____

3. Of the following, the equation of a line tangent to the graph of $x^2 + y^2 = 81$ is

    A. x=9   B. x+y=9   C. x=9y   D. x = -9y

    3.____

4. Of the following, the equation whose roots are -3 and 2 is _____ = 0.

    A. $2x^2 + 3x - 6$ B. $x^2 + x - 6$
    C. $x^2 - x + 6$ D. $x^2 + 6$

    4.____

5. If log r = x, then $\log \frac{r^2}{s}$ equals

    A. $\frac{2x}{\log s}$ B. 2x - 2   C. x - 2s   D. 2x - log s

    5.____

6. Which one of the following equations is MOST NEARLY correct?

    A. 748 watts = 1 hp   B. 746 watts = 1 hp
    C. 746 hp = 1 watt   D. 3.14 watts = 1 hp

    6.____

7. The magnitude of the emf induced in a conductor by a magnetic field is NOT affected by which one of the following?

    A. Number of turns in the conductor
    B. Strength of the magnetic field
    C. Direction of the magnetic field
    D. Relative motion between the magnetic lines of force and the conductor

    7.____

8. The power delivered to a D.C. circuit is the product of the _____ circuit.

    A. voltage and the current flowing in that
    B. resistance and the current flowing in that
    C. voltage and the resistance of the
    D. voltage, the resistance, and the current flowing in that

    8.____

9. In radio circuits, when intermediate frequency transformers are used with fixed capacitors for tuning, the inductance of the coils is normally varied by

    9.____

A. moving an iron core inside the coil
B. changing the distance between the coils
C. changing the number of turns in the coils
D. varying the cross-sectional area of the coil

10. As a load is applied to a shunt motor, the speed of the armature _____ , thus _____ the cemf and _____ the current.

    A. increases; decreasing; increasing
    B. increases; decreasing; decreasing
    C. decreases; decreasing; increasing
    D. decreases; increasing; decreasing

11. Manufacturers have increased the shelf life of primary cells by covering the zinc electrode with

    A. iron filings   B. copper
    C. mercury   D. lead

12. The open-circuit voltage of a cell is GREATER than the closed-circuit voltage by an amount equal to the

    A. external resistance times the current
    B. internal resistance times the current
    C. voltage drop across the load
    D. current times the open-circuit voltage

13. An analogy is often drawn between the properties related by Ohm's Law in an electrical system and similar properties in a water supply system.
    In this analogy, voltage is associated with the

    A. rate of flow in the pipe
    B. amount of water in the system
    C. size of the pipe in the water system
    D. difference in pressure between two points in the water supply system

14. Capacitors are often used in radio circuits to block the flow of

    A. A.C. but to pass D.C.   B. D.C. but to pass A.C.
    C. D.C. and A.C.   D. neither A.C. nor D.C.

15. When a series L-C-R circuit is resonant, the current

    A. lags the applied voltage by 90°
    B. is in phase with the applied voltage
    C. leads the applied voltage by 90°
    D. is 180° out-of-phase with the applied voltage

16. In any A.C. circuit containing an induction coil, a condenser, and a resistance, the only power that is actually dissipated is that which is absorbed by the

A. induction coil
B. condenser
C. resistance
D. induction coil and condenser

17. The principle utilized in the D'Arsonval galvanometer in measuring electric current is the

    A. ability of an electric current to exert a torque
    B. heating effect of an electric current
    C. interaction of two magnetic fields
    D. ability of a voltage to produce a current

18. Eddy currents in a transformer are reduced by

    A. using low-resistance copper windings
    B. coating the core with insulating compound
    C. using a soft silicon steel as a core
    D. using a laminated core

19. Which one of the following is the definition of a henry?
    The

    A. quantity of electricity transferred in 1 second by a current of 1 ampere
    B. electrical power required to do 1 joule of work in 1 second
    C. energy expended in 1 second by an electric current of 1 ampere in a resistance of 1 ohm
    D. inductance of a circuit in which a current change of 1 ampere per second causes a cemf of 1 volt

20. The impedance of a series circuit containing both resistance and capacitance is equal to the _____ of the resistance and the capacitive reactance.

    A. sum
    B. sum of the squares
    C. square root of the difference of the squares
    D. square root of the sum of the squares

21. The PRINCIPAL advantage of electrolytic capacitors is their

    A. large amount of capacitance and small size
    B. low power loss as compared with paper capacitors
    C. adaptability for use in high-voltage (30,000 volts) circuit
    D. adaptability to any circuit without regard to polarity

22. If the resultant of two equal A.C. voltages is zero, the

    A. two voltages are in phase
    B. first voltage leads the second voltage by 90°
    C. second voltage leads the first voltage by 90°
    D. two voltages are out of phase by 180°

23. Assume that a variometer consists of two coils with inductances L1 and L2 of 9 henrys and of 4 henrys, respectively. What is the variation in the total inductance of the variometer when L2 is arranged first to oppose and then to aid the magnetic field of L1? (Assume K = 1.)
_____ to _____ henrys.

   A. 0; 9   B. 4; 13   C. 5; 13   D. 1; 25

24. A 5-hp motor, operating on a 110-volt D.C. line, consumes 3.3 kilowatts of electrical power in an hour.
This motor requires a current of _____ ampere(s).

   A. .03   B. 15   C. 30   D. 150

25. A 6-volt battery source is used to furnish filament power to a 1.4 volt radio tube that draws .05 ampere or current. To avoid burning out the tube, what size of limiting resistor should be used in series with tube filaments?
A _____ -ohm resistor with a power rating of _____ .

   A. 92; .23 watt or greater
   B. 92; less than .23 watt
   C. 120; .3 watt or greater
   D. 120; less than .3 watt

26. If 4.2 kilowatts are supplied to a motor which delivers 4 horsepower, what is the efficiency of the motor?

   A. 17.76%   B. 71.04%   C. 78.33%   D. 95.23%

27. What is the frequency of an 8-pole A.C. generator that makes 1200 revolutions per minute?
_____ cycles per second.

   A. 10   B. 80   C. 600   D. 4800

28. A three-phase A.C. generator is wye connected.
If the coil voltage of the generator is 100 volts, the line voltage is _____ volts.

   A. 57.7   B. 100   C. 173   D. 200

29. The rotor of an induction motor turns at a speed of 580 rpm when the synchronous speed of the motor is 600 rpm.
The slip of the motor is

   A. 3.33%   B. 3.48%   C. 29%   D. 30%

30. Assume that 4 amperes of current flows through a solenoid that contains a total of 30 turns evenly spaced over a length of 6 inches.
The magnetomotive force of this coil will be

   A. dependent upon the material used for the core
   B. 20-ampere-turns-per-inch regardless of the core material
   C. impossible to determine with the information given
   D. constant as long as the length and number of turns are unchanged

31. A transformer has 600 turns on the primary and 400 turns on the secondary. If 60 volts A.C. are applied to this transformer, the induced voltage in the secondary is _____ volts.

    A. 10 B. 20 C. 30 D. 40

32. An electric fan uses an alternating effective or rms current of 20 amperes. The MAXIMUM current is CLOSEST to which one of the following? _____ amperes.

    A. 28.28 B. 31.39 C. 32.74 D. 34.14

33. A 110-volt, variable-frequency, A.C. generator is connected to a load consisting of a capacitor of 3 μf.
    If a frequency of 40 cycles per second is used, the capacitive reactance of the circuit is _____ ohms.

    A. 995 B. 1327 C. 1659 D. 1769

34. A 50-volt scale voltmeter requires .025 ampere for full-scale deflection. The ohms-per-volt value of the voltmeter is

    A. 0.025 B. 0.040 C. 4.0 D. 40.0

35. In a certain circuit, three inductances of 3 henrys, 4 henrys, and 6 henrys are connected in parallel with no magnetic coupling between the inductors.
    The total inductance of the circuit is CLOSEST to which one of the following? _____ henry(s).

    A. .75 B. 1.33 C. 13 D. 72

36. If gear A rotates clockwise at 500 rpm, gear C rotates
    A. clockwise, faster than A
    B. clockwise, slower than A
    C. counterclockwise, slower than A
    D. counterclockwise, faster than A

37.

Of the above, which provide the HIGHEST mechanical advantage?

    A. A   B. A and B   C. B and C   D. C

38. When two forces of 10 pounds and 24 pounds act upon a body at right angles to each other, the magnitude of the resultant is

    A. 26   B. 25.5   C. $\sqrt{34}$ D. 17

39. If a pulley system requires a man to pull 20 feet of rope to raise a load 5 feet, the mechanical advantage is

    A. 100   B. 50   C. 25   D. 4

40. The BEST of the following for the conversion of heat energy into mechanical energy is the _____ cycle.

    A. Otto   B. joule   C. diesel   D. Carnot

41. Absolute temperature is

    A. -273° C   B. -100° F   C. 0° C   D. 0° F

42. A four cycle engine has a compression stroke, a power stroke, an intake stroke, and an exhaust stroke.
The CORRECT sequence of strokes is

    A. compression, power, intake, exhaust
    B. power, intake, exhaust, compression
    C. intake, compression, power, exhaust
    D. power, exhaust, compression, intake

43. Which one of the following is NOT a factor in actual steam turbine efficiency? _____ losses.

    A. Radiation   B. Nozzle
    C. Evaporation   D. Bucket

44. If a steam turbine takes in steam at 350°C and exhausts it at 188°C, what is its theoretical efficiency?

    A. 53%   B. 46%   C. 26%   D. 6%

45. If the cost of one BTU is $.0002, what is the cost of raising the temperature of one ton of water from 40°F to 68°F at 100% efficiency?

    A. $11.20   B. $5.60   C. $4.00   D. $1,12

46. For measuring high temperatures, which one of the following is used?

    A. Alcohol thermometer   B. Mercury thermometer
    C. Strain thermometer   D. Pyrometer

47. According to the molecular theory, if we strike a piece of iron with a heavy hammer, the

    A. mass kinetic energy of the hammer remains the same
    B. molecules of the hammer and the piece of iron are thrown into more violent agitation

C. molecules of the iron only are thrown into more violent agitation
D. molecules of the hammer only are thrown into more violent agitation

48. In which one of the following is the unequal expansion of two metals of little or no consequence? 48._____

   A. Pendulum
   B. Balance wheel
   C. Metallic thermometer
   D. Flywheel

49. For an isothermal change, which one of the following formulas applies? 49._____

   A. $PV = K$
   B. $PV^n = K$
   C. $P = Vn$
   D. $V = K$

50. Which one of the following laws does NOT apply to gases? _____ Law. 50._____

   A. Boyle's
   B. Charles'
   C. Avogadro's
   D. Galton's

KEY (CORRECT ANSWERS)

1. D	11. C	21. A	31. D	41. A
2. C	12. B	22. D	32. A	42. C
3. A	13. D	23. D	33. B	43. C
4. B	14. B	24. C	34. D	44. C
5. D	15. B	25. A	35. B	45. D
6. B	16. C	26. B	36. A	46. D
7. C	17. C	27. B	37. C	47. B
8. A	18. D	28. C	38. A	48. D
9. A	19. D	29. A	39. D	49. A
10. C	20. D	30. B	40. D	50. D

TEST 2

DIRECTIONS: Each question or incomplete statement is followed by several suggested answers or completions. Select the one that BEST answers the question or completes the statement. *PRINT THE LETTER OF THE CORRECT ANSWER IN THE SPACE AT THE RIGHT.*

1. Which one of the following is NOT normally part of a steam power plant?

    A. Boiler feed with water pump
    B. Condensers
    C. Air compressor
    D. Blowers

2. The ramjet engine does NOT have

    A. a compressor
    B. a combustion chamber
    C. fuel nozzles
    D. an exhaust

3. Which one of the following is NOT equal to one horsepower?

    A. 150 pounds moved 220 feet in one minute
    B. 33,000 pounds moved one foot in one minute
    C. 300 pounds moved 75 feet in one minute
    D. 550 pounds moved 1 foot in one second

4. In the English system of measurement, power is USUALLY expressed in

    A. centimeters per second
    B. miles per hour
    C. foot pounds per second
    D. meters per mile

5. The power of an engine may be expressed as which one of the following?
   HP =

    A. $\dfrac{PLAN}{33,000}$
    B. $\dfrac{33,000}{PLAN}$
    C. $\dfrac{PAL}{5250L}$
    D. $\dfrac{PAL}{5250N}$

6. When a 100 lb. weight is lifted 40' in 10 minutes, how much work is done? _____ ft.lbs.

    A. 4,000
    B. 400
    C. 66
    D. none of the above

7. Which one of the following is CLOSEST to the % of radiant energy reflected by aluminum foil used as thermal insulation?

    A. 95   B. 85   C. 75   D. 65

8. Which one of the following is NOT normally part of an air conditioning system?

    A. Compressor
    B. Ducts
    C. Electric motor
    D. Differential gear

9. Which one of the following is NOT related to an indication of temperature?

    A. Centigrade
    B. Baume
    C. Kelvin
    D. Celsius

10. Lift on the wing of an airplane depends on a principle of 10.____

    A. Avogadro   B. Wright   C. Charles   D. Bernoulli

11. A screw is a form of the 11.____

    A. lever   B. pulley
    C. inclined plane   D. wheel and axle

12. Of the following, the FINEST thread is 12.____

    A. 8-36   B. 10-24   C. 1/4-20   D. 1/2-20

13. Of the following tools, the one which should be used to measure MOST accurately the diameter of a cylinder is the _____ caliper. 13.____

    A. vernier   B. inside
    C. hermaphrodite   D. outside

14. Which one of the following instruments would NOT generally be found on a piston-type airplane? 14.____

    A. Wattmeter   B. Altimeter
    C. Chronometer   D. Tachometer

15. The door knob is an example of a(n) 15.____

    A. pulley   B. inclined plane
    C. lever   D. wheel and axle

16. For a given tank volume, the shape which offers the GREATEST economy in surface area is 16.____

    A. sphere   B. cylinder   C. cube   D. pyramid

17. The flat pattern of a sheet metal cone is a 17.____

    A. triangle   B. hemisphere
    C. sector of a circle   D. circle

18. The modulus of elasticity of any metal is its 18.____

    A. index of refraction   B. index of stiffness
    C. measure of malleability   D. index of ductility

19. A wide flange beam is superior to an American standard bean of 19.____

    A. shear and bending   B. bending only
    C. shear only   D. neither shear nor bending

20. The point of maximum bending moment in a beam is located 20.____

    A. at the point of zero shear
    B. under the largest concentrated load
    C. near the center
    D. at the point of least deflection

21. The MAXIMUM internal stress in a wide flange beam occurs

    A. at the neutral axis
    B. at the extreme outer fiber
    C. uniformly throughout the section
    D. none of the above

22. Assuming a uniform cross-section area, the ideal section for a wood column is a(n)

    A. rectangle   B. square   C. octagon   D. circle

23. Torsion in a shaft is an internal stress which is a function of the

    A. torque applied   B. length of the shaft
    C. metal used   D. weight of the pulley

24. The intensity of the shearing stress in a shaft

    A. is uniform throughout the section
    B. increases from zero at the center
    C. decreases as the torque increases
    D. increases from zero at the surface

25. The principle that stress is proportional to the deformation up to the yield point is established in _____ law.

    A. Euler's   B. Hooke's   C. Pascal's   D. Newton's

26. The proportion 1: 2: 4 in concrete represents, respectively,

    A. water, cement, sand   B. sand, cement, gravel
    C. cement, water, sand   D. cement, sand, gravel

27. All steel contains iron and some

    A. carbon   B. nickel   C. vanadium   D. chrome

28. A lally column is made of

    A. cast iron pipe filled with concrete
    B. a rolled steel section
    C. cast iron
    D. steel pipe filled with concrete

29. Vermiculite is used in concrete because it

    A. retards the set
    B. has exceptional compressive strength
    C. is cheaper than crushed rock
    D. makes lightweight concrete

30. Terrazzo is composed of a cement mixture and

    A. marble chips   B. crushed limestone
    C. ceramic tile chips   D. bank run sand

31. The percentage of radiant heat loss compared to the total heat loss through the walls of an uninsulated frame house is

    A. over 65%
    B. about 50%
    C. under 35%
    D. indeterminate

32. A steel tie rod supports a load of 84,000 lbs. in tension.
    Using an ultimate stress of 63,000 psi and a safety factor of 4, the cross-section area of the rod should be CLOSEST to which one of the following?
    _____ square inches.

    A. 1/3 B. 2 1/2 C. 3 D. 5 1/3

33. The number of board feet in a 3" x 8" joist, 16 ft. in length, is

    A. 48 B. 32 C. 24 D. 16

34. In calculating the force needed to punch a rivet hole in a steel plate, the designer would have to know

    A. area of the hole and plate thickness
    B. diameter of the hole, modulus of elasticity, shearing stress
    C. plate thickness, diameter of hole, shearing stress
    D. capacity of the punch, plate thickness, modulus of rupture

35. A welding bead has a design stress of 2400 lbs. per linear inch.
    What is the safe load of a 12" weld?

    A. 14,400 B. 16,800 C. 24,000 D. 28,800

36. Contour lines on a plot plan are used to show

    A. various ground elevations
    B. the ground slope at any point
    C. where to excavate
    D. location of drainage lines

37. Which one of the following should be the heaviest line on a working drawing?
    _____ line.

    A. Plumb
    B. Object
    C. Cross-hatch
    D. Dimension

38. Of the following groups, the one which indicates three common types of pictorial drawing is

    A. isometric, cubic, oblique
    B. oblique, perspective, cubic
    C. oblique, isometric, perspective
    D. perspective, cubic, isometric

39. A sectional view does NOT

    A. show internal construction
    B. indicate kind of material
    C. require cross-hatching
    D. show hidden lines

40. Which one of the following is usually shown by a one-point perspective drawing?

    A. The elevation of a building
    B. The pictorial drawing of a plan
    C. The interior of a room
    D. A machine part

41. The moment of inertia of the illustrated rectangular wood section about its horizontal axis is

    A. 128 in⁴
    B. 128 in³
    C. 16 in⁴
    D. 16 in³

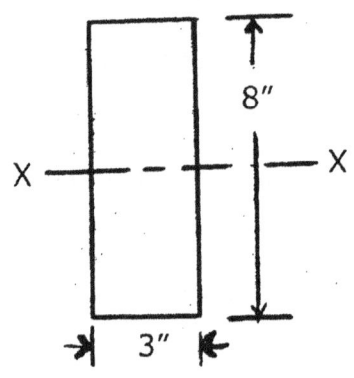

42. The reaction at A, in lbs., is
    A. 320
    B. 480
    C. 560
    D. 600

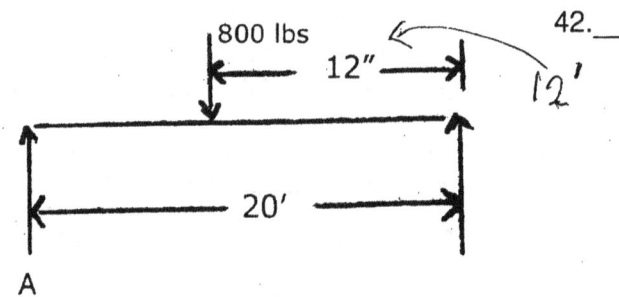

43. The distance of the center of gravity of the angle above the base in the accompanying sketch is
    A. 2.0"
    B. 1.5"
    C. 1.1"
    D. 1.0"

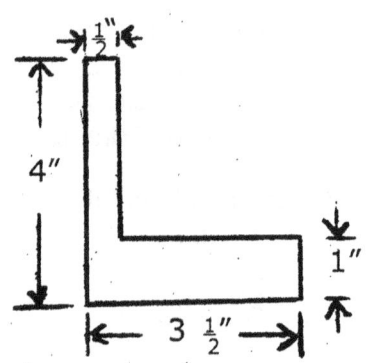

44. The rivet connection shown at the right which will shear first, assuming identical rivets and plate thickness, is
    A. I
    B. II
    C. III
    D. IV

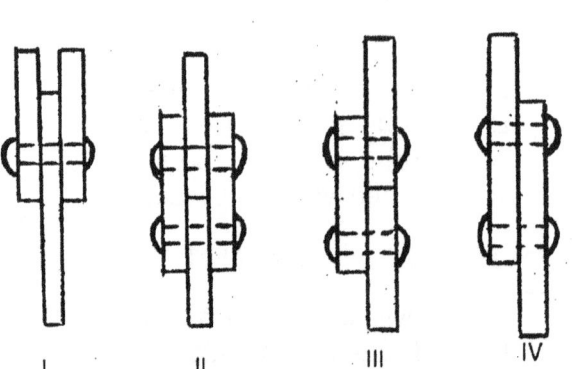

45.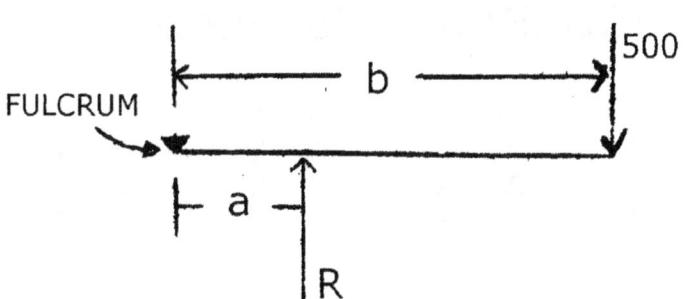

The resistance needed to keep the load in the above illustration in equilibrium is

A. $\dfrac{500b}{a}$ B. 500ab   C. $\dfrac{500a}{b}$ D. 500b

46. The rise in the cross-section of a roadway pavement, from edge to center, is USUALLY called the

A. slope   B. depth   C. elevation   D. crown

47. A device used for measuring any angle on a drawing is a

A. vernier   B. protractor
C. panimeter   D. compass

48. *Vellum* is a term used to describe a type of

A. paint   B. paper
C. ink   D. tracing cloth

49. The hardness of the pencil commonly used in making tracings on paper is MOST NEARLY

A. 2B   B. 4B   C. 2H   D. 6H

50. In orthographic representation, an auxiliary view is a view

A. of a section through the object
B. of bottom, back or left side, of top, front and right side are given
C. not parallel to any of the three principal planes of projection
D. parallel to one of the principal planes of projection and helpful in identifying the object

KEY (CORRECT ANSWERS)

1. C	11. C	21. B	31. A	41. A
2. A	12. A	22. D	32. D	42. B
3. C	13. A	23. A	33. B	43. C
4. C	14. A	24. B	34. C	44. C
5. A	15. C	25. B	35. D	45. A
6. A	16. A	26. D	36. A	46. D
7. A	17. C	27. A	37. B	47. B
8. D	18. B	28. D	38. C	48. B
9. B	19. B	29. D	39. D	49. C
10. D	20. A	30. A	40. C	50. C

TEST 3

DIRECTIONS: Each question or incomplete statement is followed by several suggested answers or completions. Select the one that BEST answers the question or completes the statement. *PRINT THE LETTER OF THE CORRECT ANSWER IN THE SPACE AT THE RIGHT.*

1. A body immersed in a fluid is buoyed up by a force equal to the weight of the fluid displaced by the body is 1._____

   A. Boyle's Law
   B. Archimedes' Principle
   C. Hooke's Law
   D. Pascal's Law

2. The angle formed by the bisectors of the two acute angles of a right triangle contains 2._____

   A. 45° B. 67 1/2° C. 105° D. 135°

3. Five pounds of water coming from a reservoir whose surface is 140 feet above a turbine possesses a potential energy of _____ ft.lbs. 3._____

   A. 28 B. 135 C. 145 D. 700

4. An example of a chemical change is 4._____

   A. freezing of water
   B. dissolving of salt
   C. formation of snow
   D. burning of paper

5. One horsepower is equivalent to _____ ft.lbs./sec.(min.). 5._____

   A. 500 B. 600 C. 30,000 D. 33,000

6. A tank 12 feet in diameter contains water to a depth of 10 feet. The pressure at the bottom of the tank is APPROXIMATELY _____ lbs. per _____ . 6._____

   A. 62.5; sq.in.
   B. 625; sq.ft.
   C. 62.5; cubic foot
   D. 625; cubic foot

7. The time required for a given quantity of oil to flow through a capillary tube under specified conditions is known as 7._____

   A. specific gravity
   B. viscosity
   C. power point
   D. capillary action

8. The conversion of rectilinear to rotary motion may be MOST easily accomplished by means of a 8._____

   A. crosshead
   B. cam
   C. slide mechanism
   D. crank

9. In the following group, the HARDEST material is 9._____

   A. iron B. bronze C. brass D. glass

10. Thermos bottles are silvered to prevent the exchange of heat by 10._____

    A. convection
    B. evaporation
    C. conduction
    D. radiation

11. The velocity divided by the time in which the change is made equals

    A. speed
    B. r.p.m.
    C. rest
    D. acceleration

12. The rate of evaporation of a boiling liquid may be increased by

    A. decreasing the surface pressure
    B. maintaining a steady heat
    C. increasing the pressure on the surface
    D. adding salt

13. Euler's formula is useful in

    A. electronics
    B. structural design
    C. metallurgy
    D. air conditioning

14. The property which enables a material to return to its original shape and dimensions is called its

    A. elasticity
    B. ductility
    C. malleability
    D. ability to be hardened

15. In graphical representation of forces, the length of the line indicates the

    A. point of application
    B. magnitude
    C. direction
    D. center of gravity

16. The acid USUALLY used in a lead storage battery is

    A. sulphuric
    B. phosphoric
    C. muriatic
    D. nitric

17. .434 pounds per square inch is the constant for

    A. weight of a cubic inch of water
    B. atmospheric pressure
    C. pressure at the bottom of a column of water 1 foot high
    D. pressure at the bottom of a column of water 27.7 inches high

18. Water reaches its maximum density at _____ °F.

    A. 10.0   B. 29.0   C. 39.2   D. 42.0

19. When the battery is fully charged, the specific gravity of the electrolyte should be

    A. 1100   B. 1275   C. 1800   D. 3200

20. When soldering galvanized iron sheet, the BEST flux to use is

    A. cut muriatic acid
    B. rosin
    C. sal ammoniac
    D. raw muriatic acid

21. Putting zinc chips in hydrochloric acid produces

    A. soldering salt concentrates
    B. killed acid
    C. hydrofluoric acid
    D. muriatic acid

22. An elastic stop nut 22._____

   A. has a fiber composition collar grooved in above the threads
   B. is made of rubber
   C. can stretch along the bolt
   D. expands more than the ordinary nut

23. The LARGEST constituent of Monel metal is 23._____

   A. copper   B. brass   C. nickel   D. steel

24. The hand brake in a sheet metal shop is used to 24._____

   A. bend metal to shape   B. roll metal to shape
   C. cut metal   D. break metal

25. A dipping solution used to clean a soldering copper is made of 25._____

   A. sal ammoniac and water
   B. nitric acid and water
   C. table salt and vinegar
   D. hydrochloric acid and water

26. Killed acid is 26._____

   A. zinc sulphate   B. copper chloride
   C. copper sulphate   D. zinc chloride

27. To anneal copper or silver, heat the metal to 27._____

   A. white hot, and cool slowly
   B. a straw color, and cool in sand
   C. a blue color, and leave it on the furnace
   D. a dull red color, and plunge into cold water

28. The addition of more tin to solder 28._____

   A. raises the melting point
   B. lowers the melting point
   C. does not alter the melting point
   D. produces a new alloy

29. A Parker Kalon screw is a _____ screw. 29._____

   A. machine   B. lag
   C. round head wood   D. sheet metal

30. A body of sand used to form a Hole in a casting is called a 30._____

   A. vent   B. core   C. sprue   D. gate

31. Core prints are used to 31._____

   A. strengthen cores
   B. locate cores in the mold
   C. make holes in castings
   D. identify patterns

32. Shrinkage allowance is seldom made for _____ sized patterns.

    A. small
    B. medium
    C. large
    D. very large

33. One-quarter inch per foot is the shrinkage allowance for

    A. type metal
    B. brass
    C. iron
    D. aluminum

34. A master pattern is a(n)

    A. metal pattern
    B. wooden pattern with double allowance for shrinkage and finish
    C. plaster pattern
    D. accurate pattern

35. The drag refers to

    A. the slow progress of the work
    B. the lower part of a flask
    C. the dross on the molten metal
    D. a part of the electric crane

36. Pitch is the

    A. distance that the propeller would advance along its axis in one revolution
    B. distance from the center of the hub to the circumference of the blade
    C. distance that the blade would travel along the helix
    D. angle of a propeller's blade

37. The term *loose piece* refers to

    A. a split pattern
    B. an undercut projecting part
    C. coping down to an irregular parting
    D. stopping off

38. The angle, in degrees, upon which the principle of the core box plane is constructed is

    A. 30   B. 45   C. 60   D. 90

39. The number of times the spindle of a lathe turns in one minute is called

    A. the surface speed
    B. the cutting speed
    C. r.p.m.
    D. centrifugal speed

40. The CHIEF element in the composition of lower grade babbit metals is

    A. brass   B. lead   C. tin   D. copper

41. Another name for silicon carbide abrasive is

    A. corrundum
    B. sandstone
    C. carborundum
    D. emery

42. Broaching is the operation performed when

    A. cutting a keyway
    B. forming gear teeth
    C. drilling holes
    D. producing the rise on a cam

42._____

43. High alloy tool steels are made in the

    A. electric furnace   B. open hearth furnace
    C. Bessemer converter   D. cupola furnace

43._____

44. The Brinnell instrument measures the hardness of steel by

    A. using a steel ball
    B. using a diamond
    C. the rebound of the hammer
    D. the penetration of acid on surface

44._____

45. Steel is a(n)

    A. compound   B. element
    C. alloy   D. virgin metal

45._____

46. The shape of the curve of a screw thread is called a

    A. cycloid   B. helix
    C. parabola   D. sine curve

46._____

47. Malleable iron is made from

    A. high carbon steel   B. cast iron
    C. low carbon steel   D. wrought iron

47._____

48. The land on the milling cutters is for the purpose of

    A. guiding the cutter   B. centering the cutter
    C. holding the cutter   D. clearance

48._____

49. The involute curve is USUALLY associated with

    A. gears   B. cams
    C. screw threads   D. drill chucks

49._____

50. If the top view of a line is horizontal and the front view oblique, then the side view is

    A. horizontal   B. oblique
    C. vertical   D. a point

50._____

KEY (CORRECT ANSWERS)

1. B	11. D	21. B	31. B	41. C
2. D	12. A	22. A	32. A	42. A
3. D	13. B	23. C	33. C	43. C
4. D	14. A	24. A	34. D	44. A
5. D	15. B	25. A	35. B	45. C
6. B	16. A	26. D	36. D	46. B
7. B	17. C	27. D	37. B	47. B
8. D	18. C	28. A	38. D	48. D
9. D	19. B	29. D	39. C	49. B
10. D	20. D	30. B	40. B	50. C

EXAMINATION SECTION
TEST 1

DIRECTIONS: Each question or incomplete statement is followed by several suggested answers or completions. Select the one that BEST answers the question or completes the statement. *PRINT THE LETTER OF THE CORRECT ANSWER IN THE SPACE AT THE RIGHT.*

1. An oblique line in the front and top views will show as a(n) 1.____

    A. point
    B. horizontal line
    C. vertical line
    D. oblique line in the side view

2. Where the front view is a point, and the top view is a vertical line, the side view is a(n) 2.____

    A. point
    B. plane
    C. oblique line
    D. horizontal line

3. An obtuse angle is _____ a right angle. 3.____

    A. greater than
    B. the same as
    C. smaller than
    D. longer than

4. An American standard bolt is dimensioned 1/2 inch - 13 N.C.-2. The number 2 represents the 4.____

    A. class of fit
    B. thickness of the head
    C. diameter of the bolt
    D. length of shank which is threaded

5. If the front view is a rectangle and the side view a vertical line, then the top view is a(n) 5.____

    A. horizontal line
    B. vertical line
    C. rectangle
    D. oblique line

6. If the projections of a line are horizontal in the front and side views, the top view is 6.____

    A. horizontal
    B. a point
    C. vertical
    D. oblique

7. Using first angle projection, the 7.____

    A. top view will appear above the ground line
    B. left side view will appear to the left of the front view
    C. front view will appear above the ground line
    D. front view will appear below the ground line

8. A pictorial drawing showing a front view and two faces with receding parallel lines at a scale of 6'-1-0" is termed 8.____

    A. cavalier
    B. oblique
    C. isometric
    D. cabinet

91

9. In sheet metal pattern drawings, the type of development in which all crease lines converge to a single point is

   A. radial-line development
   B. triangulation
   C. parallel-line development
   D. spherical development

10. The trend today is to cool large electric generators by

    A. air   B. vacuum   C. water   D. hydrogen

11. The MAIN advantage of valve seat inserts is to

    A. reduce wear on the valve face
    B. reduce frequency of valve grinding
    C. keep clearance on valve more nearly constant
    D. increase the life of the valves

12. One of the following statements is INCORRECT.
    Indicate which one it is.

    A. Liquid gasoline explodes.
    B. The carburetor is a practical application of Bernoulli's principle.
    C. Air-cooled engines are lighter in weight than water-cooled engines of equal power.
    D. The thermal efficiency of a gasoline engine is higher than that of a steam engine.

13. Absolute zero, in degrees Fahrenheit, is

    A. 0°   B. 32°   C. -273.1°   D. -459.6°

14. An engine in good condition should show a reading, in inches, of vacuum of from

    A. 16 to 19   B. 17 to 21   C. 20 to 24   D. 25 to 30

15. When the accelerator is depressed quickly, the

    A. vacuum in the intake manifold increases
    B. vacuum in the float chamber increases
    C. pressure in the float chamber increases
    D. pressure in the intake manifold increases

16. In spur gearing, the depth of the tooth space below the pitch circle is called the

    A. face of tooth   B. arc of action
    C. addendum   D. dedendum

17. The opening in the cope of a mould into which the metal is poured is called the

    A. riddle   B. riser
    C. pouring basin   D. melting zone

18. At 40° F, gasoline as used in automobiles has an APPROXIMATE specific gravity of

    A. 0.75   B. 0.96   C. 1.00   D. 1.26

19. A kilowatt hour is equal to _____ foot lbs. per minute.

    A. 2543   B. 33,000   C. 3411   D. 44,253

20. Tool steel should contain a MINIMUM of

    A. carbon   B. nickel   C. manganese   D. phosphorus

21. Using the formula: Weight of air equals $\frac{1.325 \times \text{pressure}}{\text{temperature}}$, the weight of one cubic foot of air at 100° F at 29.9 barometric pressure equals _____ lbs.

    A. .0709   B. .0807   C. .39   D. 508

22. Steam is USUALLY throttled by the use of a _____ valve.

    A. globe   B. check   C. gate   D. ball

23. The critical pressure of steam in lbs. per square inch absolute is

    A. 1880   B. 2145   C. 3206   D. 3415

24. According to thermodynamic laws, if the temperature of the working substance remains constant, it is called a(n)

    A. entropy   B. isothermal change
    C. adiabatic   D. reversible adiabatic

25. Assume 40 studs 2" x 4" 10 ft. long are required. The total number of board feet equals

    A. 133   B. 267   C. 400   D. 1600

26. A Prony brake is used to obtain

    A. I.H.P.   B. B.H.P.
    C. engine speed   D. volumetric efficiency

27. The combustion cycle of a gasoline engine is called the _____ cycle.

    A. joule   B. Otto   C. Carnot   D. diesel

28. Internal stresses in gray iron castings may be relieved by

    A. pickling
    B. heating and cooling slowly
    C. heating and quenching in oil
    D. nitriding

29. An automobile traveling at the rate of 45 miles per hour has a speed of _____ feet per second.

    A. 33   B. 44   C. 66   D. 88

30. A one-inch standard bolt having 8 threads per inch U.S. Standard has a root diameter of

    A. 0.7525   B. 0.8376   C. 0.875   D. 0.9188

31. Minus 40° C equals _____ ° F.

    A. -80   B. -25.6   C. -40   D. -72

32. Condensers are placed in parallel with fluorescent glow switches in order to

    A. reduce radio interference
    B. reduce the arc
    C. compensate the power factor
    D. increase the lamp life

33. The transistor is a device which replaces some

    A. condensers   B. resistors
    C. tubes   D. choke coils

34. An iconoscope is a device used in a

    A. radio receiver   B. telephone circuit
    C. cosmic ray recorder D. television transmitter

35. The illumination on a surface five feet away from a 75 C.P. lamp would be _____ foot candles.

    A. 1 1/2   B. 3   C. 9   D. 15

36. Holding one pole of a permanent magnet near the filament of an alternating current lighted lamp will

    A. lessen the brilliancy
    B. brighten the brilliancy
    C. have no visible effect
    D. cause the filament to vibrate

37. The BEST choice of an A.C. motor to produce a high starting torque would be a

    A. synchronous
    B. split phase
    C. shaded pole
    D. wound rotor induction motor

38. The purpose of oil in transformers is to

    A. lubricate the core
    B. prevent electrolysis between the core and the winding
    C. cool the winding
    D. reduce magnetic noises

39. The speed of an induction motor is determined by the line frequency and the

    A. number of conductors in the shots
    B. size of the winding
    C. size of the magnet wire used
    D. number of poles

40. The purpose of the cathode bias resistor is to   40.____

    A. make the cathode negative with respect to the ground
    B. grid negative with respect to the cathode
    C. grid negative with respect to the ground
    D. plate positive with respect to the grid

41. The speed of a squirrel cage motor may be reduced by   41.____

    A. *inserting* a line resistance
    B. *inserting* a line reactance
    C. *increasing* the number of poles
    D. *decreasing* the number of poles

42. If the total resistance of the wire wound on a bi-polar armature is 2 ohms, the armature resistance is _____ ohms.   42.____

    A. 1/2   B. 1   C. 2   D. 4

43. If a 220 volt induction motor were operated on 110 volts, the resulting torque with the same rotor slip would be   43.____

    A. 25%   B. 33%   C. 50%   D. 100%

44. The instrument used for measuring electrical pressure is called a(n)   44.____

    A. ammeter   B. voltmeter
    C. hydrometer   D. altimeter

45. If the cross-section area of a conductor is doubled, and its length is reduced to one-half, the resistance   45.____

    A. will be double
    B. remains the same
    C. decreases to one-half
    D. decreases to one-quarter

46. Ammeter shunts are used to   46.____

    A. increase the current through the ammeter coil
    B. supply a path of low resistance for the flow of current
    C. divide the current evenly between the instrument and the shunt
    D. reduce the error of the reading

47. For a voltage to be induced into it, a conductor MUST move   47.____

    A. in the same direction as the lines of force
    B. at right angles to the lines of force
    C. against the lines and opposite in direction
    D. in a circle about the lines of force

48. The direction of rotation of a single phase A.C. induction motor may be reversed by   48.____

    A. reversing the leads to the motor
    B. changing the starting mechanism
    C. interchanging the starting field leads
    D. shifting the position of the starting switch

49. As the speed increases, the back e.m.f. of a shunt motor 49.___

    A. decreases the current taken by the motor
    B. increases until it equals the line voltage
    C. does not change
    D. decreases

50. The MOST accurate type of ammeter is the 50.___

    A. hot wire
    B. D'Arsonval
    C. inclined coil
    D. colenoidal

KEY (CORRECT ANSWERS)

1.	D	26.	B
2.	D	27.	B
3.	A	28.	B
4.	A	29.	C
5.	A	30.	B
6.	D	31.	C
7.	B	32.	C
8.	C	33.	C
9.	B	34.	C
10.	A	35.	B
11.	B	36.	D
12.	A	37.	B
13.	D	38.	C
14.	B	39.	D
15.	D	40.	B
16.	D	41.	B
17.	B	42.	C
18.	A	43.	C
19.	D	44.	B
20.	B	45.	D
21.	B	46.	B
22.	C	47.	B
23.	C	48.	C
24.	B	49.	A
25.	B	50.	B

TEST 2

DIRECTIONS: Each question or incomplete statement is followed by several suggested answers or completions. Select the one that BEST answers the question or completes the statement. *PRINT THE LETTER OF THE CORRECT ANSWER IN THE SPACE AT THE RIGHT.*

1. The line voltage of a separately excited constant speed, shunt generator drops when a load is added because the   1._____

   A. field is weakened
   B. magnetic field is distorted
   C. armature voltage drop increases
   D. armature resistance increases

2. Eddy currents can be reduced by   2._____

   A. using alternating current
   B. increasing the voltage
   C. using rubber mounts under solenoids
   D. laminating the magnetic circuit

3. To determine the power in a two-phase lighting and power system, the proper formula to use would be _____.   3._____

4. The law that stress is proportional to deformation up to the elastic limit of the material was established by   4._____

   A. Bernoulli   B. Archimedes   C. Hooke   D. Pascal

5. A cantilever beam is   5._____

   A. one which projects beyond its support
   B. a special type of bridge truss
   C. a uniformly loaded beam
   D. an unbalanced lever

6. In a right triangle having a base of 16" and an altitude of 12", the length of the hypotenuse is _____ inches.   6._____

   A. 15   B. 20   C. 20.5   D. 28

7. Find the square root of 685 correct to the nearest tenth.   7._____

   A. 26.1   B. 26.2   C. 31.3   D. 31.4

8. A line 36" long is divided into two parts in the ratio 4 to 5. The larger part is _____ inches.   8._____

   A. 13   B. 16   C. 19   D. 20

9. The formula for the area of a circle is _____.   9._____

10. The sum of the degrees in the interior angle of a regular hexagon is   10._____

    A. 54°   B. 720°   C. 630°   D. 360°

97

11. The center of the circle circumscribed about a right triangle lies

    A. inside the triangle
    B. outside the triangle
    C. on the hypotenuse of the triangle
    D. on the bisector of the right angle

12. A working drawing has

    A. one view
    B. two views
    C. three views
    D. as many views as are needed

13. Working drawings are USUALLY drawn in

    A. isometric   B. perspective
    C. orthographic   D. oblique

14. Spontaneous combustion is caused by

    A. rubbing two substances together
    B. leaving paper or rags around
    C. using a volatile oil
    D. high kindling temperatures

15. The blast furnace produces

    A. alloy steel   B. limestone
    C. wrought iron   D. pig iron

16. The factor of safety N for a structural material is _____.

17. A 12" rule has a length, in centimeters, of APPROXIMATELY

    A. 1.4   B. 2.5   C. 30   D. 100

18. Three boards 7/8" x 8" x 12.0' long contain _____ board feet.

    A. 12   B. 16   C. 18   D. 24

19. Footings for foundation walls are commonly made of

    A. 1:2:4   B. 1:14:3   C. 1:5:5   D. 1:1:5

20. A wood joist 2" x 10" x 18.0' long contains _____ board feet.

    A. 20   B. 30   C. 33   D. 40

21. The vertical wall members in a wood frame building are called

    A. joists   B. rafters   C. posts   D. studs

22. The roof framing member extending diagonally from the outside corner of a peak to the ridge is called a

    A. jack rafter   B. trimmer
    C. common rafter   D. hip rafter

23. Batter boards are used to

    A. fasten door slats
    B. plumb a brick wall
    C. layout a construction job
    D. brace a garage door

24. The pitch of a roof is the ratio of the rise to the

    A. run of the rafter
    B. length of the rafter
    C. span of the roof
    D. length of the beam

25. In a given circle with diagram of a quadrant, indicate the length of the radius.

26. The closed expansion tank is COMMONLY used in heating systems using

    A. vacuum steam
    B. low pressure steam
    C. warm air
    D. hot water

27. The combustion cycle usually employed in the ordinary gasoline automobile engine is the _____ cycle.

    A. Carnot   B. Otto   C. joule   D. diesel

28. In hardening low carbon steel by the case hardening process, use

    A. potassium cyanide
    B. molten lead
    C. common salt
    D. oil

29. The time required for a given quantity of oil to flow through a capillary tube under specified conditions is known as

    A. specific gravity
    B. power point
    C. viscosity
    D. capillary action

30. A differential manometer can be made MOST sensitive by filling the tubes with

    A. a fluid whose density is much smaller than that of the fluid being measured
    B. air
    C. a fluid whose density is much greater than that of the fluid being measured
    D. a fluid whose density is nearly equal to that of the fluid being measured

31. The detonation process in an internal combustion engine is LEAST influenced by

    A. fuel characteristics
    B. mixture conditions
    C. exhaust conditions
    D. compression ratio

32. The conversion of rectilinear to rotary motion may be MOST easily accomplished by means of a

    A. crosshead
    B. cam
    C. slide mechanism
    D. crank

33. At high speeds, the GREATEST portion of the power developed by an automobile is used in overcoming

    A. internal friction of the running gear parts
    B. road resistance
    C. air resistance
    D. tire flexure

34. A venturi tube may be found built into a

    A. steam turbine
    B. carburetor
    C. welding machine
    D. steam engine

35. The MOST popular gasoline knock suppressor compound in use today is

    A. iso-octane
    B. tetraethyl-lead
    C. heptane
    D. butane

36. Of the following *anti-freeze* solutions, the one which is MOST effective is

    A. oil
    B. denatured alcohol
    C. distilled glycerine
    D. ethylene glycol

37. Of the following welding processes, the one which is classified as plastic welding is

    A. gas torch
    B. electric arc
    C. electric resistance
    D. thermit

38. The equation which CORRECTLY expresses the chemical reaction caused by the complete combustion of the gas used in oxyacetylene welding is

    A. $C_2H_2 + O_2 = 2CO + H_2$
    B. $CH_1 + 2O_2 = CO_2 + 2H_2O$
    C. $C_2H_2 + 2\ 1/2\ O_2 = 2CO_2 + H_2O$
    D. $C_2H_2 + O_2 = 2C + 2H_2O$

39. Activated carbon is extensively used in air conditioning to absorb odors and undesirable gases.
    Nearly all gases are absorbed EXCEPT

    A. sulphur dioxide
    B. alcohol
    C. vapor
    D. ammonia

40. To obtain a cutting speed of 80 feet per minute at the outer edge of a 1 1/8" high speed drill, it must be operated at about _____ r.p.m.

    A. 272 B. 171 C. 32.5 D. 34

41. The frequency of a 4-pole alternator depends on the

    A. number of phases
    B. type of winding
    C. rotor speed
    D. field strength

42. Power factor can be found by dividing

    A. true power by apparent power
    B. volts by amperes
    C. reactance by impedance
    D. resistance by reactance

43. The line voltage in a 3-phase, 4-wire circuit is 208 volts.
    The line to neutral voltage is _____ volts.

    A. 60 B. 208 C. 104 D. 120

44. The slip of an induction motor is the

    A. end play
    B. synchronous speed
    C. difference between the synchronous speed and the full load speed
    D. difference between the synchronous speed and the no-load speed

45. The direction of rotation of a 3-phase induction motor can be reversed by

    A. shifting the brushes
    B. switching any 2 wires
    C. reversing the D.C. field connections
    D. switching all 3 wires

46. A compensator

    A. changes D.C. to A.C.
    B. is an A.C. motor starter
    C. compensates for temperature rise
    D. regulates the speed of D.C. motors

47. Synchronous motors are used because

    A. they operate on either A.C. or D.C.
    B. of constant speed
    C. of variable speed
    D. of easy starting at full load

48. A synchronous converter when used to change D.C. to A.C. is known as a(n)

    A. rectifier   B. inverter
    C. stroboscope   D. compound motor

49. The direction of rotation of a split phase motor can be reversed by

    A. reversing the plug
    B. shifting the brushes
    C. reversing the leads to the main winding
    D. adding a slip ring

50. The direction of rotation of a repulsion induction motor can be reversed by

    A. reversing the plug
    B. shifting the brushes
    C. reversing the D.C. field winding
    D. adding a condenser

KEY (CORRECT ANSWERS)

1. C
2. D
3. E $(l_1\cos\theta_1 + l_2\cos\theta_2)$
4. C
5. A
6. B
7. A
8. D
9. πr^2
10. B
11. C
12. D
13. C
14. D
15. D
16. the number over and above the calculated load
17. C
18. D
19. A
20. B
21. D
22. D
23. C
24. C
25. $r\sqrt{x^2+y^2}$

26. D
27. B
28. A
29. C
30. A
31. C
32. D
33. C
34. B
35. B
36. D
37. C
38. C
39. D
40. A
41. C
42. A
43. D
44. C
45. B
46. B
47. B
48. B
49. C
50. B

EXAMINATION SECTION
TEST 1

DIRECTIONS: Each question or incomplete statement is followed by several suggested answers or completions. Select the one that BEST answers the question or completes the statement. *PRINT THE LETTER OF THE CORRECT ANSWER IN THE SPACE AT THE RIGHT.*

1. An unbalanced bid is a bidding device used by the contractor. An example of unbalanced bidding is to put

    A. lower unit prices in all unit price items to submit a low bid
    B. lower prices on lump sum items and higher prices on unit price items
    C. lower unit prices on secondary items and higher unit prices on primary items
    D. higher prices on items built early and lower prices on items built later

    1.____

2. Clearing and grubbing as related to excavation mean cutting trees

    A. so that 1 foot remains above ground
    B. so that 6 inches remains above ground
    C. to ground level
    D. and removing the stumps of the trees

    2.____

3. The size of a bulldozer is measured by its

    A. weight
    B. flywheel horsepower
    C. ripping capacity
    D. coefficient of traction

    3.____

4. Of the following, an important use of geotextiles is

    A. as a filter in drainage control
    B. to improve the density of soil
    C. to increase the plasticity of soil
    D. to reduce the CBR of soil

    4.____

5. A graphical procedure employing a control chart is sometimes used for statistical control in highway construction. After charts of individual tests are prepared, the upper and lower limits are usually _____ standard deviation(s) from a central value.

    A. one   B. two   C. three   D. four

    5.____

6. On a highway construction job, slope stakes are usually set on both sides of the road at intervals of _____ feet.

    A. 25   B. 50   C. 75   D. 100

    6.____

7. Earth grade stakes are usually set

    A. when the slope stakes are set
    B. at the center line of the road
    C. after final grading is completed
    D. after rough grading operations have been completed

    7.____

8. In a borrow pit, measurements for the volume of earth removed are taken usually at _____ foot intervals.

   A. 25   B. 50   C. 75   D. 100

9. In placing surveying stakes for a culvert, a stake is set at the center line of the culvert. A horizontal line on the stake gives the amount of cut or fill to the _____ of the culvert.

   A. top   B. center   C. flow line   D. subgrade

10. Aeolian soils are soils formed by

    A. glacial action
    B. volcanic action
    C. being carried by water
    D. being carried by wind

11. Specific gravity of soils are in the range of

    A. 2.3 to 2.5
    B. 2.4 to 2.6
    C. 2.5 to 2.7
    D. 2.6 to 2.8

12. Of the following soils, the one that is most highly compressible has a _____ plastic limit and _____ liquid limit.

    A. low; high
    B. low; low
    C. high; low
    D. high; high

13. In the present ASSHTO soil classification systems, soils are classified into groups. The number of basic groups are

    A. 6   B. 7   C. 8   D. 9

14. In the present AASHTO soil classification system, granular materials are primarily in Group(s)

    A. A1 only
    B. A1 and A2
    C. A1, A2, and A3
    D. A1, A2, A3, and A4

15. The optimum moisture content of a soil occurs when under a given compactive effort, the soil has a maximum

    A. void ratio
    B. plasticity index
    C. elasticity
    D. density

16. The liquid limit that separates an A4 soil from an A5 soil is

    A. 10   B. 20   C. 30   D. 40

17. As part of the soil classification in a given soil is an abbreviation NP. This is an abbreviation for no

    A. permeability
    B. plasticity
    C. peat or other organic materials
    D. porosity

18. For granular materials, the maximum allowable percent passing a Number 200 sieve is

    A. 20   B. 25   C. 30   D. 35

19.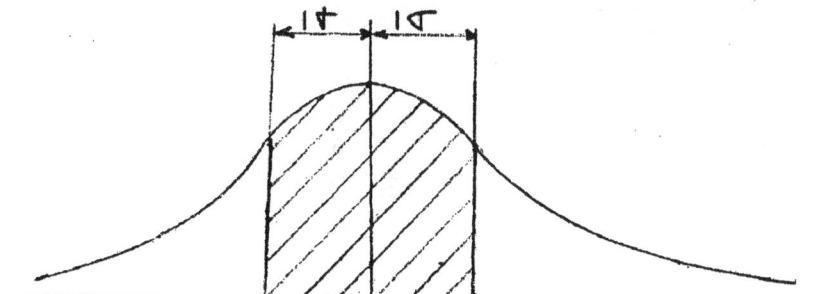

In the normal or Gauss distribution shown above, the shaded area is one standard deviation on either side of the central value covering _____ of the area under the curve.

A. 60% B. 62% C. 65% D. 68%

Questions 20-25.

DIRECTIONS: Questions 20 through 25, inclusive, refer to the diagram below of a vertical curve.

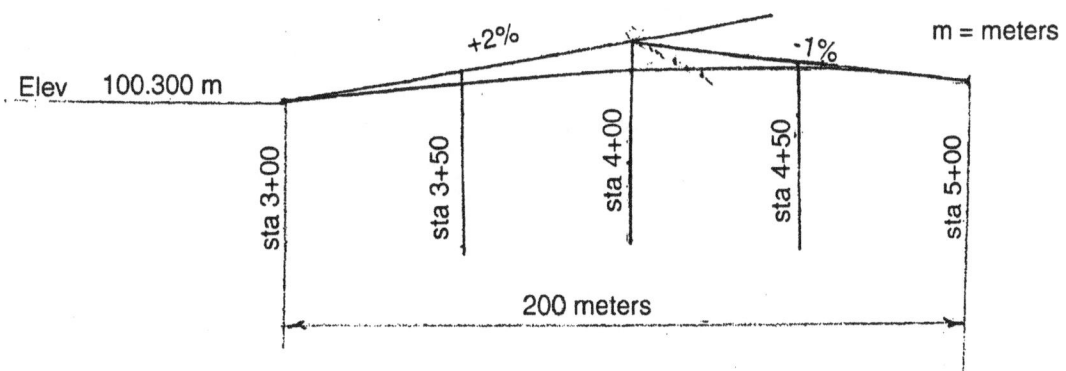

20. The elevation of the curve at Sta4+00 is _____ meters.

    A. 101.250 B. 101.350 C. 101.850 D. 102.150

21. The grade of the curve at Sta4+00 is

    A. +.5% B. +.75% C. +1.00% D. +1.25%

22. The elevation of the curve at Sta3+50 is _____ meters.

    A. 100.992 B. 101.012 C. 101.112 D. 101.212

23. The grade of the curve at Sta3+50 is

    A. 1.75% B. 1.50% C. 1.38% D. 1.25%

24. The station of the high point is

    A. 4+08.333 B. 4+16.667 C. 4+25.000 D. 4+33.333

25. The elevation of the high point is _____ meters.

    A. 101.633 B. 101.750 C. 101.833 D. 101.917

KEY (CORRECT ANSWERS)

1.	D	11.	D
2.	D	12.	A
3.	B	13.	B
4.	A	14.	C
5.	C	15.	D
6.	B	16.	D
7.	D	17.	B
8.	A	18.	D
9.	C	19.	D
10.	D	20.	B

21.	A
22.	C
23.	D
24.	D
25.	A

TEST 2

DIRECTIONS: Each question or incomplete statement is followed by several suggested answers or completions. Select the one that BEST answers the question or completes the statement. *PRINT THE LETTER OF THE CORRECT ANSWER IN THE SPACE AT THE RIGHT.*

Questions 1-3.

DIRECTIONS: Questions 1 through 3 refer to the diagram below.

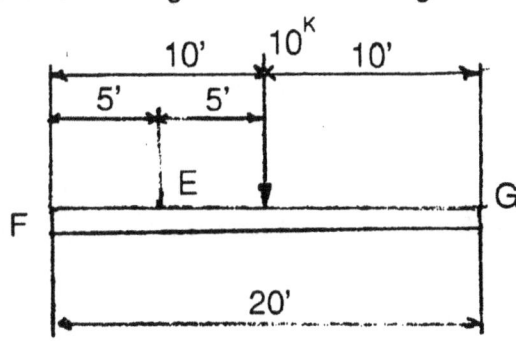

EI is constant

1. The deflection at the center of the beam is

   A. $-\dfrac{1670^{k13}}{EI}$ B. $-\dfrac{2000^{k13}}{EI}$ C. $-\dfrac{2330^{k13}}{EI}$ D. $-\dfrac{2670^{k13}}{EI}$

   1.___

2. The slope at F is

   A. $-\dfrac{200^{k12}}{EI}$ B. $-\dfrac{225^{k12}}{EI}$ C. $-\dfrac{250^{k12}}{EI}$ D. $-\dfrac{275^{k12}}{EI}$

   2.___

3. The deflection at E is

   A. $-\dfrac{966^{k13}}{EI}$ B. $-\dfrac{1046^{k13}}{EI}$ C. $-\dfrac{1096^{k13}}{EI}$ D. $-\dfrac{1146^{k13}}{EI}$

   3.___

Questions 4-7.

DIRECTIONS: Questions 4 through 7, inclusive, refer to the truss below.

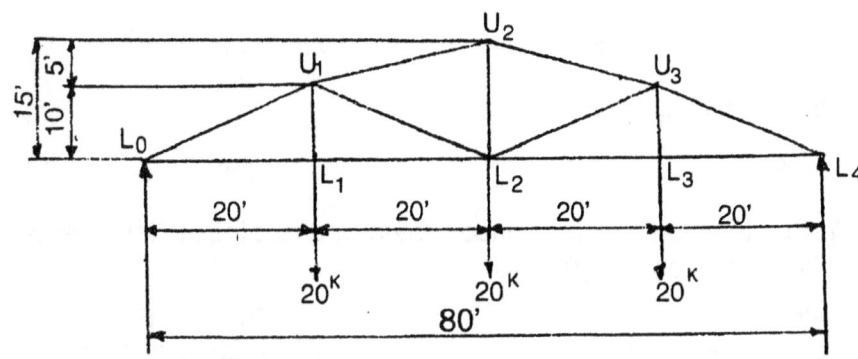

4. The load in member L_1-L_2 is   4.____

   A. $+30^k$ B. $+40^k$ C. $+50^k$ D. $+60^k$

5. The load in member U_1-U_2 is   5.____

   A. -50.9^k B. -52.9^k C. -54.9^k D. -56.9^k

6. The load in member U_1-L_2 is   6.____

   A. -3.4^k B. -5.4^k C. -7.4^k D. -9.4^k

7. The load in member U_2-L_2 is   7.____

   A. $+24.6^k$ B. $+26.6^k$ C. $+28.6^k$ D. $+30.6^k$

Questions 8-11.

DIRECTIONS: Questions 8 through 11, inclusive, refer to the diagram below of a beam with fixed ends.

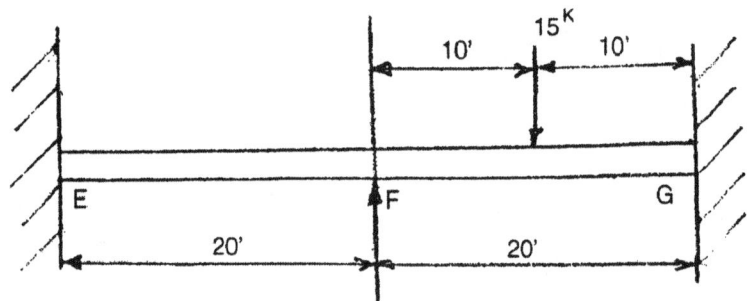

8. The moment in E is   8.____

   A. 9.4^{lk} B. 12.6^{lk} C. 14.8^{lk} D. 17.0^{lk}

9. The moment in G is   9.____

   A. 37.5^{lk} B. 40.0^{lk} C. 43.0^{lk} D. 46.9^{lk}

10. The moment at F is   10.____

    A. 14.4^{lk} B. 18.8^{lk} C. 23.2^{lk} D. 27.6^{lk}

11. The vertical reaction at E is   11.____

    A. -0.4^k B. -1.4^k C. -2.4^k D. -3.4^k

12. The former First Lady of the United States who had legislation enacted to plant wild flowers adjacent to federal highways is   12.____

    A. Rosalyn Carter   B. Barbara Bush
    C. Jackie Kennedy   D. Lady Bird Johnson

13. *Scarification* as used in the specifications means 13.____

    A. removing rust from a surface
    B. removing paint from a surface
    C. cleaning equipment
    D. loosening topsoil

14. A proposal by the contractor producing a savings to the department without impairing 14.____
    essential functions and characteristics of the facility is termed a(n)

    A. alternative suggestion
    B. design efficiency proposal
    C. value engineering proposal
    D. force account economy

15. A cubic meter is MOST NEARLY equal to _____ cubic yards. 15.____

    A. 1.31   B. 1.33   C. 1.35   D. 1.37

16. One hectare is equal to MOST NEARLY _____ acres. 16.____

    A. 2   B. 2.5   C. 3.0   D. 3.5

17. One newton is MOST NEARLY equal to _____ pounds. 17.____

    A. .12   B. .17   C. .22   D. .29

18. A metric ton is _____ pounds. 18.____

    A. 2200   B. 2400   C. 2600   D. 2800

19. A piezometer is a device that measures 19.____

    A. hydraulic pressure   B. soil compaction
    C. soil grain size   D. soil grain strength

20. Portland cement type 2 is _____ cement. 20.____

    A. high early strength
    B. low heat
    C. air entraining
    D. moderate sulfate resisting

21. Wire shall have a minimum yield strength of 240 MPa. The MPa is an abbreviation of 21.____
    _____ pascals.

    A. macro   B. micro   C. milli   D. mega

22. 7°C is, in degrees Fahrenheit, 22.____

    A. 42.6   B. 44.6   C. 46.6   D. 48.6

23. In a concrete mix, the absolute ratio of the weight of water to the weight of cement is .44. 23.____
    If a bag of cement weighs 94 pounds and there are 7.48 gallons in a cubic foot, the number of gallons of water per bag of cement for this ratio is MOST NEARLY

    A. 5.0   B. 5.5   C. 5.8   D. 6.1

24. The specifications require that when transit mixed concrete is used, approximately 90% of the design water is added followed by mixing the concrete in the drum of the truck. The remainder of the design water may be added

    A. after half the load is emptied
    B. to meet the water cement ratio requirement
    C. if the mix is not uniform
    D. to attain a suitable slump

25. For highways, the minimum median width in a divided highway is _____ feet.

    A. 2   B. 3   C. 4   D. 5

KEY (CORRECT ANSWERS)

1. A
2. C
3. D
4. D
5. C

6. C
7. B
8. A
9. D
10. B

11. B
12. D
13. D
14. C
15. A

16. B
17. C
18. A
19. A
20. D

21. D
22. B
23. A
24. D
25. C

EXAMINATION SECTION

TEST 1

DIRECTIONS: Each question or incomplete statement is followed by several suggested answers or completions. Select the one that BEST answers the question or completes the statement. *PRINT THE LETTER OF THE CORRECT ANSWER IN THE SPACE AT THE RIGHT.*

1. The ultimate strength of a short 16" x 16" concrete column with 8 #8 steel bars with f_c = 4000 psi and f_y = 69000 psi is, in kips, MOST NEARLY
   A. 1290 B. 1320 C. 1350 D. 1380

2. Transverse ties with the vertical steel #10 bars or smaller have a minimum size of _____ bar.
   A. #2 B. #3 C. #4 D. #5

3. The capacity reduction, ϕ, for shear on a concrete beam section is
   A. .75 B. .80 C. .85 D. .90

4. The balanced steel ratio occurs when the steel
   A. and concrete fail simultaneously
   B. fails before the concrete
   C. fails after the concrete
   D. reaches its ultimate strength

5. The minimum requirement of $p = \frac{200}{fy}$ is necessary in concrete beam design to insure that the
   A. concrete will not fail before the reinforcing steel
   B. member does not lose strength when it first cracks
   C. bonding between steel and concrete does not fail
   D. deflection of the beam is not excessive

6. In ultimate strength design, the ϕ value for flexure without axial load is the largest of all ϕ factors because
   A. the loads are less variable in bending than they are for axial loads
   B. there is more variability in shear loads than in bending moments
   C. steel has a greater coefficient of expansion than concrete
   D. there is less variability in steel strength than in concrete strength

7. If, in the design of a reinforced concrete beam section, the service moment is 40 k-ft. for dead load and 90 k-ft. for live load, the load factored moment is, in kip feet, MOST NEARLY (ϕ is not included)
   A. 190 B. 209 C. 219 D. 229

Questions 8-12.

DIRECTIONS: Questions 8 through 12, inclusive, refer to the reinforced concrete beam section shown below.

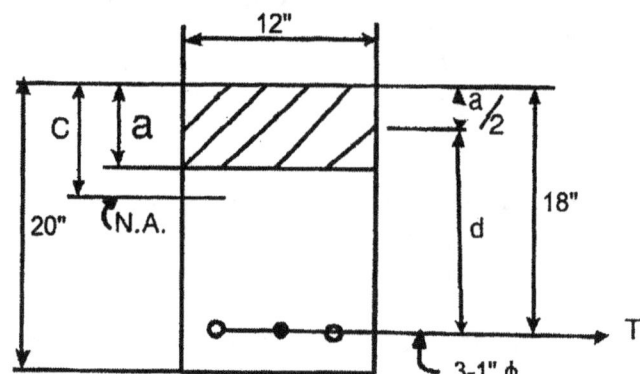

$f_c = 4000 \#/\square'$

$f_y = 60,000 \#/\square''$

Area of $1'' \phi = .79\square''$

8. The proportion of steel to concrete, p, is MOST NEARLY 8._____
   A. .011   B. .010   C. .009   D. .008

9. The maximum value of T, in kips, is MOST NEARLY 9._____
   A. 138   B. 142   C. 146   D. 150

10. The value of *a* corresponding to the maximum value of T is, in inches, MOST NEARLY 10._____
    A. 3.5   B. 3.8   C. 4.2   D. 4.6

11. The moment, in foot kips, that the beam section can carry, assuming $\phi = 0.9$, is, in foot kips, MOST NEARLY 11._____
    A. 173   B. 178   C. 183   D. 188

12. The value of *c* is, in inches, MOST NEARLY 12._____
    A. 3.7   B. 3.9   C. 4.1   D. 4.3

13. Granite is the type of rock that is 13._____
    A. silicious   B. igneous
    C. sedimentary   D. metamorphic

14. In a trial batch of concrete, the fine aggregate has a weight of 148 pounds. It has 6% of its weight in water. The specific gravity of the fine aggregate is 2.65. 14._____
    The absolute volume of the fine aggregate, in cubic feet, is MOST NEARLY
    A. .84   B. .82   C. .80   D. .78

15. The optimum concrete mix for a given structural element having a given water-cement ratio would have a 15._____
    A. maximum allowable size of coarse aggregate and a minimum allowable slump
    B. minimum allowable size of coarse aggregate and a minimum amount of slump

C. maximum allowable size of coarse aggregate and a maximum allowable slump
D. minimum size of coarse aggregate and a maximum slump

16. Bulking of sand
    A. varies inversely with the water content
    B. is greater with coarse sand than with fine sand
    C. decreases when there is high moisture in the atmosphere
    D. is a maximum when the water content is about 6% by weight

    16.____

17. A medium-curing cutback asphalt would MOST likely contain as a solvent
    A. gasoline   B. naphtha
    C. an oil of low volatility   D. kerosene

    17.____

18. The PRIMARY reason for using cutback asphalt is that it
    A. gives a harder riding surface
    B. is more resistant to softening at high outdoor temperatures
    C. requires little or no heat during placing
    D. does not age as rapidly as ordinary asphalt

    18.____

19. Emulsified asphalt is an emulsion primarily of asphalt and
    A. toluene   B. water   C. kerosene   D. naphtha

    19.____

Questions 20-22.

DIRECTIONS: Questions 20 through 22 are to be answered on the basis of the 400' vertical curve shown below.

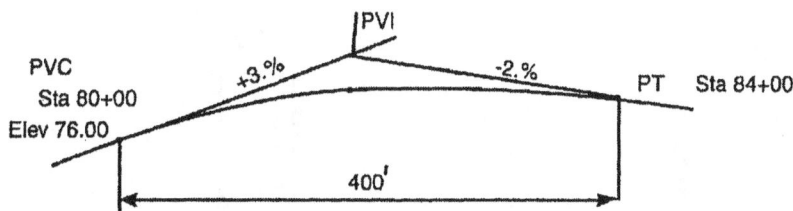

20. The elevation of the vertical curve at Sta 82+00 is, in feet, MOST NEARLY
    A. 79.25   B. 79.50   C. 79.75   D. 80.00

    20.____

21. The station at the high point of the vertical curve is MOST NEARLY
    A. 82+20   B. 82+40   C. 82+60   D. 82+80

    21.____

22. The elevation of the high point of the vertical curve is, in feet, MOST NEARLY
    A. 79.60   B. 79.70   C. 79.80   D. 79.90

    22.____

23. If a 1° central angle of a circle intercepts an arc of 100', the radius of the circle is, in feet, MOST NEARLY
    A. 5709   B. 5729   C. 5749   5769

    23.____

4 (#1)

24. A circular horizontal curve has a radius of 1600' and a tangent length of 950'. The length of the curve from PC to PT is, in feet, MOST NEARLY
   A. 1714.6   B. 1724.6   C. 1734.6   D. 1744.6

25.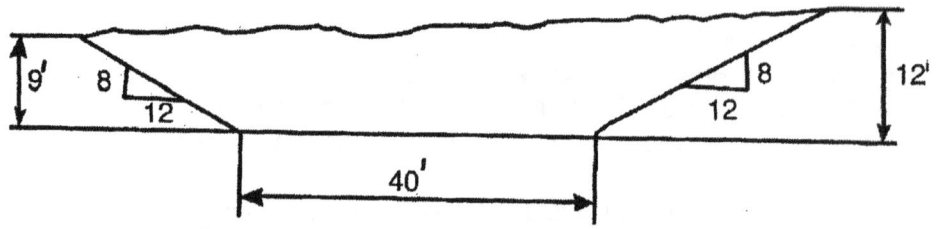

The cross-section of an area in cut in a highway excavation is shown above. the area of the cut is, in square feet, MOST NEARLY
   A. 562   B. 582   C. 602   D. 622

KEY (CORRECT ANSWERS)

1.	B	11.	A
2.	B	12.	C
3.	C	13.	B
4.	A	14.	A
5.	B	15.	A
6.	D	16.	D
7.	B	17.	D
8.	A	18.	C
9.	B	19.	B
10.	A	20.	B

21. B
22. A
23. B
24. A
25. A

TEST 2

DIRECTIONS: Each question or incomplete statement is followed by several suggested answers or completions. Select the one that BEST answers the question or completes the statement. *PRINT THE LETTER OF THE CORRECT ANSWER IN THE SPACE AT THE RIGHT.*

1. The water pressure in the pipe as shown by the manometer at the right is, in pounds per square inch, MOST NEARLY
   A. 5.5
   B. 5.9
   C. 6.3
   D. 6.7

1.

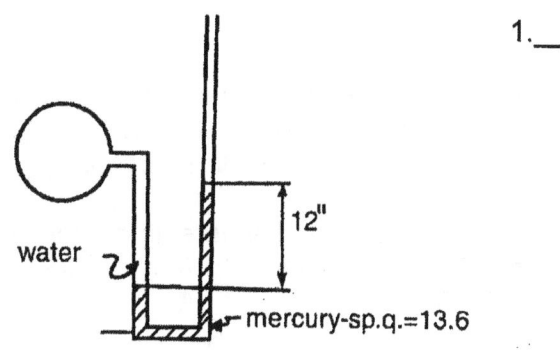

2. The theoretical discharge over a rectangular weir of length L is $Q = cL\sqrt{2qHx}$, where x is
   A. ½   B. 1   C. ³/₂   D. 2

2.____

3. If one cubic foot of water per second under a head of 80' is delivered to a turbine, the horsepower that the turbine can deliver, assuming no losses, is
   A. 5   B. 7   C. 9   D. 11

3.____

Questions 4-5.

DIRECTIONS: Questions 4 and 5 are to be answered on the basis of the diagram below of the 3" outlet from a tank of water.

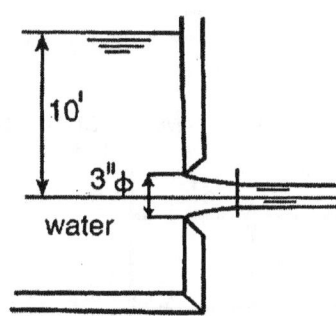

4. The velocity of the water at the point of discharge is, in feet per second, MOST NEARLY
   A. 22   B. 25   C. 28   D. 30

4.

5. The discharge rate, in cubic feet per second, is MOST NEARLY
   A. .50   B. .75   C. 1.00   D. 1.25

5.

6. When a sewer is built using vitrified clay pipe, construction starts from the _____ elevation with the bell facing _____.
   A. highest; downward
   B. highest; upward
   C. lowest; downward
   D. lowest; upward

7. A sewer that runs along a waterfront and carries sewage into a sewage treatment plant is known as a(n) _____ sewer.
   A. outfall   B. intercepting   C. relief   D. combined

8. The change in temperature, in degrees Fahrenheit, that will cause a 100 foot steel tape to lengthen .01 feet is MOST NEARLY
   A. 5   B. 10   C. 15   D. 20

9. A map is drawn to a scale of 1 inch equals 200 feet. Contours are drawn at intervals of 2 feet.
   If the distance between two adjacent contours measures ½ inch, the slope of the surface is MOST NEARLY
   A. 2%   B. 3%   C. 4%   D. 5%

10. The angle ϕ at E caused by a moment M at E is
    A. $\dfrac{ML}{EI}$
    B. $\dfrac{ML}{2EI}$
    C. $\dfrac{ML}{3EI}$
    D. $\dfrac{ML}{4EI}$

Questions 11-12.

DIRECTIONS: Questions 11 and 12 are to be answered on the basis of the following diagram.

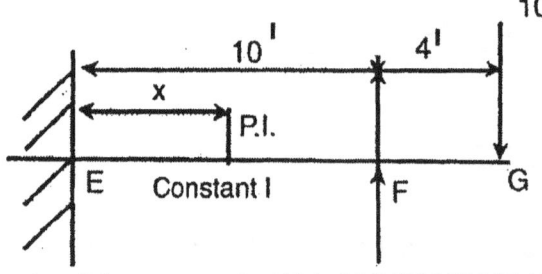

11. The magnitude of the moment at E is MOST NEARLY
    A. 20^{lk} B. 23^{lk} C. 27^{lk} D. 30^{lk}

12. The vertical reaction at E is, in kips, MOST NEARLY _____ downward.
    A. 6^K B. 5^K C. 4^K D. 3^K

3 (#2)

13. The distance x from the point E to the point of inflection is, in feet, MOST NEARLY 13.____
 A. 4.33 B. 4.00 C. 3.67 D. 3.33

Questions 14-15.

DIRECTIONS: Questions 14 and 15 are to be answered on the basis of the cantilever beam shown below.

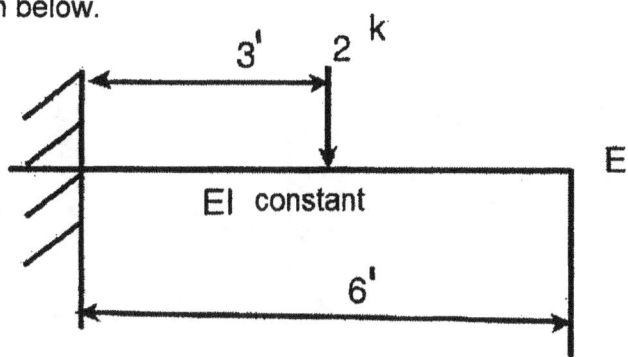

14. The deflection at the end E of the cantilever beam shown above is 14.____
 A. $30^{k13/EI}$ B. $34^{k13/EI}$ C. $40^{k13/EI}$ D. $45^{k13/EI}$

15. The slope of the beam at E is 15.____
 A. $6^{k12/EI}$ B. $9^{k12/EI}$ C. $12^{k12/EI}$ D. $15^{k12/EI}$

16. With both ends of the beam EF fixed, the magnitude of the fixed end moment at E is, in foot-kips, 16.____
 A. 18
 B. 21
 C. 24
 D. 270

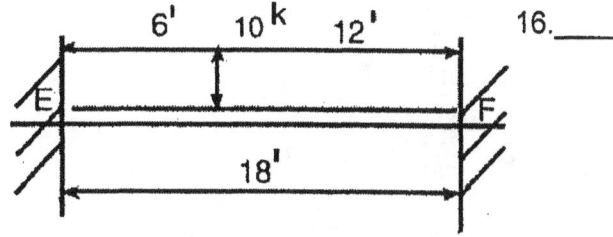

17. The conjugate beam for the beam shown at the right would be 17.____

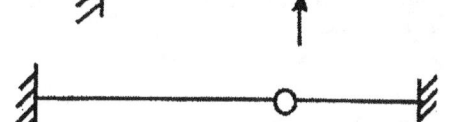

A.
B.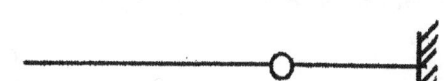

C.
D.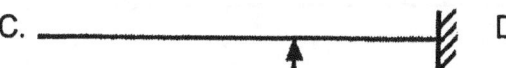

117

18. The deflection at the center of the beam shown at the right is

    A. $\dfrac{PL^3}{16EI}$
    B. $\dfrac{PL^3}{32EI}$
    C. $\dfrac{PL^3}{48EI}$
    D. $\dfrac{PL^3}{64EI}$

    18.____

    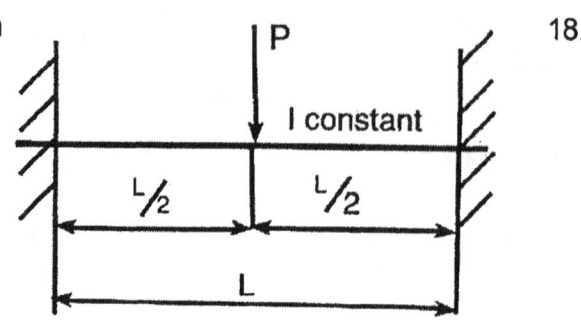

19. The deflection at the center of the beam shown at the right is

    A. $\dfrac{PL^3}{48EI}$
    B. $\dfrac{PL^3}{96EI}$
    C. $\dfrac{PL^3}{192EI}$
    D. $\dfrac{PL^3}{184EI}$

    19.____

    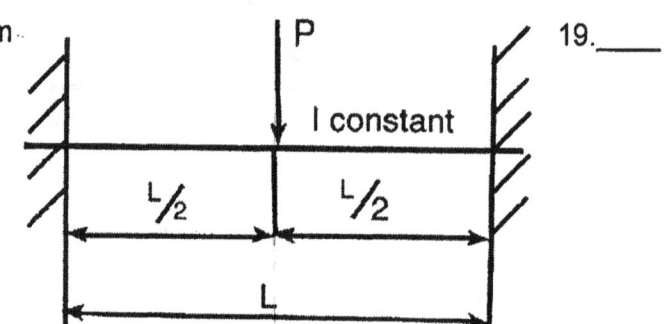

20. The offset deflection on the fixed end beam in terms of L, M, E, and I is

    A. $\dfrac{ML^2}{6EI}$
    B. $\dfrac{ML^2}{8EI}$
    C. $\dfrac{ML^2}{10EI}$
    D. $\dfrac{ML^2}{12EI}$

    20.____

    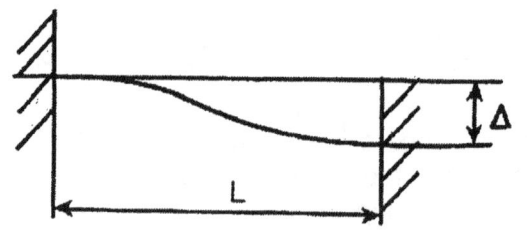

21. If the deflection on a beam is $\dfrac{KPL^3}{EI}$, where K is dimensionless, L is in feet, P is in kips, E is in kips per square inch, and I is in inches^4, the constant that the resulting product must be multiplied by in order to have the deflection in inches is

    A. 12   B. 12^2 C. 12^3 D. 12^4

    21.____

22. The maximum moment on the beam shown at the right, in foot-kips, is

    A. 16.5
    B. 18.5
    C. 20.5
    D. 22.5

    22.____

    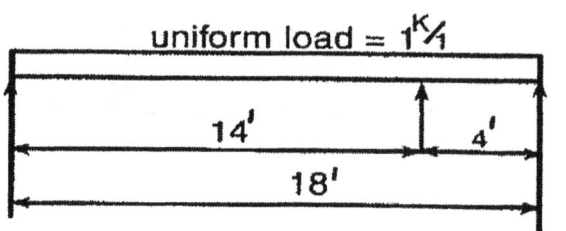

Questions 23-24.

DIRECTIONS: Questions 23 and 24 are to be answered on the basis of the beam EF shown below with a triangular loading.

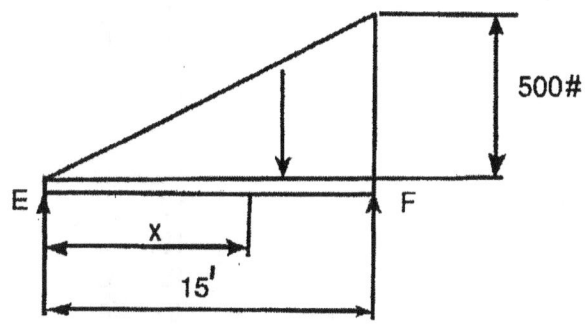

23. The distance x to the point of shears is, in feet, MOST NEARLY
    A. 8.00   B. 8.33   C. 8.66   D. 9.00

24. The maximum moment on the beam is, in foot-kips, MOST NEARLY
    A. 6.82   B. 7.22   C. 7.62   D. 8.03

25. The change in length of member EF due to the 10000 pound loads is, in inches, MOST NEARLY
    A. .032
    B. .043
    C. .056
    D. .067

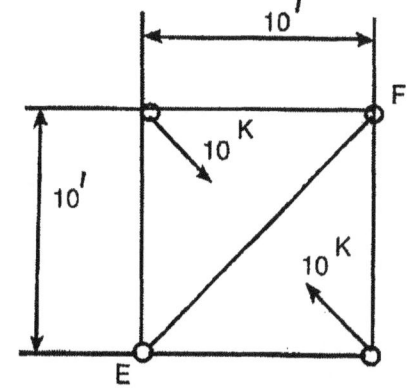

E = 30,000K/□"
Cross-section area of EF = 1 square inch

KEY (CORRECT ANSWERS)

1.	A	11.	A
2.	C	12.	A
3.	C	13.	D
4.	B	14.	D
5.	B	15.	B
6.	D	16.	D
7.	B	17.	D
8.	C	18.	C
9.	A	19.	C
10.	C	20.	A

21. C
22. C
23. C
24. B
25. C

TEST 3

DIRECTIONS: Each question or incomplete statement is followed by several suggested answers or completions. Select the one that BEST answers the question or completes the statement. *PRINT THE LETTER OF THE CORRECT ANSWER IN THE SPACE AT THE RIGHT.*

Questions 1-5.

DIRECTIONS: Questions 1 through 5, inclusive, are to be answered on the basis of the bent with rigid connections at E, F, G, and H.

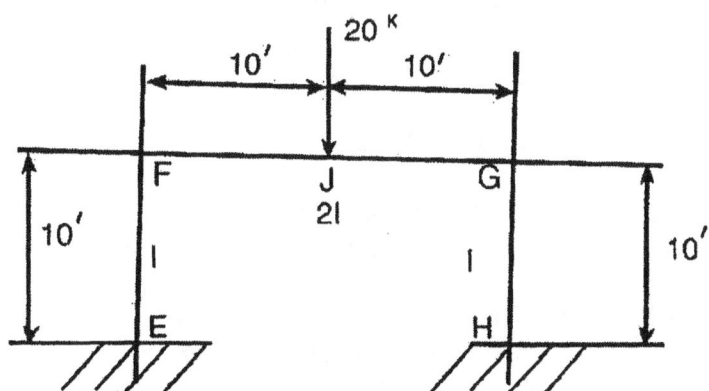

1. The vertical reaction at E is, in kips, MOST NEARLY
   A. 5   B. 7.5   C. 10   D. 12.5

2. The magnitude of the moment at F on beam FG is, in foot-kips, MOST NEARLY
   A. 25   B. 27.5   C. 30   D. 35

3. The magnitude of the moment at E on beam EF is, in foot-kips, MOST NEARLY
   A. 12.5   B. 13.8   C. 15   D. 17.5

4. The horizontal reaction at E is, in kips, MOST NEARLY
   A. 2.6   B. 3.0   C. 3.4   D. 3.8

5. The moment, in foot-kips, at J is
   A. 65   B. 70   C. 75   D. 80

Questions 6-11.

DIRECTIONS: Questions 6 through 11, inclusive, are to be answered on the basis of the following truss.

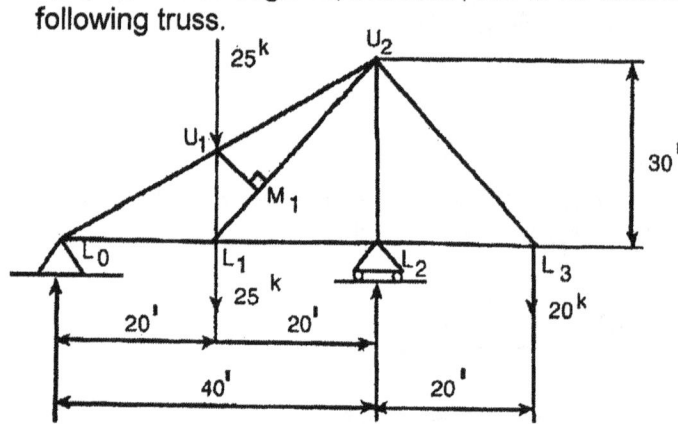

6. The length of the member U_1-M_1 is MOST NEARLY
   A. 8.3 ft.   B. 8.6 ft.   C. 8.9 ft.   D. 9.2 ft.

7. The load in member U_1-M_1 is MOST NEARLY
   A. 0
   B. 15k compression
   C. 20k compression
   D. 25k compression

8. The load in member U_2-L_2 is MOST NEARLY _____ compression.
   A. 55^k B. 50^k C. 45^k D. 40^k

9. The load in member U_1-L_1 is MOST NEARLY _____ compression.
   A. 10^k B. 15^k C. 20^k D. 25^k

10. The load in member L_1-U_2 is MOST NEARLY _____ tension.
    A. 50k   B. 55k   C. 60k   D. 65k

11. The load in member U_1-U_2 is MOST NEARLY _____ compression.
    A. 20k   B. 25k   C. 30k   D. 35k

12. If the center support of the uniformly loaded beam settles slightly, then the
    A. reaction at F increases
    B. magnitude of the moment at F increases
    C. magnitude of the shear at G decreases
    D. reaction at E increases

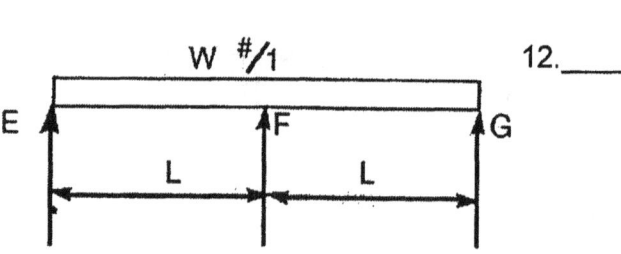

Questions 13-16.

DIRECTIONS: Questions 13 through 16, inclusive, are to be answered on the basis of the truss shown below carrying a uniform moving live load of 2 kips per foot.

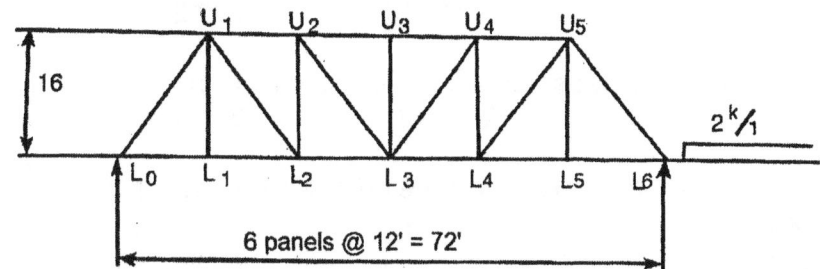

13. The type of truss shown above is known as a _____ truss.   13.____
    A. Pratt   B. Howe   C. Warren   D. Whipple

14. The influence line diagram for member U_2-L_3 is as shown in   14.____
    A.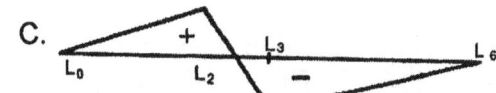
    B.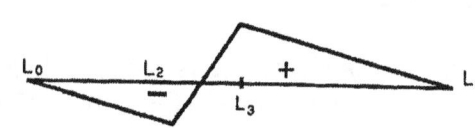
    C.
    D.

15. The ordinate on the influence line diagram for U_2-L_3 at L_3 is MOST NEARLY   15.____
    A. $3/8$ B. $1/2$ C. $5/8$ D. $3/4$

16. The maximum tensile load on U_2-L_3 caused by a $2^{k/1}$ live load coming from the right end of the truss is, in kips, MOST NEARLY   16.____
    A. 21   B. 23   C. 25   D. 27

17. The largest size weld that can be made in one pass is, in inches,   17.____
    A. $3/16$ B. $1/4$ C. $5/16$ D. $3/8$

18. The maximum allowable shearing stress on fillet welds made with E7018 welding rods is _____ kips/sq.in.   18.____
    A. 18   B. 19   C. 20   D. 21

19. The symbol for field welding is as shown in   19.____
    A. F
    B. FW
    C.
    D.

20. A 3x3/8 plate is to be welded to the back of a channel to develop the full strength of the plate in tension. The allowable tensile stress in the plate is 24 k/☐". The allowable shearing stress in the ¼ weld is 21k/☐".
    The minimum length of weld needed is, in inches, MOST NEARLY
    A. 7½   B. 9   C. 10½   D. 12

21. The minimum size fillet weld to use on a ⁷⁄₈" thick plate is, in inches,
    A. ³⁄₁₆   B. ¼   C. ⁵⁄₁₆   D. ³⁄₈

22. Shown below is a 5x5x½L to be welded to the gusset plate under the angle to carry a 60k load.

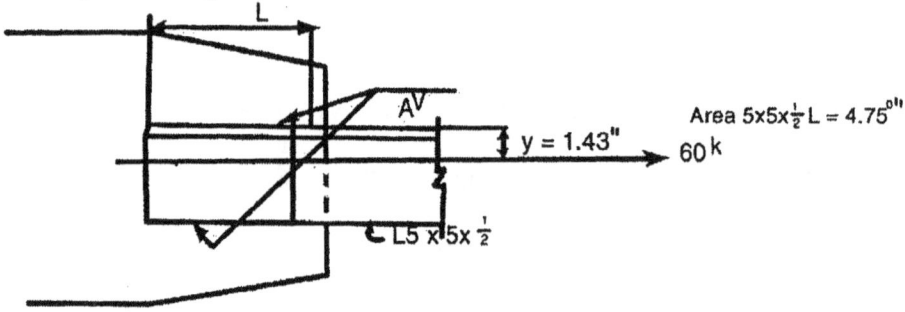

The allowable shear stress in the weld is 21k/☐". The center of gravity of the welds are to coincide with the center of gravity of L5x5x½. The length L is, in inches, MOST NEARLY
    A. 10.0   B. 11.5   C. 13.0   D. 14.5

23. Some of the bolts in a structural steel structure have square heads. The ASTM designation of these bolts would MOST likely be
    A. A307   B. A325   C. A490   D. A502

24. For high strength bolts in bearing, if Fu is the tensile strength of the steel connected by the bolts, with adequate bolts spacing, the allowable bearing stress is _____ Fu.
    A. 1.0   B. 1.25   C. 1.5   D. 1.75

25. The $\frac{d}{dx}(e^{\log x})$ is equal to
    A. e^x B. 1   C. $x \log x$ D. $\frac{1}{x}$

KEY (CORRECT ANSWERS)

1.	C		11.	B
2.	A		12.	D
3.	A		13.	A
4.	D		14.	D
5.	C		15.	C
6.	A		16.	D
7.	A		17.	C
8.	A		18.	D
9.	D		19.	D
10.	C		20.	A

21. C
22. B
23. A
24. C
25. B

TEST 4

DIRECTIONS: Each question or incomplete statement is followed by several suggested answers or completions. Select the one that BEST answers the question or completes the statement. *PRINT THE LETTER OF THE CORRECT ANSWER IN THE SPACE AT THE RIGHT.*

Questions 1-2.

DIRECTIONS: Questions 1 and 2 are to be answered on the basis of the bolted connection supporting a 15k eccentric load shown below.

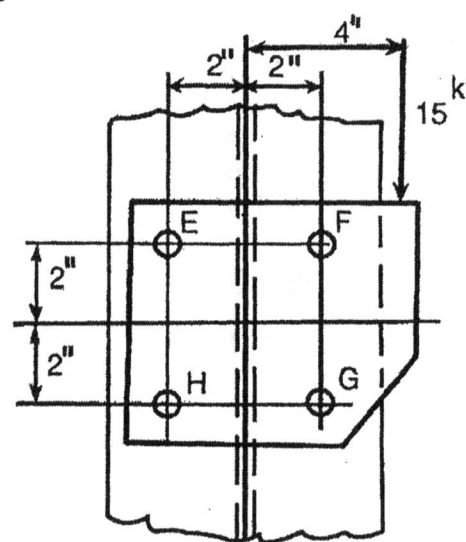

1. The bolts that carry the largest load are
   A. E and F   B. F and G   C. G and H   D. H and E

2. The maximum load on a bolt is, in kips, MOST NEARLY
   A. 7.2   B. 7.6   C. 8.0   D. 8.4

3. The value of the determinant $\begin{vmatrix} 2 & 1 & 3 \\ 1 & 5 & -6 \\ 1 & 2 & 0 \end{vmatrix}$ is
   A. +3   B. +6   C. +9   D. +12

4. $\int_0^{\pi/4} \cos x \sin^2 x \, dx$ is equal to
   A. $\frac{\sqrt{2}}{10}$ B. $\frac{\sqrt{2}}{12}$ C. $\frac{\sqrt{2}}{14}$ D. $\frac{\sqrt{2}}{16}$

1.____

2.____

3.____

4.____

2 (#4)

5. In the xy plane, the distance from point E to the line y = x + 2 is
   A. $\sqrt{2}$
   B. $2\sqrt{2}$
   C. $3\sqrt{3}$
   D. $4\sqrt{2}$

   5._____

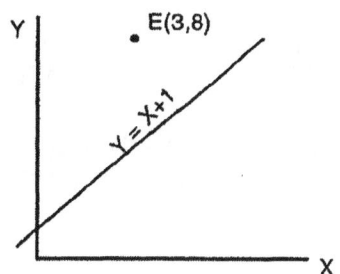

6. The area of the ellipse is $\frac{x^2}{a^2} + \frac{y^2}{b^2} = 1$
   A. $\frac{\pi ab}{4}$
   B. $\frac{\pi ab}{2}$
   C. πab
   D. $\frac{3}{2}\pi ab$

   6._____

7. Of the following matrix multiplications, the one that cannot be carried out is

   A. $\begin{bmatrix} e & f \\ g & h \end{bmatrix} \begin{bmatrix} j \\ k \end{bmatrix}$
   B. $\begin{bmatrix} e & f \\ g & h \end{bmatrix} \begin{bmatrix} j & k \end{bmatrix}$
   C. $\begin{bmatrix} e & f & g \end{bmatrix} \begin{bmatrix} h \\ j \\ k \end{bmatrix}$
   D. $\begin{bmatrix} e \\ f \\ g \end{bmatrix} \begin{bmatrix} h & j & k \end{bmatrix}$

   7._____

8. Of the following statements relating to matrix operations, the one that is NOT correct is the _____ law of _____ applies to matrices.
   A. associative; addition
   B. associative; multiplication
   C. commutative; addition
   D. commutative; multiplication

   8._____

9. The volume of revolution formed by rotating the curve y = sin x about the x axis from x = 0 to x = π is
   A. π^2
   B. $\frac{x^2}{2}$
   C. $\frac{x^2}{3}$
   D. $\frac{x^2}{4}$

   9._____

10. Based on the prismoidal formula, the volume of earth excavated in cubic yards, if one end is 6'x6', and the other end is 12'x12' and the length is 160', is MOST NEARLY
    A. 460
    B. 480
    C. 500
    D. 520

    10._____

11. The sin(arc tan $\frac{1}{\sqrt{3}}$) is equal to
    A. $\frac{2}{\sqrt{2}}$
    B. $\frac{1}{2}$
    C. $\frac{\sqrt{3}}{2}$
    D. $\frac{\sqrt{3}}{3}$

    11._____

12. The sum of the interior angles of an octagon is, in degrees, MOST NEARLY
    A. 960
    B. 1020
    C. 1080
    D. 1140

    12._____

13. The modulus of elasticity of steel in the metric system is _____ x 10^6kPa.
    A. 210
    B. 240
    C. 270
    D. 300

    13._____

14. If the density of aluminum is 173 #/cu.ft., the density of aluminum in the metric system is, in kg/m³,
    A. 2500
    B. 2590
    C. 2680
    D. 2770

    14._____

15. One pound per square inch is equal to, in newtons per square meter, 15.____
    A. 5778   B. 6180   C. 6582   D. 6984

16. The moment at E on the beam shown at the right is, in foot-kips, MOST NEARLY 16.____
    A. 28
    B. 32
    C. 36
    D. 40

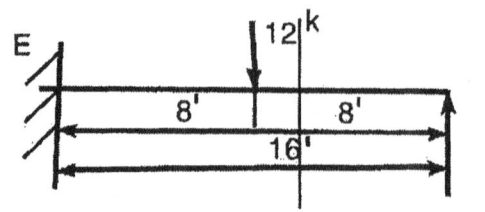

Questions 17-19.

DIRECTIONS: Questions 17 through 19 are to be answered on the basis of the simply supported beam shown below.

A wood beam 8x20# carries a uniform load (including the weight of the wood beam) of 800 #/1 including a 800# load 4 feet from the left end of a simply supported beam on a span of 16 feet as shown below.

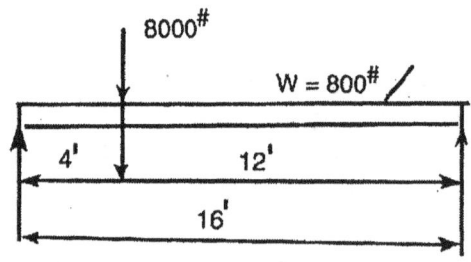 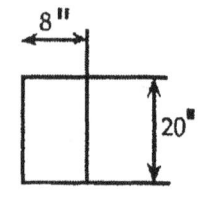

17. The of 0 shear is at a distance from the left support, in feet, MOST NEARLY 17.____
    A. 4.0   B. 4.5   C. 5.0   D. 5.5

18. The maximum bending stress is, in pounds per square inch, MOST NEARLY 18.____
    A. 900   B. 930   C. 960   D. 990

19. The maximum shearing stress is, in pounds per square inch, MOST NEARLY 19.____
    A. 116   B. 130   C. 146   D. 162

20. The cross-section area of a w 12x22 steel beam is, in square inches, MOST NEARLY 20.____
    A. 6.17   B. 6.47   C. 6.77   D. 7.07

21. A welding electrode is specified as E7018. 21.____
    Of the following statements relating to the electrode, the one that is CORRECT is the
    A. 70 relates to the tensile strength of the weld in kips per square inch
    B. 70 is the Charpy V-Notch Test requirement that must be met
    C. 1 represents the coating characteristic
    D. 8 represents the position code

22. In tall steel frame buildings, the columns are usually erected in lengths of _____ story(ies).
    A. 1 B. 2 C. 3 D. 4

23. In a L6x4x½ , the distance from the back of the 4 inch leg to the center of gravity of the angle is, in inches, MOST NEARLY
    A. 1.60 B. 1.80 C. 2.00 D. 2.20

24. In the Atterberg Test for soil, a standard brass cup is partly filled with wet soil. A groove of standard dimension is cut in the soil. The cup is lifted and dropped one centimeter 25 times.
    The purpose of this test is to determine the _____ of the soil.
    A. plastic limit
    B. plastic index
    C. shrinkage limit
    D. liquid limit

25. In the Atterberg Test for soil, the water content at which a $1/8$ inch diameter thread of soil begins to crumble when rolled under the palm of the hand is known as the _____ of the soil.
    A. plastic limit
    B. plastic index
    C. shrinkage limit
    D. liquid limit

KEY (CORRECT ANSWERS)

1. B		11. B	
2. D		12. C	
3. C		13. A	
4. B		14. D	
5. B		15. D	
6. C		16. C	
7. B		17. D	
8. D		18. D	
9. B		19. A	
10. C		20. B	

21. A
22. B
23. C
24. D
25. A

EXAMINATION SECTION
TEST 1

DIRECTIONS: Each question or incomplete statement is followed by several suggested answers or completions. Select the one that BEST answers the question or completes the statement. *PRINT THE LETTER OF THE CORRECT ANSWER IN THE SPACE AT THE RIGHT.*

NOTE: Use the following values for the physical constants:
acceleration due to gravity on the surface of the earth: g = 10 m/s speed of light in a vacuum: c = 3.0 x 10^8 m/s charge of an electron: q_e = 2.0 x 1^{-19} Coulomb

1. Which of the following is a unit of force? 1.____

   A. Newton   B. Kilogram   C. Joule
   D. Watt   E. Ampere

2. Which of the following is NOT a vector quantity? 2.____

   A. Force   B. Work   C. Torque
   D. Momentum   E. Velocity

3. From a standing start, a dragster completed a 400 meter race in 10 seconds. Assuming that the acceleration was constant, what was the FINAL speed of the dragster, in meters per second? 3.____

   A. 5   B. 20   C. 40   D. 50   E. 80

4. Referring to the graph at the right of acceleration of a given mass m as a function of time, which of the following graphs CORRECTLY shows the object's velocity as a function of time? 4.____

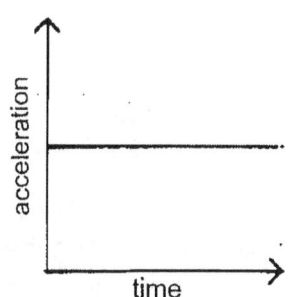

A.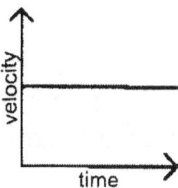

B.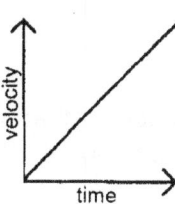

C.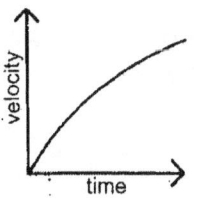

D.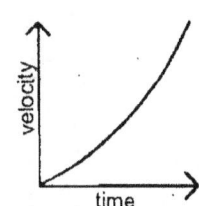

E.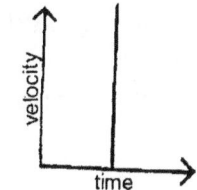

5. An object, thrown vertically upward, takes 8 seconds to reach the highest point. The INITIAL speed at the time of the upward throw is _____ meters per second.

   A. 1.25   B. 10   C. 40   D. 80   E. 320

6. In the graph at the right, what was the distance, in meters, traveled between time 10s and time 15s?
   A. 100
   B. 200
   C. 300
   D. 50
   E. 25

7. Two unequal masses produce gravitational forces on one another such that

   A. a larger force acts on the smaller mass
   B. a larger force acts on the larger mass
   C. only the smallest mass has a net force acting on it
   D. both forces are equal in magnitude
   E. the forces act in the same direction

8. In the figure at the right, mass M on a smooth, frictionless table is connected to another mass N by means of a frictionless pulley. Mass M accelerates to the right with an acceleration given by the expression a =

   A. (N/M)g   B. g   C. [N/(M+N)]g
   D. [(M-N)/(M+N)]g E. (M/N)g

9. An object is sliding along a circular path on a large, flat, frictionless surface when the string connecting the object to the circle's center breaks.
   Immediately after the string breaks, the object's trajectory will be a(n)

   A. spiral   B. straight line
   C. circular path   D. parabola
   E. ellipse

10. A student is trying to measure the acceleration of the elevator in her dorm. She stood on scale while it was at rest, and they read 500N. When the elevator accelerated, the scales read 550N.
    What is the acceleration of the elevator?

    A. 5 m/s² upward   B. 1 m/s² upward
    C. 0 m/s²   D. 1 m/s² downward
    E. 5 m/s² downward

11. An object in circular motion with constant speed has an acceleration which is

    A. zero
    B. tangent to the path
    C. pointing *in* along the radius
    D. pointing *out* along the radius
    E. perpendicular to the plane of the circle

12. The speed of a body of mass 10 kg, moving in a circle of radius 20m, is 10 m/s. The net force acting on the body is _____ N.

    A. 0   B. 5   C. 50   D. 100   E. 200

13. A bullet of mass m, moving with speed v, strikes a stationary block of mass M and becomes imbedded in it. Block and bullet then move off together with speed V, given by the expression V =

    A. (m/M)v   B. (M+m)v   C. [m/(M+m)]v
    D. [(M+m)/m]v   E. (M/M)v

14. A block of mass 10 kg has a speed of 5 m/s. Kinetic energy of the block, in joules, is

    A. 25   B. 50   C. 125   D. 250   E. 500

15. A man is asked to hold a box of mass 10 kg a distance of 2.0m above the ground for 100 seconds.
    The work done on the box during 100 seconds of holding the box is _____ J.

    A. 0   B. 100   C. 200   D. 1000   E. 10000

16. A box of mass 10 kg explodes into two pieces of masses 4 kg and 6 kg. The 4 kg piece flies away with a speed of 9 m/s.
    The speed of the 6 kg piece is _____ m/s.

    A. 0.9   B. 1.5   C. 3   D. 6   E. 13.5

17. A pendulum is swinging in simple harmonic motion with a period of 6 seconds. The maximum angle the pendulum rod makes with the vertical is suddenly *reduced* by a factor of 3.
    The period of the pendulum, in seconds, will now be

    A. 2   B. 3   C. 6   D. 18   E. 27

18. An object undergoes horizontal simple harmonic motion on a frictionless table. If the amplitude of the motion is doubled, the velocity of the object as it passes the equilibrium position will

    A. quadruple   B. double
    C. remain the same D. halve
    E. quarter

19. Which of the following properties of light remains the same when light enters the eye?

    A. Wavelength   B. Frequency   C. Speed
    D. Intensity   E. Acceleration

20. The distance between adjacent nodes in a standing wave is one-half the wavelength of the waves involved.
What is the SECOND LONGEST wavelength in m of those waves which could produce standing waves on a string of length 4m with both ends fixed?

  A. 1　　　B. 2　　　C. 4　　　D. 8　　　E. 16

KEY (CORRECT ANSWERS)

1. A	11. C
2. B	12. C
3. E	13. C
4. B	14. C
5. D	15. A
6. A	16. D
7. D	17. C
8. C	18. B
9. B	19. B
10. B	20. C

TEST 2

DIRECTIONS: Each question or incomplete statement is followed by several suggested answers or completions. Select the one that BEST answers the question or completes the statement. *PRINT THE LETTER OF THE CORRECT ANSWER IN THE SPACE AT THE RIGHT.*

1. A block of metal weighs 100N in air and 80N when completely immersed in water. The buoyant force on the block is _____ N.

    A. 100   B. 80   C. 20   D. 10   E. 8

2. An aluminum block and a lead block, each having the same volume, are submerged in a liquid.
   What can be said about the buoyant force on each block? The

    A. buoyant force on the aluminum block is greater than that on the lead block
    B. buoyant force on the lead block is greater than that on the aluminum block
    C. buoyant forces arethe same
    D. choice of answer depends on the densities of the metal blocks
    E. choice of answer depends on the density of the liquid in which the blocks are submerged

3. A thermally insulated container of negligible heat capacity contains 50g of ice (heat of fusion is 80 cal/g) at 0° C.
   If 50g of water (specific heat 1 cal/g° C) at 100° C is poured into the container, the FINAL temperature of the system will be

    A. 0° C
    B. greater than 0° C, but less than 50° C
    C. 50° C
    D. greater than 50° C, but less than 100° C
    E. 100° or greater

4. Which of the following is NOT a form of heat transfer?

    A. Conduction   B. Vaporization   C. Radiation
    D. Convection   E. Condensation

5. A hydraulic lift has a cross section of $10^3 cm^2$ on its lifting surface and a cross section of 10 cm^2 on its other surface.
   If a force of 10 Newtons is exerted downwards on this second surface, what force, in Newtons, can the lift now exert UPWARDS?

    A. 1   B. 10   C. 100   D. 1000   E. 10000

6. An ideal gas undergoes a Carnot cycle as shown at the right.
   In one complete cycle, the
   A. efficiency is 20%
   B. total change in internal energy is 200%
   C. difference in temperatures is the work done
   D. difference in the heat in and the heat out is the work done
   E. total change in internal energy is the work done

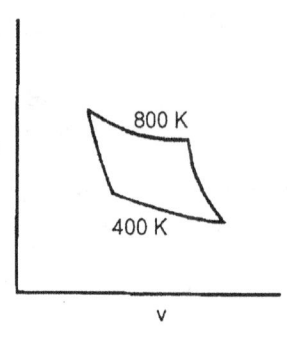

6.____

7. An excess charge is placed on the inner surface of a spherical *metal* shell. After these electrons stop being redistributed by electrical forces, they will be distributed uniformly

   A. over the shell's outer surface only
   B. over the shell's inner and outer surfaces only
   C. over the shell's inner surface only
   D. throughout the metal shell
   E. throughout the shell, but not on either surface

7.____

8. The electric field at any point along the perpendicular bisector of the line connecting two equal but opposite charges is

   A. parallel to the connecting line
   B. zero
   C. perpendicular to the connecting line
   D. at an angle of 45° to the connecting line
   E. at an angle of 60° to the connecting line

8.____

9. In an oil filled parallel plate capacitor, which of the following will definitely *increase* the capacitance?

   A. Moving the plates closer together
   B. Decreasing the area of the plates
   C. Removing the oil
   D. Increasing the voltage across the capacitor
   E. Decreasing the voltage across the capacitor

9.____

10. For the combination of resistors pictured at the right, the equivalent resistance, in ohms, which could replace this combination between points a and b is
    A. (16/9)
    B. (40/3)
    C. (9/16)
    D. 4.0
    E. 18.0

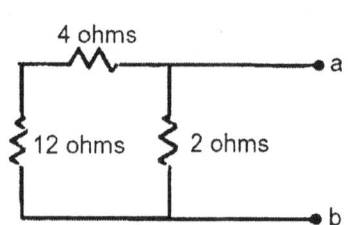

10.____

11. The heat generated when a constant current flows through a resistance R is

    A. directly proportional to R
    B. inversely of R
    C. directly proportional to R^2
    D. inversely proportional to R^2
    E. independent of R

12. Suppose that a uniform magnetic field, B, has been established in a given region. Which of the following would experience a non-zero magnetic force exerted by such a field?
    A(n)

    A. electrically neutral particle traveling perpendicularly to $\bar{B}$
    B. positively charged particle moving to the left, anti-parallel to $\bar{B}$
    C. negatively charged particle at rest in the region where $\bar{B} \neq 0$
    D. positively charged particle whose velocity makes an angle of $30°$ with the direction of $\bar{B}$
    E. negatively charged particle moving to the left, anti-parallel to $\bar{B}$

13. A coil of wire, connected to a sensitive galvanometer, is placed in the magnetic field of a strong horseshoe magnet.
    You would expect NO current to be observed in the coil when

    A. both the wire and the magnet are moved to the left at the same velocity
    B. the coil is moved and the magnet kept stationary
    C. the magnet is moved and the coil is kept stationary
    D. the coil and magnet are moved towards each other
    E. the coil and magnet are moved away from each other

14. If a lens has a positive focal length of 20 cm, at what distance from the lens, in cm, should an object be placed to form a *virtual* image 20 cm from the lens?

    A. 0   B. 10   C. 20   D. 40   E. 80

15. A ray of light is incident on a plane mirror at an angle of $40°$ to the normal. The angle the reflected ray makes with the normal is

    A. $0°$ B. $40°$ C. $50°$ D. $80°$ E. $90°$

16. A diverging lens has a focal length of -25 cm.
    If the object is placed 10 cm in front of the lens, the image is _____ the lens.

    A. 7 cm in front of   B. 7 cm behind
    C. 15 cm in front of   D. 15 cm behind
    E. 17 cm in front of

17. A screen was placed 10 cm behind a converging lens, and the object was placed 12 cm in front of the lens. The screen was illuminated but no image was formed on the screen. This means that the focal length of the lens

    A. is less than 10 cm
    B. is 22 cm
    C. is greater than 12 cm
    D. cannot be measured
    E. is between 10 and 12 cm

17.____

18. Beta particles (β-particles) are ESSENTIALLY

    A. protons
    B. neutrons
    C. electrons
    D. photons
    E. helium nuclei

18.____

19. Which type of radioactive decay does NOT change the number of protons in the nucleus?

    A. Alpha
    B. Beta
    C. Gamma
    D. Radioactive decay always changes the number of protons in the nucleus
    E. Radioactive decay never changes the number of protons in the nucleus

19.____

20. The half-life of the radioactive isotope indium-116 is 1 hour. What fraction of indium-116 will be left after 4 hours?

    A. One-half
    B. One-quarter
    C. One-eighth
    D. One-sixteenth
    E. One-thirty-second

20.____

KEY (CORRECT ANSWERS)

1. C
2. C
3. B
4. B
5. D
6. D
7. A
8. A
9. A
10. A
11. A
12. D
13. A
14. B
15. B
16. A
17. C
18. C
19. C
20. D

EXAMINATION SECTION
TEST 1

DIRECTIONS: Each question or incomplete statement is followed by several suggested answers or completions. Select the one that BEST answers the question or completes the statement. *PRINT THE LETTER OF THE CORRECT ANSWER IN THE SPACE AT THE RIGHT.*

1. The density of graphite (carbon) is 2.2 g/cm³. Accordingly, which of the following graphite samples is the LARGEST?

    A. 12 g
    B. 12 cm³
    C. 12 moles
    D. 12 atoms
    E. All are the same size

    1.____

2. How many grams of copper are produced when 1.5 g of aluminum are reacted with excess $Cu(NO_3)_2$ according to the following equation:

    $2Al + 3Cu(NO_3)_2 \rightarrow 2Al(NO_3)_3 + 3Cu$.

    (The atomic masses of copper and aluminum are 63.5 and 27.0 a.m.u., respectively.)
    1.5 x

    A. (2/3) x (27.0/63.5)
    B. (3/2) x (27.0/63.5)
    C. (2/3) x (63.5/27.0)
    D. (3/2) x (63.5/27.0)
    E. (63.5/27.0)

    2.____

3. For the reaction between A and B to form C, it is found that when one combines 0.6 moles of A with 0.6 moles of B, all of the B reacts, 0.2 moles of A remain unreacted, and 0.4 moles of C are produced.
    What is the balanced equation for this reaction?

    A. $A + 2B \rightarrow C$
    B. $A + 3B \rightarrow 2C$
    C. $3A + 3B \rightarrow 2C$
    D. $3A + 2B \rightarrow 3C$
    E. $2A + 3B \rightarrow 2C$

    3.____

4. If 3.00 g of a nitrogen-oxygen compound is found to contain 2.22 g of oxygen, what is the percentage of nitrogen in the compound?

    A. (3.00/2.22)(100/1)
    B. ((3.00 + 2.22)/3.00)(100/1)
    C. ((3.00 - 2.22)/2.22)(100/1)
    D. ((3.00 - 2.22)/3.00)(100/1)

    4.____

5. A 10.0 liter sample of oxygen at 100° C and 1 atm is cooled to 27° C and expanded until the pressure is 0.5 atm.
    Find the final volume of the oxygen.

    A. (10.0)(1/.5)(27/100)
    B. (10.0)(1/.5)(373/300)
    C. (10.0)(.5/1)(373/300)
    D. (10.0)(1/.5)(300/373)
    E. (10.0)(.5/1)(300/373)

    5.____

6. When the volume of a gas is decreased at constant temperature, the pressure increases because the molecules

    6.____

A. move faster
B. move slower
C. become heavier
D. become lighter
E. strike a unit area of the container more often

7. Which of the following types of bonding is found in diamond?

A. Covalent
B. Hydrogen
C. Van der Waal's
D. Metallic
E. Ionic

8. The molar volume of copper (63.5 g/mole) at 25° C is 7.09 cm^3 mole^{-1}. Which of the following is the density of copper at 25° C in g cm^{-3}?

A. (63.5)/(7.09)
B. (63.5)(7.09)
C. (7.09)/(63.5)
D. 7.09
E. ((63.5)/(7.09))(25)

9. A strong acid can be distinguished from a weak acid of the same concentration by the fact that the strong acid

A. neutralizes a base
B. is a better conductor of electricity
C. turns blue litmus paper red
D. reacts with a metal to liberate hydrogen
E. none of the above

10. Which of the following is NOT a colligative property (a property based on the number of particles present)?

A. Boiling point elevation
B. Sublimation energy
C. Vapor pressure lowering
D. Freezing point depression
E. Osmotic pressure

11. Which of the following will be the final volume in mL when 400 mL of 0.6 M HCl is diluted to 0.5 M HCl?

A. (400/1)(0.5/0.6)
B. (400/1)(0.6/0.5)
C. ((0.6 - 0.5)/1)(400/1)
D. ((1,000 - 400)/1)(0.5/0.6)
E. (0.6/0.5)((1,000 - 400)/1)

12. Chlorine bleaches are solutions that contain approximately 5% NaClO. These solutions are

A. slightly acidic
B. strongly acidic
C. neutral
D. slightly basic
E. strongly basic

13. What is the hydroxide ion concentration [OH⁻] of a solution having a pH of 5.0?

    A. 5×10^{-5} M
    B. 5×10 M
    C. 1×10^{-5} M
    D. 1×10^{-9} M
    E. 5×10^{-9} M

14. The solubility product of CuI is 5.1×10^{-12}.
    How many moles of Cu⁺ will be in equilibrium with CuI in 1.0 liter of a 0.01 M KI solution?

    A. 5.1×10^{-6}
    B. 2.3×10^{-6}
    C. 5.1×10^{-12}
    D. 2.3×10^{-5}
    E. 5.1×10^{-10}

15. For the reaction:
    $AgCl_{(s)} + 2NH_{3(aq)} \rightleftharpoons Ag(NH_3)_2^+ + Cl^-$,
    the equilibrium constant $K = 4 \times 10^{-3}$, which of the following statements is TRUE? [K_{sp} for AgCl is 1.0×10^{-10}]

    A. The addition of NH₃ decreases the solubility of AgCl.
    B. AgCl is more soluble in aqueous NH₃ than in water.
    C. AgCl is more soluble in an aqueous solution containing Cl⁻ than in water.
    D. AgCl is less soluble in aqueous NH₃ than in water.
    E. None of the above

16. What is the equilibrium constant expression, K, for the gaseous reaction:
    $O_2 + 4HCl \rightleftharpoons 2H_2O + 2Cl_2$?
    K =

    A. $\dfrac{[H_2O]^2[Cl_2]^2}{[O_2][HCl]^4}$
    B. $\dfrac{[H_2O][Cl_2]}{[O_2][HCl]}$
    C. $\dfrac{[O_2][HCl]^4}{[H_2O]^2[Cl_2]^2}$
    D. $\dfrac{2[H_2O]2[Cl_2]}{[O_2]4[HCl]}$
    E. $\dfrac{2[H_2O]^2 2[Cl_2]^2}{[O_2]4[HCl]^4}$

17. What would be the heat of formation, ΔHf, for NO₂ gas if one considers the equations for the following reactions where all substances are gases?

    $\dfrac{1}{2}N_2 + \dfrac{1}{2}O_2 \rightarrow NO$ $\qquad \Delta H°_f = +21.6$ kcal

    $NO_2 \rightarrow NO + \dfrac{1}{2}O_2$ $\qquad \Delta H° = 13.5$ kcal

    A. -28.7 kcal
    B. -8.1 kcal
    C. 35.1 kcal
    D. 28.7 kcal
    E. 8.1 kcal

18. Which one of the following processes is accompanied by a decrease in entropy?

    A. Freezing of water
    B. Evaporation of water
    C. Sublimation of carbon dioxide
    D. Shuffling a deck of cards
    E. Heating a balloon filled with a gas

19. Rates of reactions are USUALLY studied by

    A. measuring the concentration of the reactants or products as a function of time
    B. calculating the free energy change for the reaction
    C. measuring the heat evolved under different conditions
    D. measuring the amount of each reactant in the reaction
    E. calculating the entropy change for the reaction

20. Suppose a solution, which is initially 0.60 M in compound X, undergoes a decomposition reaction. After 10 seconds, the concentration of X is 0.40 M.
    Which of the following is the average rate of decomposition of X in mol/L sec?

    A. 0.020   B. 0.040   C. 0.10   D. 0.20   E. 0.50

21. Which of the following is the number of hydrogen ions in the balanced reaction: $H_2SO_3(aq) + IO_3^-(aq) \rightarrow SO_4^{2-}(aq) + I^-(aq) + H^+(aq)$?

    A. 2   B. 4   C. 6   D. 8   E. 10

22. Given the following half-cell reactions:

    $Cl_2(g) + 2e^- \rightarrow 2Cl^-(aq)$ $E° = +1.36v$

    $Cu^{2+}(aq) + 2e- \rightarrow Cu(s)$ $E° = +.34v$

    what is the value of E° for the following reaction:
    $Cu^{2+}(aq) + 2Cl^-(aq) \rightarrow Cu(s) + Cl_2(g)$?

    A. -2.38v   B. -1.70v   C. -1.02v   D. +1.02v   E. +1.70v

23. Which of the following represents the change in oxidation state of nitrogen during the chemical reaction:
    $2NO + 3S + 4H_2O \rightarrow 2HNO_3 + 3H_2S$?

    A. 1   B. 2   C. 3   D. 4   E. 5

24. The ion $^9_4Be^{2+}$ has _____ protons, _____ neutrons, and _____ electrons.

    A. 4; 5; 4
    B. 4; 5; 2
    C. 5; 4; 2
    D. 5; 4; 4
    E. none of the above

25. The correct Lewis formula for a nitrate ion (NO_3^-) is

$$\left[\begin{array}{c} \ddot{\underset{|}{O}} \\ \ddot{\underline{O}} - N = \ddot{O} \end{array} \right]^-$$

Which of the following are the oxygen-nitrogen-oxygen bond angles in this ion closest to?

A. 90°　　B. 109°　　C. 120°　　D. 150°　　E. 180°

26. Which of the following is the ground state electron configuration for $^{24}_{12}Mg^{2+}$?

A. $1s^2 2s^2 2p^6 3s^2$
B. $1s^2 2s^2 2p^6$
C. $1s^2 2s^2 2p^6 3s^2 3p^2$
D. $1s^2 2s^2 2p^4 3s$
E. $1s^2 2s^2 2p^6 3s^2 3p^6 3d^4 4s^2$

27. Antimony (Sb) has a smaller atomic radius than strontium (Sr) because of

A. increased electron shielding
B. the lanthanide contraction
C. increased metallic character
D. increased nuclear to electron attraction
E. the difference in number of neutrons in their nucleus

28. Which of the following compounds would have the MOST polar bonds?

A. BH_3　　B. CH_4　　C. NH_3　　D. H_2O　　E. PH_3

29. The LEAST electronegative element can be found in the _____ corner of the periodic table.

A. upper left　　　　　　　B. upper right
C. lower left　　　　　　　D. lower right

30. In the nuclear reaction: $^{14}_{7}N + ^{4}_{2}He \rightarrow ^{17}_{8}O + X$, the symbol X represents which of the following?

A. $^{4}_{2}He$　　B. $^{1}_{0}n$　　C. $^{0}_{-1}e$　　D. $^{0}_{+1}e$　　E. $^{1}_{1}H$

KEY (CORRECT ANSWERS)

1.	C	16.	A
2.	D	17.	E
3.	E	18.	A
4.	E	19.	A
5.	D	20.	A
6.	E	21.	C
7.	A	22.	C
8.	A	23.	C
9.	B	24.	B
10.	B	25.	C
11.	B	26.	B
12.	D	27.	D
13.	D	28.	D
14.	E	29.	C
15.	B	30.	E

EXAMINATION SECTION
TEST 1

DIRECTIONS: Each question or incomplete statement is followed by several suggested answers or completions. Select the one that BEST answers the question or completes the statement. *PRINT THE LETTER OF THE CORRECT ANSWER IN THE SPACE AT THE RIGHT.*

1. Vaporization is an example of a process for which at all temperatures.   1._____

    A. ΔH and ΔG are positive
    B. ΔH and ΔS are positive
    C. ΔS and ΔG are positive
    D. ΔH and ΔS are negative
    E. ΔH and ΔG are negative

2. Which of the following elements is MOST electronegative?   2._____

    A. Li   B. K   C. C   D. Ge   E. N

3. What is the percentage of oxygen by weight in $Ba(HCO_3)_2$ (259g/mol)?   3._____

    A. 9.6%   B. 18.5%   C. 24.2%   D. 37.1%   E. 49.0%

4. What species is missing in the following nuclear equation?   4._____

    $^{235}_{92}U + ^{1}_{0}n \rightarrow ^{103}_{42}Mo + 2^{1}_{0}n + ?$

    A. $^{131}_{50}Sn$ B. $^{132}_{50}Sn$ C. $^{131}_{52}Te$ D. $^{132}_{52}Te$ E. $^{132}_{51}Sb$

5. Two tanks of gas with identical volumes are filled at one atmosphere pressure and at the same temperature.   5._____
   If one tank contains H_2 and the other contains O_2, then

    A. both tanks contain the same mass of gas
    B. both tanks contain the same number of gas molecules
    C. both gases have the same density
    D. the molecules in both tanks are traveling at the same average speed
    E. the average kinetic energy in the H_2 tank is greater than in the O_2 tank

6. A solution of potassium acetate ($KC_2H_3O_2$) in water is   6._____

    A. basic because acetic acid molecules are formed
    B. basic because KOH molecules are formed
    C. acidic because acetic acid molecules are formed
    D. acidic because KOH molecules are formed
    E. neutral because potassium acetate is a salt

7. In an aqueous solution, the following equilibrium reactions are present: 7._____

    $Ag(NH_3)_2^+ \rightleftarrows Ag^+ + 2NH_3$

    $NH_3 + H_2O \rightleftarrows NH_4^+ + OH^-$

    If the soluble salt, AgNO, is added to the solution, the following changes in concentration take place:

A. [NH$_3$], [NH$_4^+$], and [OH$^-$] decrease
B. [NH$_3$] increases; [NH$_4^+$] and [OH$^-$] decrease
C. [NH$_4^+$] increases; [NH$_3$] and [OH$^-$] decrease
D. [NH$_4^+$] and [OH$^-$] increase; [NH$_3$] decreases
E. [NH$_3$] and [OH$^-$] increase; [NH$_4^+$] decreases

8. If an isotope of an element has an atomic number of 45 and a mass number of 103, another isotope of the element could have

A. 58 neutrons
B. fewer than 45 protons
C. more than 45 protons
D. 57 neutrons
E.

9. The conjugate acid of HPO$_4^{2-}$, in water solution is

A. H$^+$
B. H$_3$PO$_4$
C. H$_4$PO$_4^+$
D. PO$_4^{3-}$
E. H$_2$PO$_4^-$

10. Calculate the heat of reaction, $\Delta H°$, for the reaction
C$_3$H$_8$(g) + 5O$_2$(g) → 3CO$_2$(g) + 4H$_2$O(1)
The necessary values for, in Kcal/mole, are
H$_2$O(1) = -68.3, CO$_2$(g) = -94.0, C$_3$H$_8$(g) = -24.8

A. 1(-24.8) - 3(-94.0) - 4(-68.3)
B. -94.0 - 68.3 + 24.8
C. -24.8 - 94.0 - 68.3
D. 3(-94.0) + 4(-68.3) - 1(-24.8)
E. 3(-94.0) + 4(-68.3) + 1(-24.8)

11. If a solution which is initially 1.00M in compound X undergoes a decomposition reaction for 20.0 sec at an average rate of 0.020 mol/1. sec, the new concentration of X will be _____ M.

A. 0.10   B. 0.40   C. 0.60   D. 1.0   E. 1.4

12. A gaseous mixture of 10 mole % nitrous oxide (N$_2$O), 20 mole % oxygen (O$_2$), and 70 mole % nitrogen (N$_2$) has a total pressure of 800 mm.
What is the partial pressure, in mm, of the nitrous oxide?

A. 800 x 0.10   B. 800/0.10   C. 0.10/800
D. 800 x 0.90   E. 800/0.90

13. The simplest empirical formula for a compound was determined to be CH$_2$O, and its molecular weight was found to be 60g/mol.
How many atoms of hydrogen are in a molecule of this compound?

A. 2   B. 3   C. 4   D. 5   E. 6

14. In the following reaction, identify the oxidizing agent and the reducing agent:

    $4\ Zn + NO_3^- + 7\ OH^- \rightarrow NH_3 + 4\ ZnO_2^{2-} + 2\ H_2O$

    The oxidizing agent is _____ ; the reducing agent is _____ .

    A. Zn; NO_3
    B. NO_3; Zn
    C. OH^-; Zn^-
    D. Zn; OH^-
    E. NO_3^-; OH^-

15. What is the ionization constant of a weak acid whose hydronium ion concentration is 3.0 x 10^{-5} in an 0.02M solution?

    A. 1.8×10^{-11}
    B. 3.0×10^{-10}
    C. 3.0×10^{-3}
    D. 4.5×10^{-12}
    E. 4.5×10^{-8}

16. Which one of the following 0.15m aqueous solutions has the LOWEST freezing point?

    A. KCL
    B. $Al_2(SO_4)_3$
    C. CH_3OH
    D. C_2H_5OH
    E. NaOH

17. The boiling point of any liquid is

    A. 100° C
    B. the temperature at which as many molecules leave the liquid as return to it
    C. the temperature at which the vapor pressure is equal to the external pressure
    D. the temperature at which no molecules can return to the bulk of the liquid
    E. the temperature at which the intermolecular forces are at their maximum

18. A gaseous sample contains 0.02000 moles of N_2. How many atoms of nitrogen are in this sample?

    A. 0.02000
    B. 0.04000
    C. 6.02×10^{23}
    D. 12.04×10^{25}
    E. 24.08×10^{21}

19. In which of the following compounds does sulfur have an oxidation number of +2?

    A. Na_2S
    B. Na_2S_2
    C. $Na_2S_2O_3$
    D. Na_2SO_3
    E. Na_2SO_4

20. In which solvent should NaCl be MOST soluble?

    A. CH_3OH (methyl alcohol)
    B. C_8H_{18} (octane)
    C. $(C_2H_5)_2O$ (diethyl ether)
    D. CCl_4 (carbon tetrachloride)
    E. C_6H_6 (benzene)

21. A common oxidation number of +2 exists for most period four transition metals because

    A. the elements are filling in the d orbitals
    B. of a d orbital screening effect
    C. the +2 oxidation state is always the most stable
    D. the 4s orbital fills before the 3d orbitals in these elements
    E. the 4s electrons are more easily removed than 3d electrons during ionization

22. If the rate of a reaction is second order with respect to component A, how will the rate change if the concentration of A is tripled?
    It will

    A. double
    B. triple
    C. be six times as great
    D. be nine times as great
    E. be reduced to one-third its original value

23. An element has the electron configuration as follows:
    $1s^2 2s^2 2p^6 3s^2 3p^6 3d^{10} 4s^2 4p^3$
    This element

    A. is a transition element
    B. belongs to the halogen family
    C. has 33 neutrons
    D. belongs to Group V
    E. is an alkaline earth metal

24. When the following oxidation-reduction reaction is balanced, what is the correct stoichiometric coefficient for Sn^+ ? $Sn^{2+} + H^+ + Cr_2O_7^{2-} \rightarrow Sn^{4+} + Cr^{3+} + H_2O$

    A. 1   B. 2   C. 3   D. 4   E. 6

25. Which one of the following is the CORRECT chemical symbol for a particle containing 6 protons, 8 neutrons, and 7 electrons?

    A. N   B. C^+ C. C^- D. O^+ E. O^-

26. Select the one element below with a partially filled d-orbital subshell.
    A. Pb   B. Mg   C. Se   D. Cr   E. Al

27. What mass of NaOH (40.0g/mol) should be weighted out to make 2.50 liters of 1.50M NaOH?

    A. 40g   B. 60g   C. 100g   D. 120g   E. 150g

28. The solubility of Ag_2CrO_4 in water is x mol/L. Its solubility product constant, Ksp., is

    A. $4x^3$ B. $4x^2$ C. $2x^2$ D. $2x^3$ E. x^2

29. The amount of heat it takes to raise the temperature of 1 gram of any substance by 1 degree Celsius is ALWAYS

    A. the entropy of the substance
    B. the exothermic capacity of the substance
    C. the free energy of the substance
    D. the specific heat of the substance
    E. one (1) calorie

30. If 200 mL of 1.60M NaOH are diluted with water to a volume of 350 mL, the new concentration of the solution is   30._____

    A. (200/350)(1/1.60)   B. (200/350)(1.60/1)   C. (1.60/1)(200/550)
    D. (350/200)(1.60/1)   E. (350/200)(1/1.60)

KEY (CORRECT ANSWERS)

1.	B	16.	B
2.	E	17.	C
3.	D	18.	E
4.	A	19.	C
5.	B	20.	A
6.	A	21.	E
7.	A	22.	D
8.	D	23.	D
9.	E	24.	C
10.	D	25.	C
11.	C	26.	D
12.	A	27.	E
13.	C	28.	A
14.	B	29.	D
15.	E	30.	B

BASIC FUNDAMENTALS OF CHEMICAL MEASUREMENT

CONTENTS

	Page
1. QUALITATIVE CHEMICAL TESTS	1
2. ACIDITY AND ALKALINITY	1
3. HALOGENS	3
4. NITROGEN COMPOUNDS	3
5. SULFUR COMPOUNDS	4
6. METAL PROCESSING	5
7. CONTAMINANTS	5
8. OTHER PROCESSES	6
9. ACTIVITIES	7

BASIC FUNDAMENTALS OF CHEMICAL MEASUREMENT

CHEMICAL MEASUREMENT

1. QUALITATIVE CHEMICAL TESTS

   Chemical measurement is one of the major measurement categories of concern to Inspection and Quality Control. Some of the most common are reviewed in this section.

2. ACIDITY AND ALKALINITY

   The degree of acidity or alkalinity (pH) of a solution or mixture is important to many situations. The concentration of hydrogen ions present in a solution is a function of the concentration of acid and degree of ionization. This definition applies equally to bases and by suitable consideration of the chemical equilibria involved to hydrolysis accompanied by ionization of a product which gives hydrogen or hydroxyl ions.

   If an acid is present or added, the amount of hydrogen ion is increased and the amount of hydroxyl ion correspondingly reduced according to the laws of mass action.

$$\frac{C_H \times C_{OH}}{C_{H_2O}} = \frac{10^{-7} \times 10^{-7}}{1} = 10^{-14}$$

Where: C_H = Concentration of Hydrogen Ion
C_{OH} = Concentration of Hydroxyl Ion
C_{H_2O} = Concentration of Water

The value of C_H is commonly expressed as the pH value, which is the logarithmetic value, $\log_{10} 1/C_H$.

Measurement of pH values are commonly made of chemical processing solutions, effluents, soils, food stuffs, and other chemicals where acidity or alkalinity is important.

pH values may be determined by use of pH papers and the hydrogen electrode, antimony electrode, colorimetry, quin hydron electrode or glass electrode.

pH is measured in a scale starting at 7.0 ranging downwards towards 1.0 as being extremely acid and upward towards 13.0 as being extremely basic or alkaline. A pH of 7.0 means neutrality, that is the $C_H = C_{OH}$. Pure or distilled water approaches of pH of 7.0.

Sources of error in pH measurement include temperature of sample and standard, contamination of the test solution, degree of buffering required to reduce turbility caused by contaminants, degree of dissolved salts, type of colorimetric indicator used and calibration of electronic equipment used.

Typical areas of application include:

    Metal cleaner solution control
    Degreasing solution control
    Household cleaner manufacture quality control
    Soap purity quality control
    Food preservatives purity control
    Textile finishing materials quality control
    Dye stuffs quality control
    City water supply purity control

3. HALOGENS

The presence of halogens, chlorine, fluorine, bromine and iodine is important to many chemical reactions or processes. Methods of analysis include the following:

1. Silver nitrate is added to precipitate white curdy silver chloride from nitric acid solutions of soluble chlorides.

2. Silver bromide, pale yellow in color and silver iodine, yellow in color, are generally insoluble in ammonium, hydroxide solutions.

3. Silver bromide is slowly soluble and silver iodine hard to dissolve in ammonium hydroxide solutions.

4. Concentrated ammonium carbonate solutions dissolve silver chloride, whereas silver bromide is very slightly soluble and silver iodine insoluble.

Tests for presence of halogens require only commonly used laboratory equipment such as flasks, beakers, gram scales, distilled water, bunsen burner. Reagent grade chemicals must be used for test solutions.

Sources of error in precipitation methods such as used for detecting halogens include, unclean flasks or beakers, impure (not distilled) water, too low temperature of the test solutions, and interpretation of color indications.

Typical areas of application include:

Photographic emulsions quality control
Bleach manufacture quality control
Dye stuff manufacture quality control
Reagent grade chemicals purity control
City water supply purity control
Precious metal recovery control

4. NITROGEN COMPOUNDS

The presence of nitrogen compounds, sometimes referred to as combined nitrogen, is important to many chemical reactions and processes.

Methods of analysis include the following:

1. Ammonia is a nitrogen compound. Presence of ammonia gaseous solutions can be readily detected by its strong pungent odor. Another convenient test is to add eight

percent sodium hydroxide solution to the test solution and place moistened red litmus paper in the vapors and heat the mixture slowly. The litmus paper will turn blue in color if ammonia is present.

2. Nitrates contain ammonia. A convenient test for presence of nitrogen in an unknown solution is to combine one part unknown solution with ten parts concentrated sulfuric acid in a test tube. Then carefully add a saturated solution of ferrous sulfate by letting it flow down the tube wall. Do not mix solutions. Formation of a brown ring at the junction of the solutions indicates presence of nitrogen in nitrates. Nitrates are commonly used in fertilizers and explosives.

3. Amines contain ammonia. A convenient general test for presence of nitrogen in amines is to warm one milliliter of a test solution with two drops of chloroform and two milliliters of a strong alcoholic solution of potassium hydroxide. A very distinctive, strong, and disagreeable odor of carbylamine results if amines are present in the test solution. Standard laboratory apparatus is needed. Amines are commonly used as chemical reagents and are commonly found in nature in such things as fish oil and their derivatives.

5. SULFUR COMPOUNDS

The presence of sulfur compounds such as sulfates, sulfites, sulfides, and thiosulfate are important to many chemical reactions and processes.

Methods of analysis include the following:

1. Soluble sulfates may be identified by the barium sulfate precipitation method. Dissolve a test sample in water, make the solution acidic to litmus by adding 1:1 hydrochloric acid, heat to boiling, add a few drops of ten percent barium chloride solution and mix. Sulfate is indicated by a finely divided barium sulfate precipitate. Standard laboratory apparatus is needed. Soluble sulfates are commonly used as chemical reagents and are used in fertilizers and pharmaceuticals.

2. Insoluble sulfates must first be converted to soluble sulfates. For this purpose fuse a test sample with anhydrous sodium carbonate in a crucible. Let the melt cool and dissolve it in water. Filter to obtain a clean solution of soluble sulfate. Verify presence of soluble sulfate as described in the above paragraph.

6. METAL PROCESSING

The presence of metallic elements in minerals or ores is of primary interest in such processes as recovery of gold, silver, nickel, copper, iron, or tin. Identification of these metals in minerals or ores involves a series of tests in sequence whereby precipates are produced of the metals with various salts added to solutions of the mineral or ore.

The methods of test are many and only one example will be shown to explain the general approach.

1. Silver, mercury and lead commonly occur in the same ore or mineral. Fuse the sample with sodium carbonate, dissolve in water acidified with 1:3 hydrochloric acid, heat slowly, filter while hot and allow the filtrate to cool. Reserve the liquid for further testing. Lead is indicated if a fine white precipitate developed. The residue on the filter is silver chloride or mercurous chloride or both. Wash with hot water and then 1:5 ammonium hydroxide solution. A black residue indicates presence of mercury. Acidify the ammonical solution with hydrochloric acid, a white precipitate indicates presence of silver.

2. Standard laboratory apparatus is used. Errors can readily occur in these tests if impure reagents are used or unclean apparatus is used. Careful prevention of contamination is necessary to ensure accurate results.

7. CONTAMINANTS

The presence of contaminants in public and industrial water supplies is an important matter requiring chemical analysis and control.

Some of the more common tests made are as follows:

1. Municipal water supplies are primarily checked for bacteriological content and activity. In addition, color, turbidity, dissolved solids, hardness, alkalinity, or acidity, iron, manganese, fluoride, free chlorine and pH are determined. Occasionally, a complete mineral content is determined.

2. Of these tests, color, turbidity and pH are qualitative in nature, i.e., exact numbers are not of concern. Color comparisons of a test sample are viewed under good illumination with water color standard solutions. Less or more color in the test sample indicates comparative amounts of the known chemicals in the color standard.

3. Turbidity comparisons are made in a similar manner as color comparisons. Water turbidity standards contain known levels of minerals or other additives usually in a fine collodial state suspended in the water. Test samples are viewed under good illumination and compared for amount of turbidity present.

4. pH determinations were discussed earlier.

5. Errors in these tests primarily occur through unintentional contamination of test samples and to a lesser degree in judgement of color and/or turbidity levels or differences.

8. OTHER PROCESSES

The separation and identification of various cations by use of the paper chromatographic analysis method is an important quality control tool. Chromatographic techniques are capable of separating mixtures containing as many as fifty components with similar properties. This method gives strong proof if a certain cation is present or absent in a test solution.

The separation and identification of three cations will illustrate the method. The objective is to detect presence of silver, mercury, and lead in a nitrate solution suspected of containing these cations.

1. Modern laboratories employ very sophisticated and complex equipment such as the Gas Chromograph, the Spectrometer and the Electron Microscope to separate and identify chemicals in test materials and solutions. The principles and operation of these devices would be appropriate if their use is available.

2. Obtain three strips of regular laboratory filter paper six inches by one inch. One each strip draw a line with a pencil one inch from each end, place a dot in the center of one of the lines in each strip; and crease the strips along their lengths.

3. Place a drop of the nitrate solution on the pencil dot of each strip, allow to dry and place a second drop on the spots and allow to dry.

4. Fill three six-inch test tubes with one-half inch of distilled water, immerse the filter strips with the dot end down. Keep the tubes vertical and be careful to not splash the water. The water will then start to climb

the filter paper by capillary action. When the water rises to the upper line on the paper, remove the paper and allow to dry.

5. Immerse the strips one at a time in a six-inch test tube filled nearly to the top with potassium chromate solution. Remove them after two to three minutes and pass two of the strips one by one over 15 M NH_4OH vapors from a beaker in a hood. Observe the colors carefully, some mixing of colors may occur. Orange indicates lead present. Black indicates mercury. A spot of brick red on the third paper occurring after exposure to the potassium chromate solution indicates presence of silver. Exposure to the ammonia vapor will fade the brick red spot.

6. Comparative tests may be made to help in the color discrimination using individual solutions of lead, silver and mercurous nitrate.

9. ACTIVITIES

Determination Of Approximate pH Value

Colometric Determination of pH Values

If the approximate value of the pH of a solution is unknown, the order of its magnitude must first be approximated in order to select the correct indicator for a more accurate evaluation. As a rule a few simple tests will supply this information. For example, if a solution remains colorless after a few drops of phenolphthalein are added, it indicates the pH is less than 8.0. If a second test is made with methyl orange and the solution assumes the color of the indicator (orange), it means the pH is greater than 4.5. Therefore, the solution has a pH value between 4.5 and 8.0. Additional tests using indicators with pH values between 4.5 and 8.0 can be used to establish a closer estimate of the true pH value. The following tabulation lists the various readily available indicators for this test method.

pH Indicators

	pH Range	Solvent	Acid	Alkaline
Thymol Blue	1.2-2.8	0.1% sol. in water	Red	Yellow
Methyl Yellow	2.9-4.0	"	Red	Yellow
Methyl Orange	3.1-4.4	"	Red	Orange
Bromophenal Blue	3.0-4.6	"	Yellow	Blue Violet
Bromocresol Green	3.8-5.4	"	Yellow	Blue
Methyl Red	4.4-6.2	"	Red	Yellow
Chlowphenal Red	4.8-6.4	"	Yellow	Red
Bromophenal Red	5.4-7.0	"	Yellow	Red
Bromothymol Blue	6.0-7.6	"	Yellow	Blue
Phenal Red	6.4-8.0	"	Yellow	Red
M Cresol Purple	7.4-9.0	"	Yellow	Purple
Thymol Blue	8.0-9.6	"	Yellow	Blue
Phenolphthalein	8.0-9.8	"	Colorless	Red

Solutions with pH value less than 7.0 are acidic and solutions with pH values greater than 7.0 are alkaline. Distilled water has a pH of 7.0.

Improving Estimate Of True pH Value

When the approximate value of pH is known, 3.5 or 10 cc (depending on amount of solution available) are measured out by means of a graduated cylinder and transferred into a Pyrex or other hard glass test tube. A measured amount of an indicator solution for some pH value between 4.5 and 8.0 is added carefully from a pipette of 1cc volume which is graduated in 0.01 cc. As a rule, 0.1 to 0.2 cc of a 0.1% indicator solution to 10 cc of liquid will be the proper amount. Then these buffer solutions (8 to 10 cc), the pH of which overlaps that of the unknown are taken and treated in exactly the same way. The following tabulation lists buffer solutions used for this test method.

STANDARD BUFFER SOLUTIONS

pH				
1.0	48.5 ml.	0.2 NHCL +	25 ml. 0.2 N KCl	dil. to 100 ml.
1.2	32.5 ml.	"	"	"
1.4	20.75 ml.	"	"	"
1.6	13.15 ml.	"	"	"
1.8	8.3 ml.	"	"	"
2.0	5.3 ml.	"	"	"
2.2	3.35 ml.	"	"	"
2.2	46.70 ml.	0.1 N HCl +	50 ml. 0.1M $KHC_8H_4O_4$	dil. to 100 ml.
2.4	39.60 ml.	"	"	"
2.6	32.95 ml.	"	"	"
2.8	26.42 ml.	"	"	"
3.0	20.32 ml.	"	"	"
3.2	14.70 ml.	"	"	"
3.4	9.90 ml.	"	"	"
3.6	5.97 ml.	"	"	"
3.8	2.63 ml.	"	"	"
4.0	0.40 ml.	0.1 N Na OH +	50 ml. 0.1 M $KHC_8H_4O_4$	dil. to 100 ml.
5.0	23.85 ml.	"	"	"
6.0	5.70 ml.	0.1 H Na OH +	50 ml. 0.1 M KH_2PO_4	dil. to 100 ml.
7.0	29.63 ml.	"	"	"
8.0	46.80 ml.	"	"	"
9.0	21.30 ml.	0.1 N Na OH +	50 ml. 0.1 M H_3BO_3	dil. to 100 ml.
10.0	43.90 ml.	"	"	"

Compare color of sample with the several tubes of buffer solution. The buffer solution which most closely matches the color of the sample provides a good second approximation of the sample solution pH value. A second improved approximation of the pH value may be made in a similar manner using another pH indicator lying between 4.5 and indicator used above, or between 8.0 and the same indicator, and a third improved approximation may then be made in a similar manner. This process may be repeated until all ranges of indicators and buffers have been used.

Chemical Measurement (Quantitative)

To prepare yourself in quantitative methods, activities are presented since they are considered necessary in skills development.

1. Exercise in the Use of the Balance.

   Discuss use of the balance in determination of weight relationship involved in chemical changes and analysis. Practice in weight measurement is important before attempting chemical analysis experiments. Measurement error probabilities and significances should be presented.

2. Separations of Solids and Liquids

   Many chemical analyses require separation of solids and liquids. Methods include formation of precipitates, gravity filtration, centrifuging and decantation. Practice in these methods are required. Use water solutions of silver chloride acidified with HCl, Borium Chloride acidified with sulfuric acid, and Aluminum Hydroxide reacted with Aluminum Nitrate. Use unknown composition samples and calculate weight units per volume using solid precipitates obtained.

3. Determination of the Percentage of Oxygen in Air.

   Since air is a mixture of gases, it is possible to expose a measured volume of air to a chemical subtance that removes (absorbs) the oxygen and leaves the other components unchanged. By measuring the decrease in volume occasioned by the removal of oxygen, it is possible to calculate percentage of oxygen in the original sample of air. A suggested method is to absorb oxygen from air in a mixture of three parts pyrogallic acid and 22 parts potassium hydroxide solution (measure parts by volume) and measure loss of air volume to determine percentage oxygen in the air. Standard laboratory equipment is required.

4. Determination of "Hardness" in Natural Waters

   Natural waters contain dissolved salts that cause the water "hardness." The degree of hardness relates to the "soap consuming power" of the water. The "harder" the water, the more it consumes soap. A hardness value for the water can be expressed in terms of the amount of soap consumed until a stable lather is produced. Mix a 100 ml. of water with a standard soap solution added in .5 ml. increments and agitate vigorously each time. Continue additions until a stable lather is obtained. Divide the number of milliliters of soap required by 100 to obtain a "hardness value" of the water.

5. The Ammonia Content of a "Household Ammonia"

   A typical quantitative chemical analysis measurement used for quality control of the manufactured product. Household ammonia is prepared by passing ammonia gas (NH_3) into water. Ordinarily, one volume of water dissolves about 800 volumes of NH_3. Ammonia reacts with water (H_2O) to form NH_4OH ammonia hydroxide. The law requires Household ammonia sold in stores contain not less than 9.5 percent NH_3. Weight and titrate an ammonia solution sample with 3.g of HCl per ml. solution, use methyl red indicator. When the end point is reached, calculate the percent ammonia (NH_3) from the weight of HCl in the standard solution used divided by the weight of the ammonia sample.

$$\% NH_3 = \frac{\text{Mil of HCl Used} \times .3 \text{ gm/mil}}{\text{Grams of Ammonia Solution Tested}} \times 100$$

   Repeat test five times and calculate the upper control limit (UCL) and lower control limit (LCL) as follows:

$$\bar{R} = \frac{\text{Highest Reading} - \text{Lowest Reading}}{5}$$

   $UCL = D_4 \bar{R}$ Where: $D_4 = 2.114$ for sample size 5

   Central Line $= \bar{R}$ $D_3 = 0$ for sample size 5

   $LCL = D_3 \bar{R}$

   A control chart could then be initiated and used to check future production lot quality. The range of 5 samples taken at a later date would not exceed the $UCL = D_4 R$ as long as the process producing the ammonia solution remained unchanged.

6. The Acid Content of Vinegar for Household Use.

   This must not be less than four percent weight expressed as acetic acid. Vinegar is a rather complex mixture that is produced by fermentation of apple cider, corn sugar, or grape juice. The principal chemical changes involved are formation of ethyl alcohol (C_2H_5OH) and the oxidation of the alcohol to acetic acid ($HC_2H_3O_2$) by "Bacterium acetic" and related organisms. Acid content is determined by titration samples with standard sodium hydroxide solution.

   The procedure is quite simple and easily accomplished with normal laboratory equipment.

Wash a burette thoroughly with distilled water. Fill it exactly to the zero mark with a 0.1 gm NaOH per mil. solution. Weigh a clean dry 250 ml. beaker to the nearest 0.1 gm. Add 20 ml. of vinegar. Weigh filled beaker to nearest 0.1 gm. to determine weight of vinegar. Add 20 ml. of distilled water and two drops of phenolphthalein indicator solution.

Titrate the sample of vinegar with the standard sodium hydroxide from the burette. The first appearances of a permanent pink coloration denotes the end-point in titration. Record the initial and final burette readings and calculate the percent acid as follows:

Weight of beaker	_____ gm.
Weight of beaker + sample	_____ gm.
Weight of sample (2-1)	_____ gm.
Initial burette reading	_____ ml.
Final burette reading	_____ ml.
Volume of NaOH solution used	_____ ml.
Conc. of NaOH solution used	_____ gm./ml.
Weight of NaOH in the volume of NaOH solution used	_____ gm.
Weight of $HC_2H_3O_2$ neutralized by weight of NaOH	_____ gm.
Percent of acid found (9 divided by 8)	_____ %

Control charts for range R and upper and lower control limits may be prepared in a similar manner as described above for percent of NH_3 in "household ammonia."

7. Chemical Analyses of Food Products

These are vital to control quality and safeguard the consumer's health. To illustrate the kinds of tests made, those performed in tomato paste are outlined below: (Test method details are not presented in this outline. Instructors are referred to such references as the "International Chemical Series - Technical Methods of Analysis," by Griffin, McGraw-Hill Company.)

a. Total Solids - Evaporate to dryness and weigh.

b. Insoluble Solids - Dilute, centrifuge, dry and weigh residue.

c. Soluble Solids - Subtract percentage of insoluble solids from total solids to obtain percentage of soluble solids.

d. Sand - mix sample with water, let stand 5 minutes, decant off supernatant liquid into second beaker, let stand 5 minutes, decant into a third beaker. Repeat starting with first beaker, fill with water, mix, let stand 5 minutes, decant into the second beaker and so on. Finally, decant all supernatant from the third beaker and discard. Dry, ignite and weigh residue in third beaker to obtain amount of sand.

e. Sodium Chloride - Determine Chlorine volmetrically by the Volhorant method using nitric acid solution of the ash obtained by igniting a 10 gm. sample in a crucible. Calculate percentage of NaCl using
NaCl = AgCl x 0.4078
1cc).1 N $AgNO_3$ = 0.005845 gm. NaCl.

f. Other tests made include reducing sugars, sucrose, total acids, volatile acids, butyric acid and fixed acids.

PHYSICAL FORMULAS

CONTENTS

		Page
1.	Weight Density	1
2.	Liquid Pressure	1
3.	Total Force	1
4.	Mechanical Advantage of Any Machine	1
5.	Mechanical Advantage of Hydraulic Press	1
6.	Specific Gravity of a Solid or Liquid	1
7.	Specific Gravity of a Solid	1
8.	Specific Gravity of a Liquid	2
9.	Boyle's Law	2
10.	Hooke's Law	2
11.	Factor of Safety	2
12.	Composition of Forces	2
13.	Resolution of Force of Gravity	3
14.	Coefficient of Friction	
15.	Speed	3
16.	Accelerated Motion	3
17.	Accelerated Motion	3
18.	Accelerated Motion	3
19.	Accelerated Motion	3
20.	Newton's Second Law of Motion	3
21.	Force and Acceleration on Bodies of Known Weight	3
22.	Impulse and Momentum	4
23.	Centrifugal Force	4
24.	Pendulum	4
25.	Pendulum	4
26.	Work	4
27.	Power	4
28.	Horsepower	4
29.	Potential Energy	5
30.	Kinetic Energy	5
31.	Variation of Mass with Velocity	5
32.	Machines	5
33.	Machines	5
34.	Lever	5
35.	Pulley	5

CONTENTS (Continued)

		Page
36.	Wheel and Axle	5
37.	Inclined Plane	6
38.	Screw	6
39.	Compound Machine	6
40.	Worm Wheel	6
41.	Differential Pulley	6
42.	Temperature Conversion	6
43.	Linear Expansion	7
44.	Kelvin Temperature	7
45.	Charles' Law	7
46.	Boyle's and Charles' Laws Combined	7
47.	Heat Exchange	7
48.	Sound Wave Formula	7
49.	Intensity of Sound	8
50.	Resonance in Tubes	8
51.	Illumination	8
52.	Images in Mirrors and Lenses	8
53.	Images in Mirrors and Lenses	8
54.	Index of Refraction	8
55.	Light Wave Formula	9
56.	Simple Magnifier	9
57.	Compound Microscope	9
58.	Refracting Telescope	9
59.	Ohm's Law	9
60.	Laws of Resistance	9
61.	Resistances in Series	9
62.	Resistances in Parallel	9
63.	Quantity of Electric Charge	10
64.	Electric Power	10
65.	Electric Power	10
66.	Laws of Electrolysis	10
67.	Cell Formula	10
68.	Cells in Series	10
69.	Cells in Parallel	10
70.	Joule's Laws	11
71.	Capacitive Reactance	11
72.	Inductive Reactance	11
73.	Impedance	11
74.	Ohm's Law for A.C. Circuits	11
75.	Range of Television Station	11

PHYSICAL FORMULAS

1. **WEIGHT DENSITY**

    $D = \dfrac{w}{V}$

    D is density; w is weight; V is volume

2. **LIQUID PRESSURE**

    $p = hD$
    p is pressure; h is depth; D is density

3. **TOTAL FORCE**

    (1) Horizontal Surfaces
    $F = AhD$
    F is total force; A is area; h is depth; D is density

    (2) Vertical Surfaces

    $F = \dfrac{AhD}{2}$

    F is total force; A is area; h is depth; D is density

4. **MECHANICAL ADVANTAGE OF ANY MACHINE**

    Mechanical Advantage $= \dfrac{w}{F}$

    w is weight supported; F is force applied

5. **MECHANICAL ADVANTAGE OF HYDRAULIC PRESS**

    Mechanical Advantage $= \dfrac{w}{F} = \dfrac{A}{a} = \dfrac{D}{d}$

    w is weight supported; F is force applied; A is area of large piston; a is area of small piston; D is diameter of large piston; d is diameter of small piston

6. **SPECIFIC GRAVITY OF A SOLID OR LIQUID**

    Sp. Gr. $= \dfrac{\text{density of substance}}{\text{density of water}}$

7. **SPECIFIC GRAVITY OF A SOLID**

    (1) Denser than Water

    Sp. Gr. $= \dfrac{\text{weight in air}}{\text{buoyant force of water}}$

(2) Less Dense Than Water

$$\text{Sp. Gr.} = \frac{w}{w' - w''}$$

w is weight of solid in air; w' is combined weight of solid in air and sinker in water; w" is combined weight of both solid and sinker in water

8. SPECIFIC GRAVITY OF A LIQUID

   (1) Bottle Method

   $$\text{Sp. Gr.} = \frac{\text{weight of liquid}}{\text{weight of water}}$$

   (2) Loss-of-Weight Method

   $$\text{Sp. Gr.} = \frac{\text{buoyant force of liquid}}{\text{buoyant force of water}}$$

   (3) Hydrometer Method

   $$\text{Sp. Gr.} = \frac{\text{depth rod sinks in water}}{\text{depth rod sinks in liquid}}$$

9. BOYLE'S LAW

$$pV = p'V'$$

p is original pressure; V is original volume; p' is new pressure; V' is new volume

10. HOOKE'S LAW

$$\text{Elastic Modulus} = \frac{\text{stress}}{\text{strain}}$$

11. FACTOR OF SAFETY

$$\text{Factor of Safety} = \frac{\text{maximum load}}{\text{rated load}}$$

12. COMPOSITION OF FORCES

The resultant of two forces acting at an angle upon a given point is equal to the diagonal of a parallelogram of which the two force vectors are sides. The equilibrant equals the magnitude of the resultant, but acts in the opposite direction.

13. RESOLUTION OF FORCE OF GRAVITY

Object Resting on Inclined Plane
$W : W_p = l : h$

W is weight of object; W_p is force tending to pull object down plane; l is length of plane; h is height of plane

14. COEFFICIENT OF FRICTION

    $u = \dfrac{f}{N}$

    u is coefficient of friction; f is force of friction; N is force normal to surface

15. SPEED

    Average Speed = $\dfrac{\text{distance traveled}}{\text{elapsed time}}$

16. ACCELERATED MOTION

    $v = at$, or $v = gt$

    v is final velocity; a is acceleration, or g is acceleration due to gravity; t is time

17. ACCELERATED MOTION

    $s = \frac{1}{2}at^2$, or $s = \frac{1}{2}gt^2$

    s is total distance; a is acceleration; or g is acceleration due to gravity; t is time

18. ACCELERATED MOTION

    $v = \sqrt{2as}$, or $v = \sqrt{2gs}$

    v is final velocity; a is acceleration, or g is acceleration due to gravity; s is total distance

19. ACCELERATED MOTION

    $s = \frac{1}{2}a(2t-1)$, or $s = \frac{1}{2}g(2t-1)$

    s is distance traversed in a given second; a is acceleration, or g is acceleration due to gravity; t is the number of the given second

20. NEWTON'S SECOND LAW OF MOTION

    $F = ma$

    F is force; m is mass; a is acceleration

21. FORCE AND ACCELERATION ON BODIES OF KNOWN WEIGHT

    $F : w = a : g$

    F is force; w is weight; a is acceleration; g is acceleration due to gravity

22. IMPULSE AND MOMENTUM

$Ft = mv$

F is force; t is time; the product Ft is impulse; m is mass; v is velocity; the product mv is momentum

23. CENTRIFUGAL FORCE

$$\text{Centrifugal Force} = \frac{mv^2}{r}$$

m is mass; v is velocity; r is radius of path

24. PENDULUM

$t : t' = \sqrt{l} : \sqrt{l'}$

t is period of first pendulum; t' is period of second pendulum; l is length of first pendulum; l' is length of second pendulum

25. PENDULUM

$$t = 2\pi \frac{\sqrt{l}}{g}$$

t is period; l is length; g is acceleration due to gravity

26. WORK

$W = Fs$

W is work; F is force; s is distance

27. POWER

$$P = \frac{W}{t}$$

P is power; W is work; t is time

28. HORSEPOWER

$$hp = \frac{Fs}{550t}$$

hp is horsepower; F is force in pounds; s is distance in feet; t is time in seconds

29. **POTENTIAL ENERGY**

    P.E. = mgh

    P.E. is potential energy; m is mass; g is acceleration due to gravity; h is vertical distance

30. **KINETIC ENERGY**

    K.E. = ½mv²

    K.E. is kinetic energy; m is mass; v is velocity

31. **VARIATION OF MASS WITH VELOCITY**

    $$m = \frac{m_0}{\sqrt{1 - \frac{v^2}{c^2}}}$$

    m is mass at velocity, v; m_0 is mass at zero velocity; c is speed of light

32. **MACHINES**

    F X s_f = w X s_w

    F is acting force; s_f is distance acting force moves; w is resisting weight; s_w is distance resisting weight moves

33. **MACHINES**

    Efficiency = $\frac{\text{useful work}}{\text{total work}}$

34. **LEVER**

    Mechanical Advantage = $\frac{EF}{RF}$

    EF is length of effort arm; RF is length of resistance arm

35. **PULLEY**

    nF = w

    n is number of strands supporting movable block; F is acting force; w is resisting weight

36. **WHEEL AND AXLE**

    Mechanical Advantage = $\frac{C}{c} = \frac{D}{d} = \frac{R}{r}$

    C, D, and R are circumference, diameter, and radius, respectively, of wheel; c, d, and r are circumference, diameter, and radius, respectively, of axle

37. INCLINED PLANE

(1) When Force Acts Parallel to Plane

Mechanical Advantage = $\dfrac{l}{h}$

l is length of plane; h is height of plane

(2) When Force Acts Parallel to Base of Plane

Mechanical Advantage = $\dfrac{b}{h}$

h is base of plane; h is height of plane

38. SCREW

Mechanical Advantage = $\dfrac{2\pi r}{d}$

r is length of arm on which force acts; d is pitch of screw

39. COMPOUND MACHINE

Total Mechanical Advantage = mechanical advantage (machine 1) x mechanical advantage (machine 2) x mechanical advantage (machine 3), etc.

40. WORM WHEEL

Mechanical Advantage = $\dfrac{nl}{r}$

n is number of teeth in gear wheel; l is radius of wheel on which force acts; r is radius of axle on which weight acts

41. DIFFERENTIAL PULLEY

Mechanical Advantage = $\dfrac{2C}{C - c}$

C is circumference of large wheel; c is circumference of small wheel

42. TEMPERATURE CONVERSION

(1) Centigrade to Fahrenheit

$t_F = 9/5 t_C + 32$

t_F is Fahrenheit temperature; t_C is Centigrade temperature

(2) Fahrenheit to Centigrade

$t_C = 5/9(t_F - 32)$

t_C is Centigrade temperature; t_F is Fahrenheit temperature

43. LINEAR EXPANSION

$\Delta l = al(t - t_o)$

Δl is increase in length; a is coefficient of linear expansion; l is original length; t is final temperature; t_o is original temperature

44. KELVIN TEMPERATURE

$T = t_C + 273$

T is Kelvin temperature; t_C is Centigrade temperature

45. CHARLES' LAW

$$\frac{V}{V'} = \frac{T}{T'}$$

V is original volume; V' is new volume; T is original Kelvin temperature; T' is final Kelvin temperature

46. BOYLE'S AND CHARLES' LAWS COMBINED

$$\frac{pV}{T} = \frac{p'V'}{T'}$$

p is original pressure; V is original volume; T is original Kelvin temperature; p' is final pressure; V' is final volume; T' is final Kelvin temperature

47. HEAT EXCHANGE

$Q = mc\Delta t$

Q is amount of heat required; m is mass of substance; c is specific heat of substance; Δt is change in temperature

48. SOUND WAVE FORMULA

$V = f\lambda$

v is velocity of wave; f is frequency; λ is wavelength

49. INTENSITY OF SOUND

$$B = 10 \log \frac{I}{I_o}$$

B is intensity of sound wave; I is energy of threshold of hearing; 10^{-16} watt/cm^2

50. RESONANCE IN TUBES

   (1) Closed Tube

   $$\lambda = 4(l + 0.4d)$$

   λ is wavelength; l is length of closed tube; d is diameter of tube

   (2) Open Tube

   $$\lambda = 2(l + 0.8d)$$

   λ is wavelength; l is length of open tube; d is diameter of tube

51. ILLUMINATION

$$E = \frac{I}{R^2}$$

E is illumination; I is intensity; R is distance from source to illuminated surface

52. IMAGES IN MIRRORS AND LENSES

$$S_o : S_i = D_o : D_i$$

S_o is object size; S_i is image size; D_o is object distance; D_i is image distance

53. IMAGES IN MIRRORS AND LENSES

$$\frac{1}{D_o} + \frac{1}{D_i} = \frac{1}{f}$$

D_o is object distance; D_i is image distance; f is focal length

54. INDEX OF REFRACTION

$$u = \frac{\sin \theta_i}{\sin \theta_r}$$

u is index of refraction; θ_i is angle of incidence; θ_r is angle of refraction

55. LIGHT WAVE FORMULA

$C = f\lambda$

c is velocity of light; f is frequency; λ is wavelength

56. SIMPLE MAGNIFIER

Magnifying Power = $\dfrac{25 \text{ cm}}{f \text{ cm}} = \dfrac{10 \text{ in}}{f \text{ in}}$

f is focal length of lens in units indicated

57. COMPOUND MICROSCOPE

Magnifying Power = $\dfrac{25L}{f_e f_o}$

L is length of tube in centimeters; f_e is focal length of eyepiece in centimeters; f_o is focal length of objective in centimeters

58. REFRACTING TELESCOPE

Magnifying Power = $\dfrac{f_o}{f_e}$

f_o is focal length of objective; f_e is focal length of eyepiece

59. OHM'S LAW

$I = \dfrac{V}{R}$

I is current; V is potential difference; R is resistance

60. LAWS OF RESISTANCE

$R = \dfrac{pl}{d^2}$

R is resistance; p is resistivity; l is length in feet, d is diameter in mils

61. RESISTANCES IN SERIES

$R = R_1 + R_2 + R_3 \ldots$

R is total resistance; R_1, R_2, R_3, etc. are individual resistances

62. RESISTANCES IN PARALLEL

$\dfrac{1}{R} = \dfrac{1}{R} + \dfrac{1}{R} + \dfrac{1}{R} \ldots$

R is joint resistance; R_1, R_2, R_3, etc. are individual resistances

63. **QUANTITY OF ELECTRIC CHARGE**

    $Q = It$

    Q is amount of charge; I is current; t is time

64. **ELECTRIC POWER**

    $P = IV$

    P is power; I is current; V is potential difference

65. **ELECTRIC POWER**

    $P = I^2 R$

    P is power; I is current; R is resistance

66. **LAWS OF ELECTROLYSIS**

    $m = zIT$

    m is mass; z is electrochemical equivalent; I is current; t is time

67. **CELL FORMULA**

    $I = \dfrac{E}{R_e + R_i}$

    I is current; E is emf of cell; R_e is external resistance; R_i is internal resistance

68. **CELLS IN SERIES**

    $I = \dfrac{nE}{R_e + nR_i}$

    I is current; n is number of cells; E is emf of one cell; R_e is external resistance; R_i is internal resistance

69. **CELLS IN PARALLEL**

    $I = \dfrac{E}{R_e + \dfrac{R_i}{n}}$

    I is current; E is emf of one cell; R_e is external resistance; R_i is internal resistance; n is number of cells

70. **JOULE'S LAWS**

    $W = I^2Rt$

    W is energy; I is current strength; R is resistance; t is time

71. **CAPACITIVE REACTANCE**

    $X_c = \dfrac{159{,}000}{fc}$

    X_c is capacitive reactance in ohms; f is frequency in cycles; c is capacitance in microfarads

72. **INDUCTIVE REACTANCE**

    $X_l = 2\pi fL$

    X_l is inductive reactance in ohms; f is frequency in cycles; L is inductance in henrys

73. **IMPEDANCE**

    $Z = \sqrt{R^2 + (X_l - X_c)^2}$

    Z is impedance; R is resistance; X_l is inductive reactance; X_c is capacitive reactance

74. **OHM'S LAW FOR A.C. CIRCUITS**

    $I = \dfrac{V}{Z}$

    I is current; V is voltage; Z is impedance

75. **RANGE OF TELEVISION STATION**

    $D = 1.23\sqrt{H}$

    D is range in miles; H is height of antenna in feet

ENGINEERING FUNDAMENTALS

TABLE OF CONTENTS

	Page
I. PHYSICS	1
A. Mass, Weight and Inertia	1
B. Force	1
C. Speed, Velocity and Acceleration	1
D. Energy	2
E. Work	2
F. Power	3
G. Laws of Gases	3
H. Pressure and Vacuum	4
I. Gage Pressure	4
J. Atmospheric Pressure	4
K. Vacuum	5
L. Absolute Pressure	5
II. PRINCIPLES OF HYDRAULICS	7
III. PRINCIPLES OF PNEUMATICS	8
A. Heat	8
B. Units of Measurement	9
C. Sensible Heat and Latent Heat	10
D. Temperature	11
E. Combustion	12
IV. METALS	14

NOTES AND RESOURCES

ENGINEERING FUNDAMENTALS

This part is designed to acquaint you with various laws and phenomena of nature. Included is information pertaining to matter and energy, force and motion, heat and temperature, pressure, combustion, the laws of perfect gases, and some fundamental information about metals. The information provided here is general in nature; but it has been included to give you a better understanding of how or why engineering machinery operates or produces work. As you study this part, remember that anything that occupies space and has weight is called MATTER.

I. PHYSICS

The forces of physics and the laws of nature are at work in every single piece of machinery or equipment aboard ship. It is by these forces and laws that the machinery and equipment produce work.

A. MASS, WEIGHT, AND INERTIA

The physical principles of mass and inertia are involved in the design and operation of the heavy flywheels and bull gears that are at work in the ship's engineering plant. The great mass of the wheel tends to keep it rotating once it has been set in motion. The high inertia of the wheel keeps it from responding to small fluctuations in speed and thus helps to keep the engine running smoothly.

The mass and the weight of an object are not the same. The mass of an object is the quantity of matter which the object contains. The weight of the object is equal to the gravitational force with which the object is attracted to the earth. Inertia is that physical property which causes objects that are at rest to remain at rest, unless they are acted upon by some external force; and which causes objects moving at a constant velocity to continue moving at this constant velocity, and in the same direction, until acted upon by some external force.

B. FORCE

Force is what makes an object start to move, or speedup, or slow down; or keep moving against resistance. This force may be either a push or a pull. You exert a force when you push against a truck, whether you move the truck, or only try to move it. You also exert a force when you pull on a heavy piano, whether you move the piano, or only try to move it. Forces produce or prevent motion, or have a tendency to do so.

A tendency to prevent motion is the frictional resistance offered by an object. This frictional resistance is called frictional force. While it can never cause an object to move, it can check or stop motion. Frictional force wastes power, creates heat, and causes wear. Although frictional force cannot be entirely eliminated, it can be reduced by using lubricants.

C. SPEED, VELOCITY, AND ACCELERATION

Speed is defined as the distance covered per unit of time. Velocity is speed in a certain direction. Acceleration is the rate at which velocity changes. If, for example, the propeller shaft rate of rotation increases from stop to 100 revolutions per minute (rpm) in 20 minutes, the acceleration is 5 rpm. In other words, the velocity has increased 5 revolutions per minute, during each minute, for a total period of 20 minutes. A body with uniform motion has no acceleration. When the velocity of an object changes by the same amount each second or minute, you have uniform acceleration. Uniform deceleration is obtained when the decrease in velocity is the same each second or minute.

D. ENERGY

Energy may be described as the ability to do work. In the physical sense, work is done when a force acts on matter and moves it. We use heat energy to turn a steam turbine, and electric energy to drive motors. The mechanical energy of the pistons in an automobile engine is transmitted to the wheels by the crank shaft, transmission, drive shaft, differential gears, and rear axles. Nuclear energy is used to generate electric power and to drive naval ships.

Perhaps the most common definition of energy is given as "the capacity for doing work." However this is not quite a complete statement because energy can produce other effects which could not be considered as work. For example, heat can flow from one object to another without doing any work; yet heat is a form of energy and the process of heat transfer produces an effect. Therefore, a better definition of energy states that energy is the capacity for producing an effect.

Energy is normally classified according to the size and nature of the objects or particles with which it is associated. So we say that mechanical energy is the energy associated with large objects—usually things that are big enough to see—such as pumps and turbines. Thermal energy is energy associated with molecules. Chemical energy is energy that arises from the forces which bind the atoms together in a molecule. Chemical energy is released whenever combustion or any other chemical reaction takes place. Electrical energy, light waves, and radio waves are examples of energy that are associated with particles smaller than atoms. Nuclear energy is obtained from splitting the atoms. Each of these types of energy (mechanical, thermal, etc.) must also be classified as either (1) stored energy, or (2) energy in transition.

Stored energy is thought of as energy that is actually contained in or stored in an object. There are two kinds of stored energy: potential energy and kinetic energy. Potential energy is energy in an object waiting to be released; while kinetic energy is energy that has been released. For example, potential energy exists in a rock resting on the edge of a cliff, water behind a dam, or steam behind a turbine throttle valve.

Kinetic energy exists because of the velocities of two or more objects. If you push the rock, open the gate of the dam, or open the turbine throttle valve, something will move. The rock will fall, the water will flow, and the steam will jet through the turbine nozzle valves. Thus the potential energy is converted to kinetic energy.

Energy in transition exists when the rock hits the ground, the water hits the bottom of the dam or the paddles of a water wheel, or when the steam hits the blades of the turbine rotor.

In the examples just discussed, an external source of energy was used to get things started. External energy was used to push the rock, open the gate of the dam, or to open the throttle valve. Thus you can see that one energy system affects another energy system. There is a tremendous amount of chemical energy stored in fuel oil; but it will not raise the steam in the boiler until some external energy has been expended to start the oil burning.

Energy can be measured. The most common measurement of expended energy is in work units of foot-pounds. When an object has been moved through a resisting force, work has been done.

E. WORK

The turbines and other power equipment used aboard ship are important because they do work. WORK is defined as the result of force moving through distance. The unit of measure for work is the FOOT-POUND (ft-lb).

The two parts of this unit are the POUND OF FORCE and the FOOT OF DISTANCE.

Force is measured in pounds. The gravitational pull on an object weighing 1 pound is a force of 1 pound. If you lift a 1-pound weight from ground level to a height of 1 foot, you exert a force of 1 pound through a distance of 1 foot and 1 foot-pound of work is done in the process. A force of 100 pounds is required to raise a 100-pound anvil; if you lift it to the top of a 30-inch bench, the work done is 2 1/2 ft x 100lb = 250 ft-lb. Work (in foot-pounds), therefore, equals the force (in pounds) times the distance (in feet).

Now suppose you want to move the anvil across the deck without lifting it. It will take a considerable force to slide the anvil let us say 60 pounds. If you slide it 10 feet, you do 600 foot-pounds of work. Here the force of 60 pounds is required to overcome the resisting force of friction between the anvil and the deck. A great deal of the work done by any machine is the overcoming of the many frictional forces which resist the motion of the parts.

F. POWER

The ship's main engines are frequently called the POWER PLANT; and they are commonly rated according to how much power they can develop. For example, it might take one man 10 hours to load 20,000 pounds of ammunition on a truck, whereas a crane could do the same job in 5 minutes. The amount of work done is the same, but the crane is much more powerful than the man. It can do the work faster. POWER, then, relates to work and time. It is the TIME RATE of doing WORK. If we assume that the ammunition is raised an average height of 6 feet, the work done is equal to 6 ft x 20,000 lb or 120,000 ft-lb. Considering the man also as a machine, the power of each of the two machines is found by dividing this amount of work by the time required in each case. Expressing 10 hours in minutes, the man would work at the rate of 120,000 ft-lb ÷ 600 min = 200 ft-lb per min. The computed power of the crane would be 120,000 ft-lb ÷ 5 min = 24,000 ft-lb per min or 400 ft-lb per sec.

The most common unit of power is known as the HORSEPOWER. One horsepower is equivalent to 550 ft-lb per second, or 33,000 ft-lb per minute. Thus, if a lifting machine raises a weight of 100 pounds at the rate of 250 ft-lb per second, the machine is exerting only 0.454 of a horsepower (250 ft-lb ÷ 550 ft-lb = 0.454 hp).

If a crane hoists 2,000 pounds of cargo to a height of 30 feet in 5 seconds, how much horsepower is developed? Here is how to get the answer:

$$\text{Power} = \frac{\text{work}}{\text{time}} = \frac{2,000 \text{ lb} \times 30 \text{ ft}}{5 \text{ sec}}$$

$$= 12,000 \text{ ft-lb per sec}$$

$$\text{Horsepower} = \frac{12,000 \text{ ft-lb per sec}}{550 \text{ ft-lb per sec}} = 21.8$$

Or suppose a turbine has a known horsepower of 37,500 at rated capacity, and you want to know how much work it does. You find out by multiplying the developed horsepower by the hours in operation. This gives HORSEPOWER-HOURS, which is a measure of work for main propulsion machinery.

G. LAWS OF GASES

The energy transformation of major interest in the shipboard engineering plant is the transformation from heat to work. To see how this transformation occurs, we need to consider the pressure, temperature, and volume relationships which hold true for gases. In the middle of the 17th century, an English scientist, Robert Boyle, made some interesting discoveries concerning the relationship between the pressure, the temperature, and the volume of gases. In 1787, Jacques Charles, a Frenchman, proved that all gases expand the same amount when heated one degree if the pressure is kept constant. The relationships that these two men discovered are : summarized as follows:

1. When the temperature is held constant, increasing the pressure on a gas causes a pro- portional decrease in volume. Decreasing the pressure causes a proportional increase in volume.

2. When the pressure is held constant, increasing the temperature of a gas causes a proportional increase in volume. Decreasing the temperature causes a proportional decrease in volume.

3. When the volume is held constant, increasing the temperature of a gas causes a proportional increase in pressure. Decreasing the temperature causes a proportional decrease in pressure.

Suppose we have a boiler in which steam has just begun to form. With the steam stop valves still closed, the volume of the steam remains constant while the pressure and the temperature are both increasing. When operating pressure is reached, and the steam stop valves are opened, the high pressure of the steam causes the steam to flow to the turbines. The pressure of the steam thus provides the potential for doing work; the actual conversion of heat to work is done in the turbines.

H . PRESSURE AND VACUUM

Because pressure is very important to the engineering plant, it is necessary that you understand the relationships between gage pressure, atmospheric pressure, vacuum, and absolute pressure. These relationships are indicated in figure 3-1.

I .Gage Pressure

Gage pressure is the pressure actually shown on the dial of a gage which registers pressures at or above atmospheric pressure. Gage pressure is usually shown in pounds per square inch (psi); but it may be shown in inches of water, mercury, or other liquid. A reading of 1 inch of water means that the exerted pressure is able to support a column of water 1 inch high, or that a column of water in a U-tube would be displaced 1 inch by the pressure being measured. Similarly, a gage pressure reading of 12 inches of mercury means that the measured pressure is able to support a column of mercury 12 inches high. Gages are calibrated in inches of water

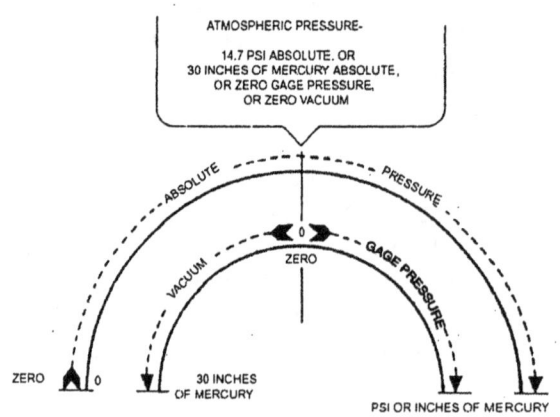

Figure 3-1.—Relationships between vacuum, gage pressure, absolute pressure, and atmospheric pressure.

when they are to be used for the measurement of very low pressures. Inches of mercury may be used when the range of pressures to be measured is somewhat higher, since mercury is about 14 times as heavy as water.

Note that a gage pressure reading of zero means that the pressure being measured is exactly the same as the existing atmospheric pressure. A gage reading of 50 psi means that the pressure being measured is 50 psi IN EXCESS OF the existing atmospheric pressure.

J. Atmospheric Pressure

Atmospheric pressure, or the pressure exerted by the weight of the air in the atmosphere, is measured with a BAROMETER (fig. 3-2). A barometer is similar to a manometer (see chapter 9), except that the indicating tube is sealed at the top. A barometer may be made by filling a tube with mercury and then inverting it so that the open end rests in a container of mercury which is open to the atmosphere. The absence of pressure at the closed end of the tube permits atmospheric pressure, acting upon the surface of the mercury in the open container, to hold the mercury in the tube at a height which corresponds to the pressure being exerted.

Normally, at sea level, atmospheric pressure will hold the column of mercury at a height of approximately 30 inches. Since a column of mercury 1 inch high exerts a pressure of 0.49 pounds per square inch, a 30-inch column of mercury exerts a pressure which is equal to (30 x 0.49) 14.7 pounds per square inch. Thus we can say that atmospheric pressure (zero gage pressure) at sea level is 14.7 psi, or 14.7 pounds per square inch absolute (psia). Notice, however, that this figure of 14.7 psi is the STANDARD for atmospheric pressure. Since fluctuations from this standard are shown on the barometer, the term BAROMETRIC PRESSURE is used to describe the atmospheric pressure which exists at any given moment. As a rule, you can use the term ATMOSPHERIC PRESSURE and the value 14.7 psi in place of the actual barometric pressure; but there may be times when it will be important to know the ACTUAL (barometric) pressure, in order to make precise measurements of gage pressure or vacuum.

K. Vacuum

A space in which the pressure is LESS than atmospheric pressure is said to be under VACUUM. The amount of vacuum is expressed in terms of the difference between the pressure in the space and the existing atmospheric pressure. Vacuum is measured in inches of mercury that is, the number of inches a column of mercury in a U-tube would be displaced by a pressure equal to the DIFFERENCE between the pressure in the vacuum space and the existing atmospheric pressure.

Vacuum gage scales are marked from 0 to 30. When a vacuum gage reads zero, the pressure in the space is the same as the existing atmospheric pressureor, in other words, there is no vacuum. A vacuum gage reading of 30 inches of mercury would indicate a nearly perfect vacuum. In actual practice, it is impossible to obtain a perfect vacuum; and the highest vacuum gage readings are seldom over 29 inches of mercury.

L. Absolute Pressure

Absolute pressure is atmospheric pressure PLUS gage pressure, or atmospheric pressure MINUS vacuum. For example, if gage pressure is 300 psi, absolute pressure is 314.7 psi; or if the measured vacuum is 10 inches of mercury, absolute pressure is approximately 20 inches of mercury. It is important to note that the amount of PRESSURE in a space under vacuum can be expressed only in terms of absolute pressure.

Sometimes it is necessary to convert a reading from inches of mercury to pounds per square inch. Figure 3-1 gives you all the information you need to make this conversion. Since atmospheric pressure is equal to 14.7 psi or to 30 inches of mercury, it is easy to see that 1 inch of mercury is equal to (14.7 psi divided by 30) 0.49 psi. Now convert your gage reading to absolute pressure (in inches of mercury) and then multiply this figure by 0.49 psi. For example, to convert a vacuum gage reading of 14 inches of mercury to psi, you would proceed as follows:

1. Convert 14 inches of mercury VACUUM to ABSOLUTE PRESSURE. Absolute pressure is atmospheric pressure MINUS vacuum (30 inches -14 inches = 16 inches).

2. Multiply the absolute pressure in inches of mercury by 0.49. Since 1 inch of mercury is equal to 0.49 psi, 16 inches of mercury is equal to (16 x 0.49 psi) 7.8 psi (about 8 psi). Remember that this answer is in terms of ABSOLUTE PRESSURE.

As you can see, it is also easy to convert psi to inches of mercury. Since atmospheric pressure is equal to 14.7 psi OR to 30 inches of mercury, 1 psi is equal to (30 inches of mercury divided by 14.7) 2.04 inches of mercury. For example, 10 psi absolute is equal to (10 x 2.04 inches of mercury) 20.4 inches of mercury absolute.

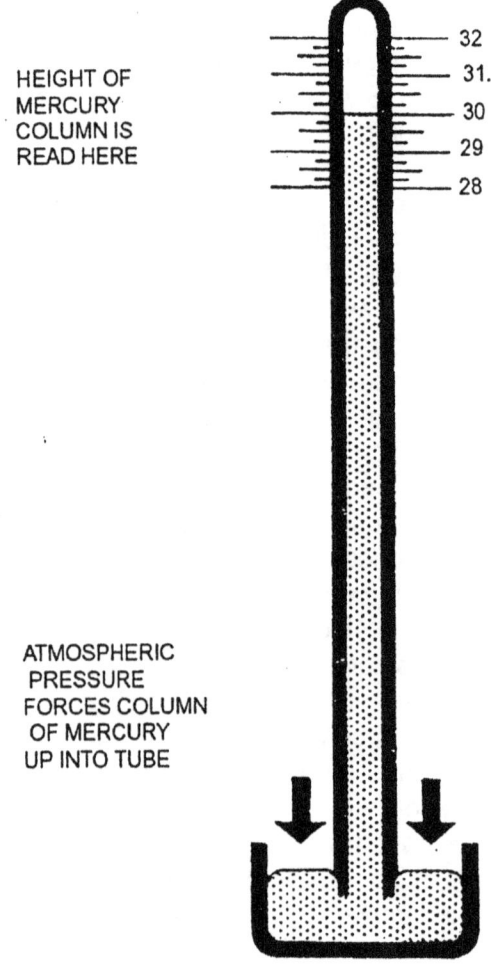

Figure 3-2.—Operating principle of mercurial barometer.

In order to interpret the reading on a pressure gage, you must know the LOCATION of the gage in relation to the line in which the pressure is being measured. As a general rule, pressure gage connections are led from the top of the pressure line. Occasionally, however, it is necessary to locate a pressure gage at some distance BELOW the pipe; then the reading on the gage will indicate the pressure being measured PLUS the pressure exerted by the weight of the column of liquid above the gage. The required correction should be made in calibration of the gage; but if it has not been made in calibration, it must be made in the interpretation of the gage reading.

Correction for a head of liquid should be made as follows:

1. Measure the vertical distance from the center of the gage to the line in which the pressure is being measured.

2. For each foot of the distance measured, subtract from the gage reading the weight of a column of liquid 1 foot high and 1 inch square in cross section. If you are measuring pressure on a steam or water line, you must correct for a head of water. Since a column of water 1 foot high and 1 inch square in cross section weighs 0.433 pounds, you subtract 0.433 psi from the gage reading for each foot of drop. (CAUTION: The weight of each liquid is different, and must be determined before you can make this correction.)

For example, to correct a pressure gage reading for a head of water, assume that a steam pressure gage is connected 10 feet BELOW the steam line. The steam cools and condenses in the gage connection line, filling the connection line with water. The uncorrected gage reading is 250 psi. Multiply 0.433 psi by 10, and then subtract the resulting figure from 250 psi;
   (1) 0.433 psi x 10 = 4.33 psi
   (2) 250 psi - 4.33 psi - 245.67 psi

Thus the true pressure in the steam line is 245.67, or approximately 246 psi.

It is sometimes necessary to connect a water pressure gage at some distance ABOVE the point at which the pressure is being measured; then the reading on the gage will show the pressure being measured MINUS the pressure required to support the column of water up to the gage. To correct the reading, you must ADD the weight of the column of water-that is, you must add 0.433 psi to the gage reading for each foot of rise.

For example, assume that a water pressure gage is connected 5 feet ABOVE the point at which the pressure is being measured. The gage reading is 30 psi. To obtain the actual pressure at the point of measurement, you must add (5 x 0.433 psi) 2.17 psi to the gage reading. Thus the actual pressure is 32.17 psi.

II. PRINCIPLES OF HYDRAULICS

The word hydraulics is derived from the Greek word for water (hydor) plus the Greek word for flute (aulos). The term "hydraulics" originally covered a study of the physical behavior of water at rest and in motion. However, the meaning of the term "hydraulics" has been broadened to cover the physical behavior of all liquids, including the oils that are used in present day hydraulic systems.

During the period before World War I, the Navy began to apply hydraulics extensively to naval mechanisms. Since that time, naval applications have increased to the point where many ingenious hydraulic devices are used in the solution of problems of gunnery, navigation, and aeronautics. Aboard ship today the applications of hydraulics include anchor windlasses, power cranes, steering gear, remote controls, power drives for the elevating of guns and training of mounts and turrets, powder and projectile hoists, recoil systems, gun rammers, and airplane catapults.

The foundations of modern hydraulics began in 1653 when Pascal discovered that "pressure set up in a liquid acts equally in all directions." This pressure acts at right angles to the containing surfaces.

In figure 3-3 if the liquid standing on a square inch (A) at the bottom of the tank weighs 8 pounds, a pressure of 8 pounds is exerted in every direction at A. The liquid resting on A will push equally downward and outward. But the liquid on every other square inch of the bottom surface is also pushing downward and outward in the same manner.

When we apply a force to the end of a column of confined liquid, the force is transmitted not only straight through to the other end, but also equally in every direction throughout the column-forwards, backwards, and sidewaysso that the containing vessel is literally filled with pressure. This is the reason that aflat fire hose takes on a circular cross-section when it is filled with water under pressure. The outward push of the water is equal in every direction. Water will leave the hose at the same velocity, through leaks, regardless of where the leaks are in the hose.

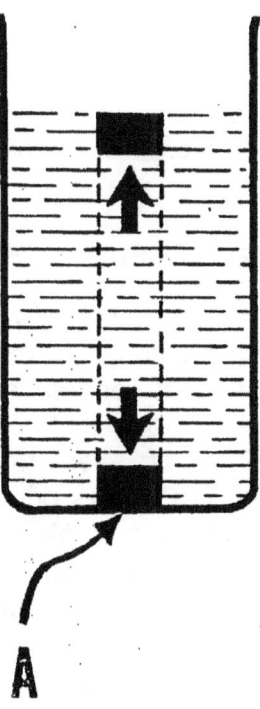

Figure 3-3.—Illustration showing principle of Pascal's law.

Let us now consider the effect of Pascal's law in the system shown in figure 3-4. If the force at piston A is 100 pounds and the area of the piston is 10 square inches, then the pressure in the liquid must be 10 pounds per square inch (psi). This pressure is transmitted to piston Bso that for every square inch of its area, piston B will be pushed upward with a force of 10 pounds. In this example we are merely considering a liquid column of equal cross-section so that the areas of the pistons are equal. All we have done is to carry a 100-poundforce around a bend; however, the principle illustrated is the basis for practically all mechanical hydraulics.

The same principle may be applied where the input piston is much smaller than the output piston or vice versa. Assume that the area of the input piston is 2 square inches and the area of the output piston is 20 square inches. If you apply a pressure of 20 pounds to the smaller piston, the pressure created in the liquid will again be 10 pounds per square inch because the force is concentrated on a smaller area. The upward force on the larger piston will be 200 pounds10 pounds for each of its 20 square inches. Thus you can see if two pistons are used in a hydraulic system, the force acting on each piston will be directly proportional to its area, and the magnitude of each force will be the product of the pressure and the area of the piston.

III. PRINCIPLES OF PNEUMATICS

Pneumatics is that branch of mechanics that deals with the mechanical properties of gases. Perhaps the most common application of these properties is the use of compressed air. Compressed air is used to transmit pressure, according to Pascal's principle, in a variety of applications. For example, in tires and air cushioned springs, compressed air acts as a cushion to absorb shock. Air brakes on locomotives and large trucks contribute greatly to the safety of railroad and truck transportation. Compressed air is used in numerous ways. For example, tools such as riveting hammers and pneumatic drills are air operated. Automatic combustion control systems utilize compressed air for the operation of the instruments. Compressed air is also used in diving bells and diving suits. Perhaps a brief discussion on the use of compressed air as an aid in the control of submarines will best explain the theory of pneumatics.

Submarines are designed with a number of tanks that may be used for the control of the ship. These tanks may be flooded with water to submerge; or they may be filled with compressed air to surface.

The compressed air for the pneumatic system is maintained in storage tanks (called banks) at a pressure of 4,500 psi. When surfacing, the pneumatic system delivers compressed air to the desired control tanks. Since the pressure of the air is greater than the pressure of the water, the water is forced out of the tank. As a result, the weight of the ship is decreased; it becomes more buoyant, and thus it will tend to rise to the surface.

A. HEAT

You undoubtedly know from experience that heat and temperature are related; however, they are not the same. Water from a water main feels cool until it has been over a fire a few minutes. It evidently must have received something from the fire. If you place two pennies together, one of which was heated by being held in the flame of a match, in a short time the two pennies will be equally warm. Again something passed into the cooler object and made it hot. That something is called heat.

Many forms of mechanical action also produce considerable quantities of heat. For example, you rub your hands together to warm them when they are cold. Matches are ignited by rubbing them on a rough surface. A Shipfitter can notice heat in a piece of metal after hammering it; and the head of a nail is heated when the nail is driven into wood.

The molecules in the nail (as in all matter) are in continual motion. The blow on the nail increases the molecular motion. The molecules in the top layer receive the impulse from the hammer, and vibrate with greater violence. The increased vibration and energy of motion is passed on to layer after layer of molecules. Thus the effect of the blow is to produce ageneral increase in the motion of the molecules. This energy of molecular motion is called heat.

Because molecules are constantly in motion, they exert a pressure on the walls of the pipe, boiler, cylinder, or other object in which they are contained. Also, the temperature of any substance arises from and is directly proportional to the activity of the molecules. Therefore, every time you read thermometers and pressure gages you are finding out something about the amount of internal energy contained in the substance. High pressures and temperatures indicate that the molecules are moving rapidly and that the substance therefore has a lot of internal energy.

HEAT is a more familiar term than internal energy, yet one that may actually be more difficult to define correctly. The important thing to remember is that heat is THERMAL ENERGY IN TRANSITION—that is, it is thermal energy that is moving from one substance or system to another.

An example will help to illustrate the difference between heat and internal energy. Suppose there are two equal lengths of pipe, made of identical materials and containing steam at the same pressure and temperature. One pipe is well insulated, the other is not insulated at all. From everyday experience you know that more heat will flow from the uninsulated pipe than from the insulated pipe. When the two pipes are first filled with steam, the steam in one pipe contains exactly as much internal energy as the steam in the other pipe. We know this is true because the two pipes contain equal volumes of steam at the same pressure and at the same temperature. After a few minutes, the steam in the uninsulated pipe will contain much less internal energy than the steam in the insulated pipe, as we can tell by measuring the pressure and the temperature of the steam in each pipe. What has happened? Stored thermal energy—internal energy—has moved from one place to another, first from the steam to the pipe, then from the uninsulated pipe to the air. The MOVEMENT or FLOW of thermal energy is what should be called heat.

B. Units of Measurement

Both internal energy and heat are usually measured using the unit called the BRITISH THERMAL UNIT (Btu). For most practical engineering purposes, 1 Btu is defined as the amount of thermal energy required to raise the temperature of 1 pound of water through 1°F.

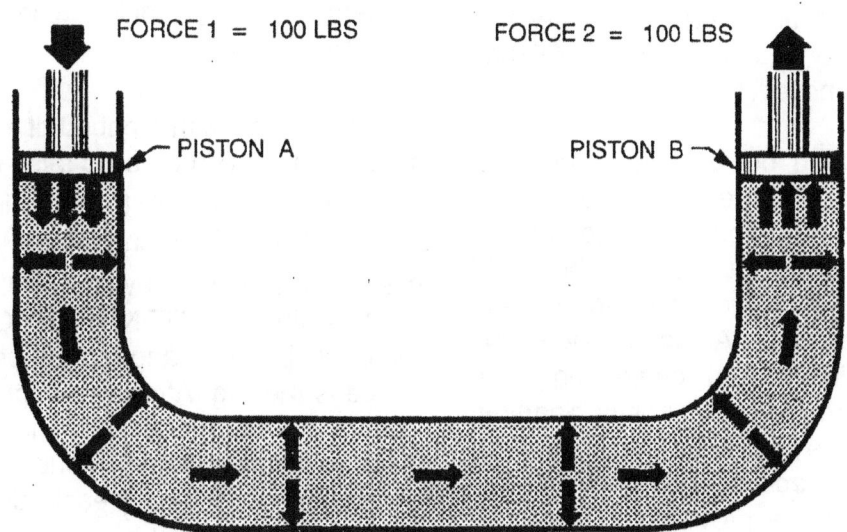

Figure 3-4.—Principle of mechanical hydraulics.

When large amounts of thermal energy are involved, it is usually more convenient to use multiples of the Btu. For example, 1 kB is equal to 1,000 Btu, and 1 mB is equal to 1,000,000 Btu.

Another unit in which thermal energy may be measured is the CALORIE, the amount of heat required to raise the temperature of 1 gram of water 1°C. One Btu equals 252 calories.

C. Sensible Heat and Latent Heat

The terms SENSIBLE HEAT and LATENT HEAT are often used to indicate the effect that the flow of heat has on a substance. The flow of heat from one substance to another is normally reflected in a temperature change in each substance the hotter substance becomes cooler, the cooler substance becomes hotter. However, the flow of heat is NOT reflected in a temperature change in a substance which is in the process of changing from one physical state (solid, liquid, or gas) to another. When the flow of heat is reflected in a temperature change, we say that SENSIBLE HEAT has been added to or removed from the substance. When the flow of heat is NOT reflected in a temperature change but IS reflected in the changing physical state of s substance, we say that LATENT HEAT has been added or removed.

Does anything bother you in this last paragraph? It should. Here we are, talking about adding and removing heat. And, furthermore, we are talking about sensible heat and latent heat as though we had two different kinds of heat to consider. As noted before, this is common (if inaccurate) engineering language. So keep the following points clearly in mind: (1) heat is the flow of thermal energy; (2) when we talk about adding and removing heat, we mean that we are providing temperature differentials so that thermal energy can flow from one substance to another; and (3) when we talk about sensible heat and latent heat, we are talking about two different kinds of EFFECTS that can be produced by heat, but not about two different kinds of heat.

The three basic physical states of all matter are SOLID, LIQUID, and GAS (or vapor). The physical state of a substance is closely related to the distance between molecules. As a general rule, the molecules are closest together in solids, farther apart in liquids, and farthest apart in gases. When the flow of heat to a substance is not reflected in a temperature change, we know that the energy is being used to increase the distance between the molecules of the substance and thus to change it from a solid to a liquid or from a liquid to a gas. You might say that latent heat is the energy price that must be paid for a change of state from solid to liquid or from liquid to gas. The energy is not lost; rather, it is stored in the substance as internal energy. The energy price is "repaid," so to speak, when the substance changes back from gas to liquid or from liquid to solid, since heat flows FROM the substance during these changes of state.

Figure 3-5 shows the relationship between sensible heat and latent heat for one substance, water, at atmospheric pressure. (The same kind of chart could be drawn up for other substances; however, different amounts of thermal energy would be involved in the changes of state.)

If we start with 1 pound of ice at 0° F, we must add 16 Btu in order to raise the temperature of the ice to 32° F. We call this adding SENSIBLE HEAT. To change the pound of ice at 32° F to a pound of water at 32°F, we must add 144 Btu (the LATENT HEAT OF FUSION). There will be no change in temperature while the ice is melting. After all the ice has melted, however, the temperature of the water will be raised as additional heat is supplied. If we add 180 Btu that is, 1 Btu for each degree of temperature between 32° F and 212 F the temperature of the water, will be raised to the boiling point. To change the pound of water at 212° F to a pound of steam at 212° F, we must add 970 Btu (the LATENT HEAT OF VAPORIZA-

TION). After all the water has been converted to steam, the addition of more heat will cause an increase in the temperature of the steam. If we add about 44 Btu to the pound of steam which is at 210° F, we can superheat it to 300° F.

The same relationships apply when heat is being removed. The removal of 44 Btu from the pound of steam which is at 300° F will cause the temperature to drop to 212° F. As the pound of steam at 212° F changes to a pound of water at 212° F, 970 Btu are given off. When a substance is changing from a gas or vapor to a liquid, we usually use the term LATENT HEAT OF CONDENSATION for the heat that is given off. Notice, however, that the latent heat of condensation is exactly the same as the latent heat of vaporization. The removal of another 180 Btu of sensible heat will lower the temperature of the pound of water from 212° F to 32° F. As the pound of water at 32° F changes to a pound of ice at 32° F, 144 Btu are given off without any accompanying change in temperature. Further removal of heat causes the temperature of the ice to decrease.

D. TEMPERATURE

The temperature of an object is a measure of how hot or cold the object is; and it can be measured by thermometers and read on their temperature scales.

The TEMPERATURE SCALES employed to measure temperature are the Fahrenheit scale and the centigrade scale. In engineering and for practically all purposes in the Navy, the Fahrenheit scale is used. It may, however, be necessary for you to convert centigrade readings to the Fahrenheit scale, so both scales are explained here.

The FAHRENHEIT SCALE has two main reference points the boiling point of pure water at 212, and the freezing point of pure water at 32. The size of the Fahrenheit degree is 1/180 of the total temperature change from 32 to 212. And the scale can be extended in either direction to higher temperatures without any limits, and (by using MINUS degrees) to lower temperatures down to the lowest temperature theoretically possible, the so-called ABSOLUTE ZERO. This temperature is -460, or 492 below the freezing point of water.

In the CENTIGRADE SCALE, the freezing point of pure water is 0 and the boiling point of pure water is 100. Therefore, 0° C and 100° C are equivalent to 32° F and 212° F, respectively. Each centigrade degree is larger than a Fahrenheit degree (since there are only 100 centigrade degrees between the freezing and boiling points of water, while this same temperature change requires 180 degrees in the Fahrenheit scale). Therefore the centigrade degree is 180/100 or 1.8 Fahrenheit degrees. In the centigrade scale absolute zero is -273.

Figure 3-6 shows the two temperature scales in comparison. This figure also introduces the simplest of the temperature measuring instruments, the liquid-in-glass THERMOMETER. The two thermometers shown are exactly alike in SIZE and SHAPE, the only difference being in the outside markings or SCALES on them. Each thermometer is a hollow glass tube which has a mercury-filled bulb at the bottom, and which is sealed at the top. Mercury, like any liquid, expands on being heated, and it will rise in the hollow tube. The illustration shows the Fahrenheit thermometer with its bulb standing in ice water (32° F), while the centigrade thermometer is in boiling water (100° C).

The essential point to remember is that the level of the mercury in a thermometer depends only on the temperature to which the bulb is exposed. If you were to exchange the thermometers, the mercury in the centigrade thermometer would drop to the level at which the mercury now stands in the Fahrenheit thermometer, while the mercury in the Fahrenheit thermometer would rise to the level at which the mercury now stands in the centigrade

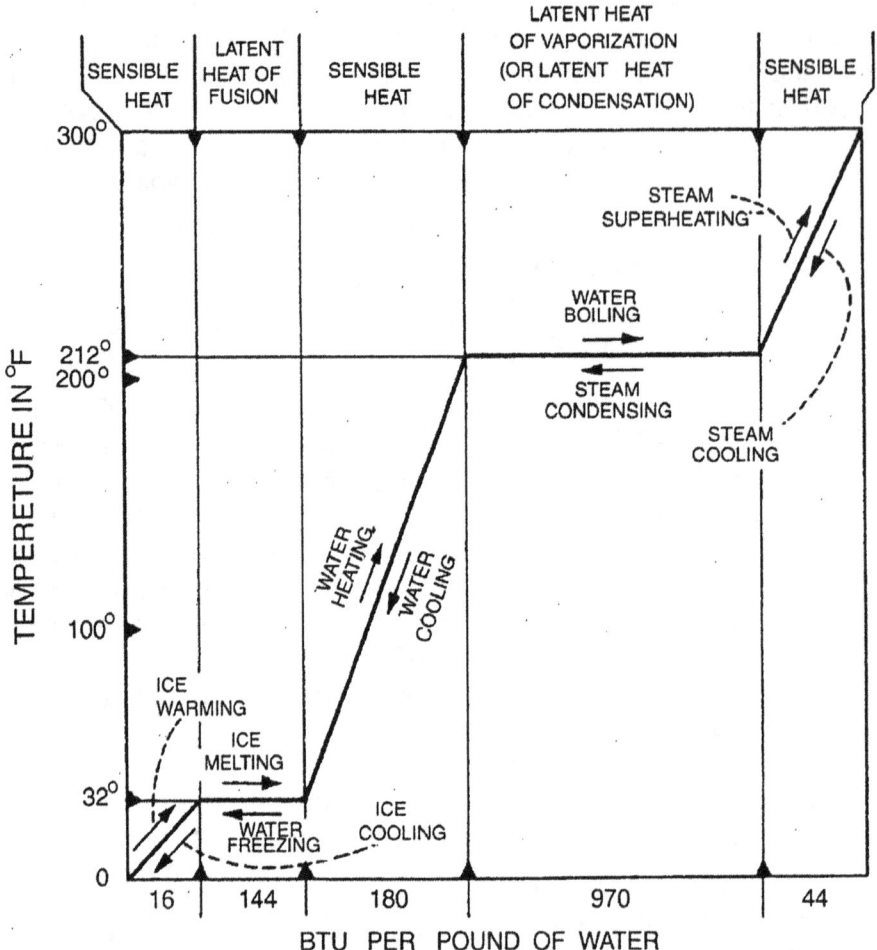

Figure 3-5.—Relationship between sensible heat and latent heat for water at atmospheric pressure.

thermometer. The temperatures would be 0° C for the ice water and 212° F for the boiling water.

If you place both thermometers in water containing lumps of ice, the Fahrenheit thermometer will read 32 and the centigrade thermometer will read 0. Heat the water slowly. The temperature will not change until the ice in the water has completely melted (a great deal of heat is required just to melt the ice), then both mercury columns will begin to rise. When the mercury level is at the +10 mark in the centigrade thermometer, it will be at the +50 mark in the Fahrenheit thermometer. The two columns will rise together at the same speed, and when the water finally boils they will stand at 100° C and 212° F, respectively. The same temperature change that is, the same amount of heat transferred to the waterhas raised the temperature 100 entigrade degrees and 180 Fahrenheit degrees, but the actual change in heat energy is EXACTLY THE SAME.

E. COMBUSTION

The term "combustion" refers to the rapid chemical union of oxygen with the fuel. The perfect combustion of fuel should result in carbon dioxide, nitrogen, water vapor, and sulphur dioxide. The oxygen furnished to the fuel, in order to burn it, is obtained from the air. Air is a mechanical mixture containing by weight 23.15 percent oxygen and 76.85 percent nitrogen. The oxygen only is used in combustion of the fuel; the nitrogen, being an inert gas, has no chemical effect upon the combustion.

The chemical combination obtained during combustion results in the liberation of heat energy, a portion of which is used to propel the ship. Actually, what happens is a rearrangement of the atoms of the chemical elements into new combinations of molecules. In other words, as the temperature of the fuel oil in the presence of oxygen is increased to the ignition point, the various chemical elements in the fuel begin to separate from each other and unite with certain amounts of oxygen, to form entirely new substances, which give off heat energy in the process. A good fuel has a high speed of combustion, thus producing a large amount of heat in a short time.

sists of bringing each particle of the fuel (heated to its ignition temperature) into contact with the correct amount of oxygen. The following factors are involved:

1. Sufficient air must be supplied.

2. The air and fuel particles must be thoroughly mixed.

3. Temperatures must be high enough to maintain combustion.

4. Enough time must be allowed to permit completion of the process.

What is known as COMPLETE COMBUSTION, however, can be achieved. This is accomplished by supplying more oxygen to the process than would be required if perfect combustion were possible. The result is that some of the excess oxygen appears in the combustion gases.

F. STEAM

Steam is water to which enough heat has been added to convert it from the liquid to the gaseous state. When heat is added to water in an open container, steam forms, but it quickly mixes with air and cools back to water that is dispersed in the air, making the air more humid. If you add the heat to water in a closed container, the steam builds up pressure. If you add exactly enough heat to convert all the water to steam at the temperature of boiling water, you get saturated steam. SATURATED STEAM is steam saturated with all the heat it can hold at the boiling temperature of water.

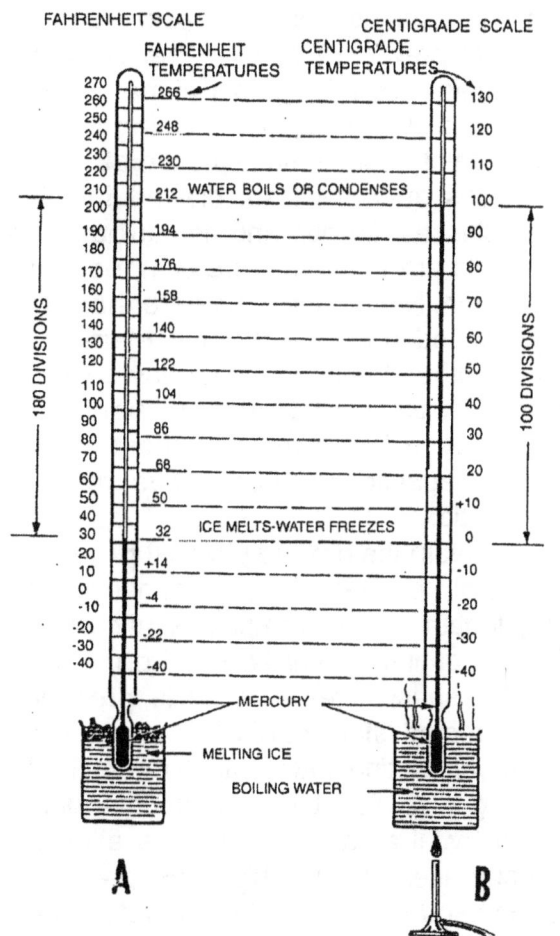

Figure 3-6.—Temperature scales: A. Fahrenheit p. scale. B. Centigrade scale.

PERFECT COMBUSTION cannot as yet be achieved in either a boiler or the cylinders of an internal combustion engine, but this is the objective. Theoretically, it is simple. It con-

The boiling temperature of water becomes higher as the pressure over the water becomes higher. Steam hotter than the boiling temperature of water is called SUPERHEATED STEAM. When steam has 250° F of superheat, the actual temperature is the boiling temperature plus 250° F. At 600 psi the boiling temperature of water is 489° F. So if steam at 600 psi has 250° F of superheat, its actual temperature is 739° F. WET STEAM is steam at the boiling temperature, but still containing some water particles. DESUPERHEATED STEAM is steam which has been cooled by being passed through a pipe extending through the steam drum; in the process the steam loses all but about 20 or 30 of its superheat. The advantage of desuperheated steam is that it is certain to be dry, and yet it is not so hot that special alloy steels would be required for the construction of the piping that carries the desuperheated steam.

IV. METALS

As you look around, you can see that not only is a ship constructed of metal, but that the boilers, piping system, machinery, and even a bunk and locker are constructed of some type of metal. No one type of metal can serve all the needs aboard ship, so many types of metals or metal alloys must be used. For some parts of a ship a strong metal must be used and on other parts a lightweight metal is needed. Some areas require special metal that can be shaped or worked very easily.

The physical properties of some metals or metal alloys make them more suitable for one use than for another. Various terms are used in describing the physical properties of metals. By studying the following explanations of these terms you should have a better understanding of why certain metals are used on one part of a ship's structure and not on another part.

STRENGTH refers to the ability of a metal to maintain heavy loads (or force) without breaking. Steel, for example, is strong, but lead is weak.

HARDNESS refers to the ability of a metal to resist penetration, wear, or cutting action.

MALLEABILITY is a property of a metal that allows it to be rolled, forged, hammered, or shaped, without cracking or breaking. Copper is a very malleable metal.

BRITTLENESS—any metal that will shatter easily is brittle. Metals such as cast iron or cast aluminum, and some very hard steels are brittle.

DUCTILITY refers to the ability of a metal to stretch or bend without breaking. Soft iron, soft steel, and copper are ductile metals.

TOUGHNESS—metal that will not tear or shear (cut) easily and that will stretch without breaking has the property of toughness.

Metal preservation aboard ship is a continuous operation since the metals are constantly exposed to fumes, water, acids, and moist salt air; all of these will eventually cause corrosion. The corrosion of iron and steel is called rusting and results in the formation of iron oxide (iron and oxygen) on the surface of the metal. Iron oxide (or rust) can be easily identified by its reddish color. (A blackish hue occurs in the first stage of rusting, but is seldom thought of as rust.) Corrosion can be reduced, or prevented, by using better grades of base metals, by adding special metals such as nickel and chromium, or by coating the surface with paint or other metal preservatives.

Metals and alloys are divided into two general classes; ferrous and nonferrous. Ferrous metals are those that are composed primarily of iron. Nonferrous metals are those that are composed primarily of some element or elements other than iron. One way to tell a common ferrous metal from a nonferrous metal, is by using a magnet; most ferrous metal is magnetic and non-ferrous metal is nonmagnetic.

To obtain the desired physical properties of a metal, elements must be alloyed (or mixed) together. For example, by alloying (or mixing) chromium and nickel with iron, a metal known as special treated steel is produced. Special treated steel (STS) has great resistance to penetrating and shearing forces and is used for gun shields, turrets, protective decks, and other vital areas. A nonferrous alloy that has many uses aboard ship is copper-nickel, which is used extensively in salt water piping systems. Copper-nickel is produced by mixing copper and nickel.